COLLEGE OF ST MARK & ST JOHN
188733

Political Behavior in the Arab States

Also of Interest

Local Politics and Development in the Middle East, edited by Louis J. Cantori and Illiya Harik

†*Rich and Poor States in the Middle East: Egypt and the New Arab Order,* edited by Malcolm H. Kerr and El Sayed Yassin

The New Arab Social Order: A Study of the Social Impact of Oil Wealth, Saad Eddin Ibrahim

†*The Government and Politics of the Middle East and North Africa,* edited by David E. Long and Bernard Reich

Food, Development, and Politics in the Middle East, Marvin G. Weinbaum

†*Religion and Politics in the Middle East,* edited by Michael Curtis

†*Islam: Continuity and Change in the Modern World,* John Obert Voll

†*The Foreign Policies of Arab States,* edited by Bahgat Korany and Ali E. Hillal Dessouki

The Problems of Arab Economic Development and Integration, edited by Adda Guecioueur

†*Survey Research in the Arab World: An Analytical Index,* Monte Palmer, Mima S. Nedelcovych, Hilal Khashan, and Debra L. Munro

Dadda 'Atta and His Forty Grandsons: The Socio-Political Organization of the Ait 'Atta of Southern Morocco, David Hart

The Two Yemens, Robin Bidwell

PROFILES OF THE CONTEMPORARY MIDDLE EAST

South Yemen: A Marxist Republic in Arabia, Robert W. Stookey

Jordan: Crossroads of Middle Eastern Events, Peter Gubser

Syria: Modern State in an Ancient Land, John F. Devlin

The Republic of Lebanon: Nation in Jeopardy, David C. Gordon

Yemen: The Politics of the Yemen Arab Republic, Robert W. Stookey

†Available in hardcover and paperback.

About the Book and Editor

Political Behavior in the Arab States

edited by Tawfic E. Farah

This vivid portrayal of political and social behavior in the Arab states offers new perspectives to the student and scholar of the Middle East. It also illustrates the effectiveness of survey research as an analytical tool for investigating political, social, and economic problems in Arab societies. The only book of its kind—dealing in a comprehensive and interdisciplinary fashion with the political and social behavior of individuals in the Arab world—it fills a gap in the materials available for courses on the Middle East.

Dr. Farah is president of the Middle East Research Group, Inc., and editor of its publication, *Journal of Arab Affairs.* He was an assistant professor of political science at Kuwait University (1975–1979), a research fellow at the Center for International and Strategic Affairs, University of California, Los Angeles (1980–1981), and is the recipient of a Fulbright research grant for the study of political culture in Kuwait, Saudi Arabia, and Egypt (1983). He has been a visiting associate professor of political science at the University of California, Los Angeles, every summer since 1978. He is author of *Aspects of Consociationalism and Modernization: Lebanon as an Exploratory Test Case* (1975) and co-author of *Research Methods in the Social Sciences* (1977) and the *Dictionary of Social Analysis* (1980).

About the Book and Author

Political Behavior in the Arab States

edited by
Tawfic E. Farah

Foreword by Malcolm H. Kerr

Westview Press • Boulder, Colorado

Published in 1983 in the United States of America by
Westview Press, Inc.
5500 Central Avenue
Boulder, Colorado 80301
Frederick A. Praeger, President and Publisher

Library of Congress Cataloging in Publication Data
Main entry under title:
Political behavior in the Arab states.
Bibliography: p.
Includes index.
1. Arab countries—Social conditions—Addresses, essays, lectures. 2. Arab countries—Politics and government—Addresses, essays, lectures. 3. Political Sociology—Addresses, essays, lectures. I. Farah, Tawfic.
HN766.A8P64 1983 306′.2′09174927 83-6868
ISBN 0-86531-524-8
ISBN 0-86531-525-6 (pbk.)

Printed and bound in the United States of America

10 9 8 7 6 5 4 3 2 1

To the people who taught us all many lessons in political behavior in the summer of 1982 and provided us with insights into politics in the Arab states—the people of Beirut.

Contents

Part III
Socialization and Alienation

Part IV
A New Arab Order?

Foreword

It is a fair guess that very few of the courses on Middle Eastern politics taught in European and American universities devote much attention to the science of political behavior. Some teachers in the field have been trained in Middle Eastern area studies, with an emphasis on learning classical Arabic, Islamic culture, and modern political history; others come from a background in comparative political development theory or international relations. The most popular topics for field research include political ideology, parties, movements, elites, bureaucracies, revolutions, wars, and whole national systems. Not only are those the topics most in keeping with a researcher's background, but they are also the ones that can most readily be studied under the restrictive conditions of most Middle Eastern countries.

Some excellent work has come out of this tradition, and some has also been written by historians and journalists. But the missing dimensions have been those of sociology and psychology, particularly as represented in survey research. The publication of this volume edited by Professor Farah will do much to fill the gap. The book's contents serve to remind us that the conduct of political affairs in the Middle East, as elsewhere, is conditioned not only—perhaps not even primarily—by the leading public issues, ideas, and personalities of the day, but also by the primordial building blocks of human motivation such as childhood experiences, family and religious affiliations, and intercultural conflict. For us to learn more about the primordial and the ordinary in the political acculturation of people in the Arab world is to start to demythologize the distorted images of the "mysterious East" that we in Europe and America have inherited over many past generations and that color our vision of what Arab politics is really all about.

Not surprisingly, many of the articles reproduced in this volume are not by political scientists but by sociologists and psychologists, and in many cases the subjects of the articles are only related to politics in a general or indirect way. This is as it should be if we consider the explicitly political level of the life of a society as a superstructure resting on unseen foundations of the individual needs, emotions, and experiences of masses of people. It is also noteworthy that of the articles specifically reporting research within a single country, many are about Lebanon and the others are scattered widely among other countries. Among those missing altogether are Algeria, Iraq, Syria, and the two Yemens, all of them countries of great potential interest but where field research is hard to come by.

Admittedly this situation could have been somewhat different, for there do exist scholars working in Egypt, Jordan, Tunisia, and elsewhere whose work is not included in the volume. But the fact remains that, on the whole, social psychology and survey research are still largely the preserves of researchers trained in or affiliated with U.S. and British universities. In the Arab world they are concentrated in a few locales of Anglo-American culture influence, such as the American University of Beirut and the American University in Cairo. It is also a sad truth that when it comes to survey research on subjects with a clear political relevance, Lebanon has been almost alone in the Arab world in offering full hospitality to foreign or domestic scholars.

In any event I must confess, as I suppose many others will also, that it came to me as a surprise to realize how much politically related behavioral research has already been carried out in the Arab world. Much more is needed in order to bring a healthier perspective to our understanding of Arab politics and so that we may see it a little less as a reflection of formal cultural norms or contemporary world ideological currents and a little more as a set of patterns of behavior of many ordinary individuals undergoing varying degrees of stress in their lives. Tawfic Farah has been prominent among those doing this kind of work through his excellent studies of political socialization among several sectors of society in Kuwait. Let us hope that in the coming years he will be joined by many others.

Malcolm H. Kerr
President
American University of Beirut

Preface

The primary focus of this book of readings is politics in the Arab states. The fifteen selections present some works of practitioners and students of political behavior in some Arab societies. Arab societies, all twenty of them, are a heterogeneous lot, and research in the area of political and social behavior is almost nonexistent in some of them. Hence, the selections are not representative of all of these societies.

Survey research is the investigator's dominant tool in the selections of this book. This tool is still in its infancy in many Arab societies. Nevertheless, survey research is becoming more common in the Arab world. Its use was formerly limited to Beirut, Cairo, and Tunis, but it is now utilized in Kuwait, where there is a Survey Research Center at Kuwait University, at the University of Qatar, and at a number of universities in Saudi Arabia and in Libya. Efforts are underway to conduct an inventory of survey research in Arab societies and attempts are being made to gather and standardize the studies that are available in Arabic, English, and French.[1] We have been able to include in this book the early pioneering works of Levon Melikian and Lutfy Diab, but many excellent studies had to be excluded because of space and resource limitations.

Some of the selections presented here might seem methodologically inelegant, and their research designs might appear primitive to practitioners of survey research in America and Europe. Yet these scholars have dared to tread in this area despite very adverse conditions: a hostile political environment, a lack of trained interviewers, the absence of telephone books, city maps, and city addresses (absolutely necessary tools for the construction of representative samples). Scholars could have been overly cautious and hence paralyzed.

The quality of this kind of research will improve with time. Experimentation is a fundamental tool of science: If we experiment we will make mistakes. The process is very messy. Robert Merton, a historian of science, describes the typical scientific paper:

> There is a rockbound difference between scientific work as it appears in print, and the actual course of inquiry. . . . The difference is a little like that between textbooks of scientific method and the ways in which scientists actually think, feel and go about their work. The books on methods

> present ideal patterns, but these tidy normative patterns . . . do not reproduce the typically untidy, opportunistic adaptations that scientists really make. The scientific paper presents an immaculate appearance which reproduces little or nothing of the intuitive leaps, false starts, mistakes, loose ends, and happy accidents that actually cluttered up the inquiry.[2]

In time, the methodology of survey research in the Arab societies will become more elegant, the research designs more elaborate. Also, the standard problems associated with validity, reliability, standardization in measurement, and measurement equivalence within and across these societies will be solved. Saad Eddin Ibrahim and others, for example, attempted this "mission impossible" in seventeen Arab societies in the late seventies with surveys about politically salient topics and produced their *Itajahat Al-Rai-Al-Am Al-Arabi Nahwa Masa'lat Al-wihda* ("Trends of Arab opinion toward the issue of unity").[3] The mere fact that Saad Eddin Ibrahim successfully undertook this task underscores the fact that, despite the many obstacles and the opposition by many regimes to survey research, it can be done.

But resistance to survey research is not limited to governments. Many scholars in Arab societies detest the method as an investigatory procedure and doubt whether it can really be detached from its Western and/or "imperialistic" origins. Recognizing the limits of survey research, as many of its practitioners do, is not enough for many critics in Arab societies.[4] They suggest that survey research is a tool of the imperialists, a "trojan horse," and hence ought not to be utilized as an instrument for the scientific study of societies. Yet these same scholars avail themselves of "imperialist" tools like "jumbo jets," telephones, telexes, and photocopy machines. Never underestimate the utility of hypocrisy.

It has been said: "If you want to understand what science is, you should look in the first instance not to its theories or its findings, and certainly not to what its apologists say about it; you should look at what the practitioners of it do."[5] In the following pages fifteen selections are presented in four parts. The first three parts focus on political behavior at the micro-level, while the fourth part presents three treatments of Arab politics on the macro-level by seasoned students of that part of the world: Malcolm Kerr, Fouad Ajami, and Saad Eddin Ibrahim.

Part I presents the pioneering work of Levon Melikian and Lutfy Diab on group affiliations of students at the American University of Beirut. In an effort to facilitate comparison across systems, two selections by Tawfic Farah are included that report the findings of two surveys (one conducted in Kuwait and one in the United States), each survey asking essentially similar questions and focusing on equivalent concepts in two different settings.[6]

Part II looks at family, religion, and social class, which are sources of conflict within Arab societies. The three papers presented in this section utilize survey research to analyze the social underpinnings of change in Qatar, the interaction of religion and politics in Egypt, and communal conflict in Lebanon.

Part III presents four selections. Edwin Terry Prothro focuses on child-rearing practices in Lebanon, and Michael Suleiman is concerned with the values advocated in Egyptian children's readers. The two remaining selections, one by Tawfic Farah and one by Mark Tessler and Jean O'Barr, are concerned with the attitudes and values of young men and women in Kuwait and Tunisia, respectively.

Part IV takes a broad look at Arab societies today. Malcolm Kerr, Fouad Ajami, and Saad Eddin Ibrahim discuss the decade of the seventies. They analyze the "heady" days of the "oil rush," the way politics was played out in the 1970s. They are not at all surprised by the outcome. In the 1970s the Arabs had a great opportunity that was wasted. The party that started with the oil rush of 1973 was over well before the Israeli tanks encircled the city of Beirut in the summer of 1982. Is there a new Arab order? This question is addressed in different ways by the three authors.

Finally, a word of appreciation is due for those to whom I owe many an intellectual debt: Malcolm Kerr, Fouad Ajami, Thomas Sorensen, Munif Abu Rish, Arne Nixon, Raphael Zariski, Michael Suleiman, James Bill, Yasumassa Kuroda, and Faisal Al-Salem. My colleagues and friends on the board of directors at the Middle East Research Group, Suhayl Bathish, Fowzi Farah, and Hassan Bissat, were always supportive and encouraged me to undertake this project. My wife, Linda, my son, Omar, and daughter, Aliya, are forever patient and understanding while I occasionally go through the process of trying to make sense of political behavior in the Arab states. Most times I fail.

T.E.F.
Fresno, California

Notes

1. See Mark Tessler, Monte Palmer, and Tawfic Farah, "Survey Research in Arab Society: A Research Proposal," presented to the National Science Foundation, 1982.
2. Quoted in Thomas J. Peters and Robert H. Waterman, Jr., *In Search of Excellence* (New York: Harper & Row, 1982), p. 48.
3. Saad Eddin Ibrahim, *Itajahat Al-Rai-Al-Am-Al-Arabi Nahwa Masa'lat Al-wihda* [Trends of Arab opinion toward the issue of unity] (Beirut: Center of Arab Unity Studies, 1980).
4. See for example Mohamad Al-Sayed Salim, "Al-Jamiat Al-Arabia wa Thahirat Al-Tabiya Al-Ilmiya" [Arab universities and scientific dependency], *Al-Mustaqbal Al Arabi,* 40 (June 1982), pp. 93–104.
5. Clifford Geertz, *The Interpretation of Cultures* (New York: Basic Books, 1973), p. 5.
6. Henry Teune, *The Logic of Comparative Social Inquiry* (New York: Wiley, 1970).

Part I

Affiliations

1
Group Affiliations of University Students in the Arab Middle East

Levon H. Melikian and Lutfy N. Diab

A. The Problem

The value to an individual of group identification and affiliation has been recognized by social scientists. The strength and permanency of such affiliations depend upon the needs which they satisfy in the individual and upon the status which they confer upon him. Hence we can assume that a hierarchy of group affiliation exists and that the groups that rank lower on this hierarchy will be more readily relinquished than the higher ranking groups.

Knowledge of the affiliation hierarchy is especially important in cultures in which affiliation to certain groups not only satisfies certain psychological needs but actually determines one's legal and social status. Such is the case in the Arab Middle East where the family, religion, and ethnic affiliations are the traditional backbones of the social structure. In a culture which is changing as rapidly as that of the Middle East affiliations to groups that are not part of the traditional culture emerge and at times are in conflict with the traditional loyalties required of the individual.

This study seeks first to determine the hierarchy of group affiliations of university students in the Arab Middle East. It also seeks to answer the question as to whether this hierarchy is affected by the sex, religion, or political orientation of the *S*s. In the third place it will seek to determine whether a major social threat, e.g., a revolution, has an effect on the hierarchy.

B. The Arab Middle East

The Arab *ME* has been an area of concern and interest not only to the traditional historian and archeologist and the ever present strategist and economist, but also to the student of human relations. Burke (1),

Reprinted with permission from *Journal of Social Psychology* 49:145–159 (1959).

in her bibliography of books and periodicals in English dealing with human relations in the area between 1945 and 1954, gives 1453 references. Of interest to this study are the observations made regarding the social structure of the area, its group and minority affiliations as well as the rapid social change that the area is undergoing, and the effect of this change on the traditional pattern. The "mosaic" nature of the culture and its ethnic divisions has been emphasized by Coon (2). The minority problems and conflicts have been presented by Hourani (5) and Ibish (6); and the problems of social structure and acculturation have been studied by Gulick (3) and Hourani (4).

The Arab *ME* is essentially an authoritarian culture (8) in which the extended patriarchal family system in one form or another is basic. The family is all-pervasive and requires the support and loyalty of its members. In return it provides its members with the essential security and support. Families as such play an important part in the politics of the area, e.g., Hashimites vs. Saudis, and many an extended family has its own organization to watch for the interest and rights of its members. The family ascribes clearly defined roles and statuses to its various members, specially to the eldest male child who comes next in importance to the parents. He has more privileges as well as more responsibilities than the rest of his siblings. In the absence of the father it is the eldest boy who becomes the family representative. Thus the family constitutes a very important social unit in the life of an individual, and its standing in society at large contributes to the prestige of its individual members.

Within this culture system religion plays an important role, not primarily as a spiritual force, but as a basic structure of society. Under the Turkish rule which lasted for roughly 500 years, religious affiliation was what determined one's legal status. "Since for Moslems and Christians alike consciousness of belonging to a religious community was the basis of political and social obligation both were conscious of not belonging to the other communities; distinctiveness led to suspicion and dislike" (4, p. 63). "The sect persisted as a social entity even after the impulse which gave it birth had died away. To leave one's sect was to leave one's whole world, and to live without loyalties, the protection of a community, the consciousness of solidarity and the comfort of normality" (4, p. 64). This emphasis on the sect and its importance was reflected in the Turkish "millet" or communal system through which one transacted his legal and civil rights with the government. It is still manifest in the personal status laws over the area where inheritance, marriage, etc., are still carried out within one's own religious community. Belonging to a religious group limited in a sense not only one's contact with others but also, until recently, the kind of occupation that was open to the individual. Studies of social distance in the area have shown that preference for one's own religious group is still strong but slowly on the decline (7). The importance of religious and sectarian identifications shows itself in everyday colloquial conversation where the word religion is used in the sense of "kind." Thus when wanting to find some information about a person one very often uses the word religion and asks "shou dino," "what is his religion," literally meaning what kind of a person is he, in spite of the fact that among the educated religious affiliation is not consciously considered to be an important factor. Students in the American University of Beirut have often objected to indicating their religious affiliation on university forms—still it plays a very subtle role. Hence membership in and affiliation to a sect or a religious group is of vital importance to the individual, not only in the psychological support that it gives but also in the social and legal status that it accords to him.

Another characteristic of the *ME* culture area is the presence of many ethnic groups. The vast majority of the population are Arabs, but minorities, such as Kurds, Armenians, Assyrians, Yazidis, Circassians, play an important part in society and raise many problems in the area. As citizens in the various countries of the area they play an important role in many respects. As members of "ethnic" minorities they are not fully assimilated in the general culture, probably because of their other affiliations, language, or ethnic origin.

Under the Turkish rule the people living in the area were all citizens of the Empire and subjects of the Turkish Sultan. There were no boundaries, no separate states, but "valayets" or administrative districts responsible to the Capital. With the advent of the Mandatory governments the area was divided into different countries, and people who had previously been subjects of the Turkish Empire now became citizens of small countries such as Palestine, Transjordan, Syria, Iraq, etc. This state of affairs introduced a new identification, a new group to which the individual was affiliated and which demanded his allegiance and loyalty. Thus an individual became a Palestinian or an Iraqi. Being born in a certain country makes the individual a citizen of that country which demands loyalty and allegiance and becomes a focus of affiliation. Hence a citizenship is based on somewhat artificially induced boundaries and not on ethnic or linguistic factors. Thus a citizen of Jordan is also an Arab and a Moslem at the same time. The reaction to this splitting up is seen, among other things, in the recent "unification" between Egypt and Syria, and the short-lived federation between Iraq and Jordan.

Since 1900, as a result of the spread of education and of political consciousness, a new force has entered the area—mainly the political party, which again demands the loyalty of some of the people. Political parties of many kinds and of all degrees of organization and effectiveness have sprung up. This focus of identification differs from the others in that the individual is free to join it or not. Unlike the others he is literally not born into it. Even though a small percentage of the population belongs to organized political parties yet the appeal is strongest with youth. University students in the *ME* are known to be the champions of different political parties and ideologies, and have at times been rabid and aggressive in their political beliefs. Most of the political parties cut across religious and political boundaries and in one form or another they aim at some form of Arab Unity. Barring the Communist and some sectarian parties, all the existing major parties include in their platform a clause calling for Arab Unity or a federation among the Arab States.

Because of the nature of the culture and its values the individual is expected to give his loyalty to and identify himself with the above groups, except for the last one, the political party. However, the fact that an individual actively joins a certain political party, in spite of the fact that this new membership often contradicts some of his previous loyalties and affiliations, means that new and important needs of the individual are being satisfied by this new group. Therefore, it might well be that the political party, and the degree to which the individual identifies with its goals and aspirations, also acts as an important reference group for the individual and thus consitutes an additional factor regulating his behavior.

C. Method

1. The Subjects

A 42-item questionnaire was prepared and administered to 138 *S*s in May, 1957, and to 69 *S*s in May, 1958. The *S*s were students at the American University of Beirut taking undergraduate courses in psychology. Over 75 percent of the *S*s in both samples came from Lebanon, Jordan, and Syria, while the remainder came from Iraq, Saudi Arabia, and Bahrain. In Table 1 is a breakdown of both samples as far as religion, sex, and political orientation.

The composition of the two samples appears to be relatively the same. No significant differences exist in the religious, sex, or political affiliation of the two samples. The age range at last birthday of the 1957 sample was from 17 to 31 with a mean of 21.32 and a standard deviation of 3.07. Even though no age data are available on the 1958 sample there is no reason to suppose that it differs significantly in this respect.

*S*s were asked to indicate whether they were members of an organized political party or subscribed to a particular political ideology. Ninety-nine *S*s who gave affirmative answers are referred to in the study as the "politically oriented," 39 who did not indicate any such affiliation or belief are referred to as the "non-politically oriented." *S*s were free to withhold the name of the party to which they belonged or the ideology to which they subscribed. The parties and ideologies indicated ranged from organized parties such as the Ba'th and *PPS* to the less defined ideologies of "Arab Nationalism," "Arab Unity," and Democracy. Economic, sectarian parties and ideologies were also indicated.

Table 1

Distribution of Respondents in 1957 and 1958

	Total	Christians	Moslems	Males	Females	Politically oriented	Non-politically oriented
1957	138	80	58	98	40	99	39
1958	69	43	26	51	18	52	17

2. The Questionnaire

Part I: The stem in each question pointed to the attainment of a goal involving affiliation with or loyalty to one of the following five major reference groups: family, religion, national (ethnic) origin, citizenship, and political party. Two additional goals, namely, the securing of either a job or a mate, were also included. The goal could be attained only by *S* giving up one of two of the above group affiliations which were presented in the form of paired alternatives as illustrated below:

1. If to show your loyalty to your nation: *(a)* You were forced to give up your religion permanently, both in private and in public, or, *(b)* You were forced to give up your family and never see them again. Which would you choose? *(a)*_____ *(b)*_____
2. If in order to join a certain political party: *(a)* You were forced to give up your religion permanently, both in private and in public, or, *(b)* You were forced to become a permanent exile from the country to which you belonged. Which would you choose? *(a)*_____ *(b)*_____

Six pairs of alternative choices were presented for the attainment of the goals of national (ethnic) affiliation, political party, and citizenship; three pairs of alternative choices for each of the goals of family and religious affiliation; and nine pairs of alternative choices for each of the goals of securing a job and having a mate. In the 42 alternative choices presented in the questionnaire a *S* could have scored a maximum of 17 on family or political party affiliation; 18 on citizenship; 20 on religion; and 12 on national (ethnic) affiliation.

The questionnaire included a data sheet to get information about the *S*'s sex, age, citizenship, ethnic background, and religious affiliation. *S*s who belonged to a political party had the option to indicate its name if they so wanted. The terms "citizenship" and "ethnic" were defined on the data sheet. The definition given to the former was "the country whose passport a person holds," and to the latter "the national background of the person." The example of a person of Italian parents living in the United States was given by way of illustration. He was described as a citizen of that country but his ethnic origin as being Italian. *S*s were instructed not to write their names on the questionnaire.

3. Scoring

The choice of an alternative in a question indicated the readiness of the *S* to give it up before the other or else it indicated a greater preference for the other alternative. In the examples from the questionnaire cited above a subject checking *(a)*—religion—will get a score of 1 for *(b)*—family. The number of scores given to each group affiliation under the same goal-seeking situation gives the *S*'s preference scores for each of the groups under that situation. The sum of the preference scores for each group under the seven goal-seeking situations gives a full picture of the *S*'s preference scores for each of the five reference groups under study.

In order to equalize the *S*'s scores for each reference group the group preference scores were divided by the number of times each group appeared as an alternative choice. Thus the family preference score was divided by 17, the political party by 17, citizenship by 18, religion by 20, and national (ethnic) by 12.

The equated scores for each *S* were then ranked in order of magnitude. Through this means we were able to calculate the number of times each group was ranked 1 to 5 by the *S*s.

D. Results

1. 1957 Sample

The results in Table 2 show the frequency of each of the five ranks given by the male and female *S*s for each of the five reference groups, as well as the median rank of each group. In order to determine whether any significant differences occur between the ranking of males and females on the five reference groups the frequencies of Ranks 1, 2, and 3 were combined into a "high" score and of Ranks 4 and 5 into a "low" score. This made a 2 × 2 contingency table available to calculate a χ^2. This combination was used throughout except in three cases where the frequencies were below 5.

No significant difference was found between the ranking of the male and female *S*s on any of the five reference groups. This indicates that sex does not appear to be a factor in the group preferences of our *S*s. If the median scores for the rank of each group are considered males seem to rank the family first on the hierarchy followed by ethnic, religion, political party, and citizenship in order of importance. Female *S*s maintain the same order for the first two but rank citizenship third and religion fourth and political party fifth. The differences in rank do not indicate a significant difference in the magnitude of the medians.

Table 3 shows the frequency of the five ranks given by Christian and Moslem *S*s for each of the five reference groups, as well as the median score for each group. No significant difference was found between Christians and Moslems in their rankings of the five reference groups. If the median score for each group is considered, Moslems rank the family first followed by religion, ethnic, political party, and citizenship in order of importance. Christians rank family first followed by ethnic, religion, political party, and citizenship in order of their importance.

Table 4 shows the frequency of each of the five ranks given by the politically oriented and the non-politically oriented *S*s for each of the five reference groups as well as the median score for each group. The only significant difference between the two groups refers to political party—the politically oriented *S*s give it a stronger preference than the non-politically oriented *S*s. The difference is significant at the .02 level

Table 2

Frequency and median score of ranks given by Male and Female *S*s for each of the five Reference Groups in 1957 and 1958

	Males *N*57 = 98 *N*58 = 51										Females *N*57 = 40 *N*58 = 18									
	PP		F		C		R		N(E)		PP		F		C		R		N(E)	
Rank	57	58	57	58	57	58	57	58	57	58	57	58	57	58	57	58	57	58	57	58
1	14	7	34	26	4	5	31	4	16	9	4	1	13	11	2	0	14	5	8	1
2	15	9	36	10	11	11	11	12	26	12	1	0	18	4	9	6	4	5	8	3
3	14	6	18	8	24	12	14	13	26	9	5	1	6	2	15	6	3	1	10	9
4	26	12	6	5	38	15	14	7	14	12	11	6	3	0	10	5	8	2	8	4
5	29	17	4	2	21	8	28	15	16	9	19	10	0	1	4	1	11	5	6	1
Median	4.3	4.5	2.1	2.0	4.5	3.8	3.5	3.7	3.2	3.5	4.9	4.1	2.4	1.8	3.6	3.5	3.7	2.8	3.4	3.6

Table 3

Frequency and median score of ranks given by Christian and Moslem *Ss* for each of the five Reference Groups in 1957 and 1958

	Christians *N*57 = 80 *N*58 = 43										Moslems *N*57 = 58 *N*58 = 26									
	PP		F		C		R		N(E)		PP		F		C		R		N(E)	
Rank	57	58	57	58	57	58	57	58	57	58	57	58	57	58	57	58	57	58	57	58
1	6	5	28	21	5	5	24	6	17	6	12	3	19	15	1	0	21	3	7	4
2	8	6	31	9	12	11	8	10	22	10	8	3	23	5	8	6	7	6	12	5
3	9	2	14	6	21	10	12	8	23	15	10	5	10	4	18	7	5	6	13	3
4	23	11	5	4	25	13	15	5	12	9	14	6	4	1	23	7	7	4	10	7
5	34	19	2	3	17	4	21	14	6	3	14	8	2	0	8	5	18	6	16	6
Median	4.7	4.8	2.4	2.1	4.1	3.5	3.7	3.7	3.0	3.4	3.9	4.2	2.4	1.8	4.1	3.9	3.2	3.6	3.8	4.1

Table 4

Frequency and median score of ranks given by Politically and Non-Politically Oriented *S*s for each of the five Reference Groups in 1957 and 1958

	Politically oriented *N*57 = 99 *N*58 = 52										Non-politically oriented *N*57 = 39 *N*58 = 17									
	PP		F		C		R		N(E)		PP		F		C		R		N(E)	
Rank	57	58	57	58	57	58	57	58	57	58	57	58	57	58	57	58	57	58	57	58
1	17	7	32	26	5	4	28	6	18	9	1	1	15	11	1	1	17	3	6	1
2	15	9	34	11	14	14	10	10	27	9	1	0	20	3	6	3	5	7	7	6
3	15	7	21	8	21	12	16	12	24	13	4	0	3	2	18	6	1	2	12	5
4	25	14	8	4	38	15	14	7	14	11	12	4	1	1	10	5	8	2	8	5
5	27	15	4	3	21	7	31	17	16	10	21	12	0	0	4	2	8	3	6	0
Median	4.1	4.2	2.5	2.0	4.2	3.7	3.7	3.8	3.2	3.6	4.1	4.3	2.3	1.7	3.7	3.7	2.5	2.8	3.5	3.5

of confidence. If the median scores are considered the politically oriented *S*s rank family first followed by nation (ethnic), religion, political party, and citizenship. For the non-politically oriented *S*s the family ranks first, followed by religion, ethnic, citizenship, and political party.

Table 5 shows the frequency of each of the five ranks given by the whole sample, as well as the median ranks. For the whole group the family ranks first, followed by ethnic, religion, citizenship, and political party in their order of importance.

2. Results 1958

The data were analyzed in the same manner and appear in Tables 2, 3, 4, and 5. No significant differences were found between males or females, Christian or Moslem *S*s, and between the politically and the non-politically oriented *S*s. Minor differences appear in the rank order of the medians except in the case of family which ranks first and political party which all rank fifth in all cases.

A comparison of the 1957 and 1958 results showed no significant differences in the frequency of each of the five ranks given to the five reference groups. The rank order of the medians for the total samples of 1957 and 1958 is the same. Both rank family first, ethnic second, religion third, citizenship fourth, and political party last.

E. Discussion

The results presented above can best be understood in the light of the cultural pattern of the Arab Middle East and of its recent social and political history. (As indicated earlier, the area is basically authoritarian in its characteristics, and has recently been subjected to external influences that have challenged the pattern and threatened to change it.)

The core group in the culture—the family—still seems to have maintained its position. Irrespective of sex, religion, or political orientation, the family ranks first in the hierarchy of groups that command the loyalties of our *S*s. It is still the main source of security in a society of conflicting loyalties and unstable values, a society in which the individual as such has not fully established himself. To win the approval of one's family and to maintain its confidence is still of primary importance. Where a conflict between other values occurs, as in the case of Moslem-Christian marriages, the main concern is not religious but the reaction of the family to such a marriage. How long will the family maintain this position? Will the increased economic independence of youth and the opening of employment opportunities for women change the order of the family in the hierarchy of group identifications? The results do not give us any answer unless we can consider the lower rank which the politically oriented *S*s give to the family as an indication of such a trend. Their median shows the possibility that they attach less importance to the family than the others. However there is no

Table 5

Frequency and median score of ranks for each of the five Reference Groups in 1957 and 1958

Rank	PP	F	C	R	N
		1957, N = 138			
1	18	47	6	45	24
2	16	54	20	15	34
3	19	24	39	17	36
4	37	9	48	22	22
5	48	4	25	39	22
Total	138	138	138	138	138
Median	4.44	2.41	4.09	3.53	3.31
		1958, N = 69			
1	8	37	5	9	10
2	9	14	17	17	15
3	7	10	18	14	18
4	18	5	20	9	16
5	27	3	9	20	10
Total	69	69	69	69	69
Median	4.59	1.33	3.70	3.61	3.53

reason to believe that the fate of the family will be different than its fate in other societies under similar conditions. In fact it may hold out longer because of its authoritarian structure. This does not imply that in other cultures the family does not rank first on the hierarchy.

The ranking of religion as second and ethnic as third by the Moslem *S*s and of ethnic as second and religion as third by Christian *S*s is worth examining. These differences can be understood when we keep in mind the role which religious and sectarian affiliation plays in the life of the region. Islam is the predominant religion in the area except for Lebanon where Christians and Moslems are equally divided. The dilemma of the Christian, according to Hourani (4), is whether he is first an Arab or a Christian. When we consider the fact that religious affiliation has been the basis for one's political and social obligations, it is possible that its importance will begin to diminish when other bases for such obligations begin to permeate the social structure. This appears to have happened with our Christian *S*s—to them ethnic or national identification ranks next to the family in importance and religion follows in the third place. It appears that they may have resolved the Arab-Christian dilemma by affiliation with the larger ethnic group that does away with having a minority status. Is it an urge to join the bandwagon and thus gain respect of the Moslems? Is it an over-identification, or is it the result of deep thinking and conviction? It may be all *three* of these, but in the case of our *S*s it is probable that the strength is due to the liberalizing and progressive influence of a college education. In some cases this may be a psychological shift; in others, and this is more probable in the case of college students, it may be a reflection of more liberalizing tendencies and more contact with the Moslem elements of the population. It is interesting to note that Western-educated Christians, such as Constantine Zurayk, Michel Aflaq, George Antonious, have been among the most outstanding advocates of Arab Nationalism. This may also be due to the possibility that religion as a deep-seated spiritual value has lost its power on our Christian *S*s. Thus the Christian *S*s resolve their religious minority status by affiliating with a greater whole. However there is another possible explanation for the importance given to national (ethnic) affiliation by our Christian *S*s. It is possible that some of our Lebanese Christian *S*s understood the term national (ethnic) as referring to a non-Arab group, e.g., Phoenicians, rather than to a non-Moslem entity.

The case of the Moslem is quite different. Religion occupies the second place in the hierarchy and nation third. This may be due to several factors. In the first place our Moslem *S*s are ethnically Arabs (the terms in the area are synonymous to the majority); thus unlike the Christian *S*s they are not presented with a dilemma or a conflict—they are sure of this identity.

To the politically oriented *S*s national identification ranks second and religion is third in the hierarchy. Political orientation in the area is generally some kind of Arab Unity and Arab Federation under the banner of Arab Nationalism. Arab Nationalism occurs in one form or another on all political platforms except in the case of one highly sectarian Christian party in Lebanon, and ranges from those groups that are strictly religious like the Moslem Brotherhood, to the most secular like the Ba'th "Renaissance" Party.

The non-politically oriented *S*s rank religion as second in importance with a median for religion that is considerably smaller than that of all the other subgroups. The identification with nationalism may seem to lessen the importance of religious affiliation, yet to those who do not have any political orientation religion may still be serving as an anchorage and a source of supporting ideology. The need for a mature ideology that will give substance to Arab Nationalism is greatly felt among the intellectuals of the area. So far it has not been supplied to any extensive degree. This is reflected in the low rank which the political party still has. To the politically oriented it ranks fourth and to the non-politically oriented it ranks fifth. It appears therefore that to strengthen political party affiliations a mature ideology has to be developed to give it a sense of direction, preferably an ideology gleaned from the cultural heritage of the area rather than one imported from East or West. Inspection of the distribution of the frequencies of each of the five ranks for the five reference groups shows that the distributions are either negatively or positively skewed except in the case of religion where the distribution is generally bimodal. This applies to all the subsamples in both 1957 and 1958. It seems that *S*s are either for or against religious affiliation. This does not refer at all to religious conviction or belief.

Citizenship appears to be the least important of the groups. It consistently ranks the last or before the last in the hierarchy except in the case of females where it ranks third. However, with the growing importance of ethnic affiliation through Arab Nationalism our *S*s do not seem to be interested in identifying themselves as Syrians or Jordanians but more as Arabs. This is reflected in the recent unifications that have taken place between various "countries" in the area. Regional differences may appear in the area, particularly in Lebanon where ethnic affiliation with Arabs is still not strong among the Christian sections of the population.

The need for further research with an exclusively Lebanese population as well as with members of specific political parties is indicated.

The results of the 1958 sample do not differ significantly from those of 1957. However, a few shifts occur in the median rank on the hierarchy which may be suggestive of certain trends. Political party affiliation drops to the bottom of the hierarchy for all subdivisions except the females and the non-politically oriented *S*s among which political party was already at the bottom. A drop is also noted for ethnic affiliation in the case of the females, Moslems, and politically oriented *S*s—while an improvement in rank for citizenship among males, Moslems, Christians, and the politically oriented *S*s is noted. Even though these changes are not significant yet they may be due to the political crisis through which Lebanon was going when the data were collected in 1958. It may indicate the possibility that political party affiliation had begun to lose its function for our *S*s and that a growing recognition of citizenship may be a reaction to the "threatened existence of Lebanon as an independent state" according to the belief of a large section of the Lebanese population. The above however is purely speculative and tentative.

The non-politically oriented *S*s show no shifting at all in their hierarchy. It seems that in a period which is marked by political and social unrest the non-politically oriented, though lost, are the least affected as far as their group preferences are concerned. They may either not be sensitive to changes and happenings around them, or it may be that because they are not committed one way or another they can afford to bide their time.

In view of the above discussion and within the limitations of this study certain tentative conclusions are made. The absence of a significant difference in the rankings of the five reference groups by males and females, Christians and Moslems, and politically and non-politically oriented *S*s suggests the absence of a relationship between these variables and the hierarchy. The data suggest the possibility that the hierarchy of group affiliations is determined by an all-pervasive cultural core that is common to sex, religion, and political ideology.

The similarity in the rank order of the median scores for all subgroups in both samples suggests the possibility that the pattern is somewhat stable.

In view of the consistency with which family was given the first rank we can legitimately say that it still is the prime source of security for our *S*s.

The suggested conclusions made above apply only to the population from which our samples were drawn, i.e., Arab undergraduates at the American University of Beirut.

For more generalized and definitive conclusions the need for further research is indicated. Larger samples in which the citizenship and political orientation of *S*s are controlled will give us more definitive results.

The present conclusions are limited and the study exploratory.

F. Summary

A 42-item forced choice type of a questionnaire was administered to a sample of undergraduate students at the American University of Beirut in 1957 and to another sample in 1958. The representation of males and females, Christians and Moslems, politically and non-politically oriented did not differ significantly in the two samples. The questionnaire was designed to find the rank order of importance of the family, religion, citizenship, ethnic, and political party. The hierarchy for both samples was similar—family ranked first with ethnic group, religion, citizenship, and political party in order of rank.

No relationship was found between the order of the hierarchy and the variables of sex, religion, and political orientation. A strong culture core was suggested as determining the hierarchy.

Acknowledgment

The authors are grateful to Professors E. Terry Prothro and Wayne Dennis for their helpful suggestions.

References

1. Burke, J. T. An Annotated Bibliography of Books and Periodicals in English Dealing with Human Relations in the Arab States of the Middle East. Beirut: American Univ. Beirut, 1956.
2. Coon, C. Caravan. New York: Holt, 1952.
3. Gulick, J. Social Structure and Culture Change in a Lebanese Village. New York: Wrenn-Green Foundation for Anthropological Research, 1955.
4. Hourani, A. H. Syria and Lebanon. London: Oxford Univ. Press, 1954.
5. ———. Minorities in the Arab World. London: Oxford Univ. Press, 1947.
6. Ibish, Y. The Minority Problems in Syria (Unpublished Master's Thesis). Beirut: American Univ. Beirut, 1953.
7. Prothro, E. T., and Melikian, L. H. Social distance and social change in the Near East. *Soc. & Soc. Res.*, 1952, **37**, 3–11.
8. ———. The California Public Opinion Scale in an authoritarian culture. *Publ. Opin. Quart.*, 1953, **17**, 352–362.

2

Stability and Change in Group Affiliations of University Students in the Arab Middle East

Levon H. Melikian and Lutfy N. Diab

Summary

A 42-item forced choice questionnaire, administered in 1957-58 to undergraduate students at the American University of Beirut, was readministered to a matched sample in 1970-71 to determine the hierarchy of group affiliations.

With the exception of a significantly higher ranking given to citizenship by males in 1970 compared to 1957, no other significant differences were found between 1957 and 1971 in the relative importance given to family, national (ethnic) origin, and citizenship by subjects in both samples, irrespective of sex, religion, and political orientation. Family still ranked first, followed by national (ethnic) affiliation, and third by citizenship. Also, the only significant within-sample difference found in 1957 was also found in 1971: namely, politically oriented subjects gave significantly higher rankings to political party affiliation than nonpolitically oriented subjects.

However, significant changes were found to occur between 1957 and 1971 with respect to political party and religion: namely, political party affiliation became significantly more important and religious affiliation became significantly less important. These changes were discussed within the context of changing social and political conditions in the Arab Middle East.

Finally, within-sample comparisons in the 1970-71 sample showed that politically oriented Palestinians were the only subgrouping who ranked national (ethnic) origin rather than family first, and they also ranked political party affiliation significantly higher than even the politically oriented other Arabs. These differences were discussed in the light of recent significant developments which had characterized the

Reprinted with permission from *Journal of Social Psychology* 93 (1974):13–21.

Palestinian community, particularly since the 1967 Arab-Israeli war. It is, however, clearly understood that our findings cannot be generalized to populations other than our subjects.

A. Introduction

Among other things, a study published previously by the authors (2) sought to determine the hierarchy of group affiliations of Arab university students in the Middle East and to assess whether such a hierarchy is affected differentially by the sex, religion, or political interest of the subjects. On the basis of data collected in 1957 and in 1958, Melikian and Diab (2) found that "family ranked first with ethnic group, religion, citizenship, and political party in order of preference. No relationship was found between the order of the hierarchy and the variables of sex, religion, and political orientation. A strong culture core was suggested as determining the hierarchy" (2, p. 159).

A number of significant events have taken place in the Arab Middle East since 1957-58, among which one could list the secession of Syria from its union with Egypt in the year 1961, the Arab-Israeli war of June 1967, and the emergence of the Palestinian Commando movements shortly thereafter, to mention only a few. In view of these highly important events in a rapidly changing society, and after more than a decade of time, the authors sought *(a)* first, to determine the persistence and/or change in the hierarchy of Arab university students' group affiliations from 1957-58 to 1970-71, *(b)* second, to see whether this hierarchy is affected by the sex, religion, or political orientation of the subjects, and *(c)* third, in the light of drastic recent developments which have been sweeping the Palestinian community since the Arab-Israeli war of June 1967, to look for possible differences in group affiliations between Palestinian Arabs and other Arabs.

Besides the above which are mainly of interest to scholars of the area, this study may be of importance to the current theories of culture change. Doob (1) in his major empirical study of the psychological consequences of "becoming more civilized" mentions the relative stability of "central" behavior, which refers to beliefs and values that serve continuing personality needs, and to "segmental" behavior which changes more readily because it is not directly involved with personality needs. Hence if we find that the family retains its primary position in the hierarchy of loyalties of our *S*s, it would provide further evidence for Doob's finding regarding the retention of traditional attitudes towards family forms and practices until or even beyond the occurrence of central change within them and their society (1, p. 112). Again, if we find an improvement in the position of the political party on the hierarchy of loyalties, it would be in line with Doob's finding regarding the antagonism towards traditional leaders as a result of central (or social) change. This study could also be of relevance to social reinforcement theories in the sense that the higher the group on the hierarchy of loyalties the greater its social reinforcement to the person.

B. Method

1. Subjects

The sample used in this study consisted of 114 undergraduate Arab students at the American University of Beirut who volunteered to respond to our call to take the questionnaire during the academic year 1970-71. Approximately 70 percent of the subjects in this sample came from Lebanon, Jordan (including Palestinians), and Syria (as compared to about 75 percent in the 1957-58 samples), while the remainder of the subjects came from Bahrain and Kuwait. Out of the total 1970-71 sample of 114 subjects, about 28 percent of the subjects identified themselves as Palestinians, and about 31 percent of the sample were Lebanese. The age range of this sample at last birthday was from 16 to 25 years with a mean of 20.47 years and a standard deviation of 2.08 (compared to an age range of 17–31 years, a mean of 21.32 years, and a standard deviation of 3.07 for the 1957 sample). Further comparisons between the 1957-58 sample and the 1970-71 sample show that while the former consisted of 59 percent Christians, 72 percent males, and 73 percent politically oriented, the latter consisted of 49 percent Christians, 68 percent males, and 72 percent politically oriented subjects, thus pointing to the lack of any appreciable differences in the composition of the samples. Furthermore, the same method used in the earlier study for obtaining subjects was followed also in the present study.

2. Procedure

The same questionnaire used in 1957-58 (2) was administered again to the sample in this study in 1970-71. In addition to obtaining background information about the subjects' sex, age, citizenship, religious affiliation, and national (ethnic) origin, subjects were also asked to indicate whether they belonged to an organized political party (or movement) or subscribed to a particular political ideology, with the option to withhold names if they so wished. Subjects who answered in the affirmative are referred to as "politically oriented," while those who stated that they neither belonged to a political party nor subscribed to a political ideology are referred to as "nonpolitically oriented."

The questionnaire consisted of 42 items or questions. Each question pointed to the attainment of a goal involving either affiliation with or loyalty to one out of five major groupings: namely, family (F), national (ethnic) origin (N-E), religion (R), citizenship (C), and political party (PP). Two additional goals were also included: namely, securing a job or having a mate, thus making up a total of seven goal-seeking situations covered by the 42 items in the questionnaire and distributed as follows: six items for each of the goals involving national (ethnic) origin, citizenship, and political party; three items for each of the goals involving family and religion; and, finally, nine items for each of the goals involving securing a job or having a mate.

For each question or item, the goal could be attained by the subject only by giving up one of two alternatives from among the five major groupings which were pitted against each other. The following two items are illustrative:

> 1. If to show your loyalty to your nation: *(a)* You were forced to give up your religion permanently, both in private and in public, or *(b)* You were forced to give up your family and never see them again. Which would you choose? *(a)*____ *(b)*____.
>
> 2. If in order to join a certain political party: *(a)* You were forced to give up your religion permanently, both in private and in public, or *(b)* You were forced to become a permanent exile from the country to which you belonged. Which would you choose? *(a)*____ *(b)*____.

In the 42 alternative forced choices presented in the questionnaire, family and political party each appeared 17 times, religion was paired 20 times, national (ethnic) origin appeared 12 times, and, finally, citizenship was paired 18 times.

The same scoring procedure used previously (2) was also followed here. Thus, the choice of an alternative in a question meant a greater preference for the other alternative. In the first item illustrated above, a subject choosing *(a)* gets a score of 1 for *(b)*—i.e., for family. The total number of scores given to each of the five major groupings under the same goal-seeking situation gives the subjects' preference scores for each of the groups under that situation. The sum of the preference scores for each of the five groupings, across the seven goal-seeking situations, gives a full picture of the subject's relative preference scores for each of the five major groupings under study. However, in order to equalize the subject's preference scores for each of the five groupings, the group preference scores were divided by the number of times each grouping appeared as an alternative choice. The ranking of the equated scores for each subject enabled us to calculate the number of times each of the five groupings was ranked 1 to 5 by the subjects and also to combine the frequencies of ranks 1, 2, and 3 into a "high" score and ranks 4 and 5 into a "low" score, thus permitting the calculation of chi-square values. Also, on the basis of the frequencies of ranks 1 to 5 given by the subjects for each of the five major groupings, median scores of ranks were computed.

C. Results

The main results of this study involve comparisons between the 1957-58 samples and the present 1970-71 sample, as well as comparisons of some subgroupings within the 1970-71 sample.

Comparisons of the rankings given by our subjects to the five major groups in 1957 and in 1971, based on the relative magnitudes of the median scores of ranks for each group, point to stability in the importance of some group affiliations, as well as to change in some others. Thus, the primary importance of the family, followed by national (ethnic) affiliation, relative to the other group affiliations, is still maintained, and even strengthened, regardless of the sex, religion, or political interest of the subjects. The changes that have taken place from 1957 to 1971 relate to the remaining three group affiliations, whereby the importance of citizenship and particularly of political party increased at the expense of religious affiliation which relatively became the least important. More specifically, political party affiliation became significantly more important (χ^2 = 8.10, significant at the .01 level when evaluated at *df* = 1) and religion became significantly less important (χ^2 = 8.74, significant at the .01 level when evaluated at *df* = 1) from 1957 to 1971 for the samples as a whole.

Dividing the subjects in 1957 and in 1971 according to sex, religion, and political orientation shows again that no significant changes have occurred between 1957 and 1971 with respect to family and to national (ethnic) affiliation, regardless of the sex, religion, or political orientation of the subjects. With respect to citizenship, the only significant difference which was found (χ^2 = 3.86, significant at the .05 level for *df* = 1) was the tendency for Arab male students to rank citizenship significantly higher in 1971 compared to 1957, while no significant differences in ranking of citizenship over the same period of time were found for females, Christians or Moslems, and politically or nonpolitically oriented subjects. However, a number of significant differences in the rankings of political party and of religion were found. Thus, on the one hand, there were significantly higher rankings given to political party in 1971, compared to 1957, by females (χ^2 = 13.14, significant at the .001 level for *df* = 1), Christians (χ^2 = 11.54, significant at the .001 level for *df* = 1), politically oriented subjects (χ^2 = 3.98, significant at the .05 level for *df* = 1), and nonpolitically oriented subjects (χ^2 = 6.11, significant at the .02 level for *df* = 1), while no significant differences were found for males and for Moslems. On the other hand, there were significantly lower rankings given to religion in 1971, compared to 1957, by males (χ^2 = 6.87, significant at the .01 level for *df* = 1), Christians (χ^2 = 8.61, significant at the .01 level for *df* = 1), and politically oriented subjects (χ^2 = 7.87, significant at the .01 level for *df* = 1), while no significant differences were found in the case of females, Moslems, and nonpolitically oriented subjects.

Dividing the subjects in 1971 according to sex, religion, and political orientation shows that the only significant difference obtained is that relevant to political party which was given significantly higher ranking by the politically oriented than by the nonpolitically oriented subjects (χ^2 = 4.21, significant at the .05 level for *df* = 1), similar to the findings arrived at for within-group comparisons in the 1957 sample. All other differences in frequencies of "high" and "low" rankings for all five groups based on subdivisions of the sample in terms of differences in sex, religion, and political orientation, both in 1957 and in 1971, were not found to be significant.

Finally, comparisons of group affiliations were made within the 1971 sample between Palestinian Arabs, both politically oriented and nonpolitically oriented, and politically oriented other Arabs. It was found that both nonpolitically oriented Palestinians and politically oriented other Arabs ranked family first in importance, followed by national (ethnic) origin, citizenship, political party; and, finally, religion was ranked last in order of preference. In contrast to this hierarchy of group affiliations, politically oriented Palestinians ranked national (ethnic) origin as first in importance, followed by family, then political party, citizenship; and, finally, religion was also considered least important.

Further comparisons between Palestinian Arabs, both politically oriented and nonpolitically oriented, and politically oriented other Arabs show that the only significant differences between these subgroupings were with respect to political party. More specifically, a larger proportion of politically oriented Palestinians gave significantly higher rankings to political party than nonpolitically oriented Palestinians (χ^2 = 3.043, significant at approximately the .09 level at *df* = 1) and than politically oriented other Arabs (χ^2 = 2.571, significant at the .05 level for *df* = 1).

D. Discussion

The results of this study indicate that stability rather than change has characterized the hierarchy of group affiliations of Arab university students from the late fifties to the early seventies.

With the exception of a significantly higher ranking given to citizenship by males in 1971 compared to 1957, no other significant differences were found between 1957 and 1971 in the relative importance given to family, national (ethnic) origin, and citizenship by subjects in both samples, and irrespective of the sex, religion, and political orientation of the subjects. Family still ranked first in commanding the loyalties of our subjects, followed by national (ethnic) affiliation as still second in importance, with a slight but not significant (except in the case of males) improvement in the ranking of citizenship which changed from fourth to third place. Also, both in 1957 and in 1971, only political party was given significantly larger rankings by politically oriented than by nonpolitically oriented subjects; all other within-sample differences, both in 1957 and in 1971, were not found to be significant.

However, significant changes were found to occur between 1957 and 1971 with respect to the relative importance of the remaining two group affiliations. Political party affiliation became significantly more important, particularly for females, Christians, and politically oriented, as well as nonpolitically oriented subjects, while religious affiliation became significantly less important, particularly for males, Christians, and politically oriented subjects. Consequently, the basic change occurring in the hierarchy of group affiliations of our subjects from 1957 to 1971 is one involving a significant decrease in the importance of religious affiliation accompanied by a significant increase in the importance of political party affiliation.

The above change in the hierarchy of group affiliations can best be understood within the context of changing social and political factors affecting the Arab Middle East in general, and the Lebanese community in particular, during the period extending from 1957-58 to 1970-71.

During the late fifties, the Arab world was polarized around the issue of Arab unity, particularly as exemplified by the United Arab Republic. In Lebanon, there was a civil war in 1958 and, though the factors involved in this war were many, it was evident that one of the warring factions was supported by the United Arab Republic and that this faction consisted predominantly, though by no means exclusively, of Moslems. The other party to the conflict, opposed to the United Arab Republic and to its policies and principles, consisted predominantly, though again not exclusively, of Christians. Thus, at the time of collecting our first set of data in 1957-58, sectarianism was so much situationally aroused and so salient a factor to most of our subjects that it ranked third in importance in the hierarchy of group affiliations of our subjects. It would be also relevant in this connection to mention that, in the eyes of many Christians, Arab unity implied a Moslem majority. Within such a general social and political context, the relative importance accorded to religious affiliation by our subjects in 1957-58 becomes quite understandable.

However, by 1970-71 the above situation has changed considerably. The decline in thrust towards Arab unity, accompanied by a unanimous concern with facing a common external enemy, contributed to the fading away of the previous polarization which characterized the Arab world in the late fifties and early sixties, and consequently helped to improve relations between the various Arab states and to render divisions along sectarian lines rather difficult to materialize, in spite of the possible benefits that some could reap from such divisions. Thus, in the late sixties and early seventies, the ebb of sectarianism was clearly apparent. It was within this general social context that our second set of data was collected in 1970-71, and the significant decrease in the importance given by our subjects to religious affiliation, which went down from third to fifth rank, becomes again understandable. Religious affiliation was not as socially reinforcing as before.

The results pertinent to comparisons between Palestinian Arabs and politically oriented other Arabs within the 1970-71 sample showed that while nonpolitically oriented Palestinians did not differ in their hierarchy of group affiliations from politically oriented other Arabs, both of these subgroupings differed from politically oriented Palestinians, whereby the latter showed stronger preferences to national (ethnic) origin and to political party affiliation. More specifically, politically oriented Palestinians were the only subgrouping who ranked national (ethnic) affiliation first rather than family; and they also ranked political party affiliation significantly higher than even the politically oriented other Arabs. When we examine closely the terms "national (ethnic) origin" and "political party affiliation" with reference to politically oriented Palestinians, it becomes clear that they both refer to highly related (though not necessarily identical) entities: namely, "Palestinian" or "Palestinian Arab" and "Palestinian Commando movement," respectively. A series of developments had characterized the Palestinian community since the 1967 Arab-Israeli war. Among these developments were such significant events as the emergence of the Palestinian Commando movements, the 1970 clamping down on Palestinians in Jordan by the government troops, the continual but interrupted clashes between Palestinians and the governments within both Lebanon and Jordan, and the continuous military raids by Israel against Palestinian refugee camps in Lebanon, Syria, and Jordan. The consequence of these events has been to crystallize the Palestinian identity and to heighten the awareness of the typical Palestinian concerning his national (ethnic) origin. In the light of these developments and their consequence, one's status as a Palestinian came to be the most important single aspect of his identity and, consequently, the one group affiliation that one considers as the most important in his whole being and the last one he would be willing to relinquish.

References

1. Doob, L. Becoming More Civilized. New Haven, Conn.: Yale Univ. Press, 1960.
2. Melikian, L. H., and Diab, L. N. Group affiliations of university students in the Arab Middle East. *J. Soc. Psychol.* 1959, **49,** 145–159.

3
Group Affiliations of University Students in the Arab Middle East (Kuwait)

Tawfic E. Farah

Summary

Family, national (ethnic) origin, and citizenship have been found to form the hierarchy of group affiliations among undergraduate students attending the American University of Beirut (AUB). Interestingly no significant differences were found between the results of the study conducted in 1957 and 1971.

A 36-item forced choice questionnaire was administered in October 1977, to a random sample consisting of 420 Arab undergraduate men and women at Kuwait University (KU). Mean age of the respondents was 21.48. Ninety-nine percent were Moslems.

The results indicate that Arab undergraduates representing 13 Arab states in addition to Palestinians attending KU ranked religion first in their hierarchy of group affiliations followed by family, citizenship, national origin, and political ideology, regardless of sex.

It is, however, understood that our findings cannot be generalized to other populations.

A. Introduction

A study published by Melikian and Diab in 1959 sought to determine the hierarchy of group affiliations of Arab university students at American University of Beirut (AUB). The authors also sought to assess whether such a hierarchy is affected differentially by sex, religion, or political interest of the *S*s. They found that "family ranked first with ethnic group, religion, citizenship, and political party in order of preference. No relationship was found between the order of hierarchy and the variables of sex, religion, and political orientation. A strong culture

Reprinted with permission from *Journal of Social Psychology* 106 (1978):161–165.

core was suggested as determining the hierarchy" (7, p. 159).

Fourteen years later the same investigators sought to determine *(a)* the persistence and/or change in the hierarchy of Arab university students' group affiliations from 1957-58 to 1970, *(b)* whether this hierarchy is affected by the sex, religion, or political orientations of the *S*s, and *(c)* possible differences in group affiliations between Palestinian Arabs and other Arabs in view of the drastic developments in the Palestinian community since the Arab-Israeli war of June 1967 (8).

We sought to replicate these two studies in a different cultural milieu. Lebanon, where the two studies were conducted, is not representative of other Arab countries. In addition the students at AUB have been the sons and daughters of Arab elites. Kuwait is also a unique Arab country (highest per capita income in the world). Yet, it is more representative of the majority of Arab countries in that it is predominantly a Moslem country. Lebanon was for a long time considered the Switzerland of the Middle East, a cosmopolitan place. Kuwait, in spite of its tremendous growth, is not.

The two institutions are also different. While AUB is a private institution, Kuwait University (KU) is not. Students in Kuwait pay nominal tuition and fees. Even though half the students at KU are Kuwaiti nationals, most other Arabs from some 15 Arab states are represented on campus. Many of these students are the children of well-to-do families but the majority are not. Before the Lebanese civil war, the well-to-do families in Kuwait who were Kuwaiti nationals or expatriates sent their children to AUB and universities in England and the United States and not to KU. This is still the case. Hence this study attempts to replicate the original two studies in a different setting. We suspected at the outset that our results would be different. This suspicion was based on the results of similar exploratory studies which have been undertaken in Kuwait and Lebanon (3, 4, 5, 6).

B. Method

1. Subjects

Every attempt was made to replicate the two previous studies, and the samples are comparable to a large degree. A stratified random sample was isolated for the purpose of this study, consisting of 420 undergraduate students at KU. The total population of the institution is 7,300 students. Master lists of the names of all students broken down by nationalities were obtained. Random samples totaling 30 each were isolated. Hence our sample includes students from Iraq, Kuwait, Saudi Arabia, the two Yemens, United Arab Emirates (U.A.E.), Egypt, Syria, Sudan, the Somali Republic, Lebanon, Jordan, Mauritania, and Palestine. Questionnaires were drawn up in Arabic. Each respondent filled out a questionnaire in his classroom. The study was conducted in October 1977 at KU. The ages of the *S*s ranged from 17 to 24 years with a mean of 21.48 years and a standard deviation of 2.09. Ninety-nine percent were Moslems and 63 percent were girls. Seventy-three percent considered themselves politically oriented.

2. Procedure

The questionnaire consisted of 36 items in addition to the usual questions which seek background information about the *S*s' sex, age, citizenship, religious affiliation, and national (ethnic) origin. Respondents were not asked to indicate if they belonged to a political party because political parties are outlawed in Kuwait. However, we allowed the *S*s to indicate on the forms if they subscribed to a particular political ideology or not. Since no names were required on the forms, we are fairly confident that most of those who subscribed to a particular ideology did indicate so. *S*s answering in the affirmative are classified as "politically oriented," the others as "nonpolitically oriented." Group affiliations were determined by a scale developed by Melikian and Diab (7, p. 149). Two items listed here are illustrative:

1. If to show your loyalty to your nation *(a)* You were forced to give up your religion permanently, both in private and in public, or *(b)* You were forced to give up your family and never see them again. Which would you choose?

2. If in order to subscribe to a political ideology *(a)* You were forced to give up your religion permanently, both in private and in public, or *(b)* You were forced to become a permanent exile from the country to which you belonged. Which would you choose?

A choice of an alternative in a question meant a greater preference for the other alternative. In the first question illustrated above, for example, a respondent choosing *(a)* gets a score of 1 for *(b),* i.e., for family. The total number of scores gives the respondents' preference scores.

C. Results

Most *S*s ranked religion first in their hierarchy of group affiliations, followed by family, citizenship (Kuwaiti, Palestinian, Syrian, etc.), national origin (Arab), and political ideology, regardless of the sex of the respondent.

Islam, the religion of most Arabs, seems to permeate the lives of our *S*s. They ranked it higher than family ($\chi^2 = 8.20$, $p < .01$). Family to our respondents, in contrast to the respondents in the Melikian and Diab studies, did not rank first but a clear second to religion ($\chi^2 = 8.36$, $p < .01$). In addition, the results do not agree with those of Melikian and Diab who found that citizenship and political party were gaining in importance at the expense of religious affiliation.

This latter finding holds true for all politically oriented respondents except for Palestinians ($\chi^2 = 3.85$, $p < .05$), Bahrainis ($\chi^2 = 3.92$, $p < .05$ level), and Southern Yemenis ($\chi^2 = 4.30$, $p < .05$). In the case of the Palestinians they ranked being Palestinian (citizenship) first, followed by political ideology, national origin, family, and religion. Politically oriented Bahrainis and Southern Yemenis ranked political ideology first, then citizenship, national origin, family, and religion.

D. Discussion

Islam was paramount in the lives of the vast majority of Arab undergraduate students attending Kuwait University. It does not seem to make any difference whether the student was from Saudi Arabia or Lebanon, a man or a woman. The only variable that seems to have made a difference was whether the *S* was politically oriented or not. Yet this variable seems to play a significant role only in the case of Palestinians, Bahrainis, and Southern Yemenis.

The Palestinians have lost Palestine but they do not seem to have lost their "Palestinianism." They identify with Palestine, a lost country and a country to be regained. They identify with each other as any persecuted minority would. To them it is apparent that one's religion, be it Islam or Christianity, did not help them in their conflict with the Israelis on the one hand and fellow Moslems (as in the case of the 1970 war in Jordan) on the other (2).

Yet this problem is not shared by politically oriented Bahraini students. Bahrain has had an active student opposition to its government in the last quarter of a century. As a result many Bahraini students tend to be highly politicized and ideological (1).

The Southern Yemenis come from a poor country. It is the only Marxist country in the Arab world. These politically oriented students are very well socialized to accept the need for a political party representing a certain ideology to develop that part of Yemen. Even though Southern Yemen is predominantly a Moslem country, the present government downplays religion (1).

Very few among our respondents immediately consider themselves Arabs. In fact they mentioned their citizenships first. It was assumed by many students of the Middle East that pan-Arabism and Arab Nationalism were forces to be reckoned with. In fact, many political parties which dominated Arab politics in the fifties and sixties were pan-Arab in nature (i.e., Nasserism, Arab Nationalist party, and Baath). Yet, inter-Arab feuding has apparently taken its toll. An Egyptian student among our respondents, for example, considered himself an Egyptian first and an Arab second. The same holds true for Palestinians, Kuwaitis, Bahrainis, etc.

Acknowledgments

This study is influenced a great deal by the pioneering work of Professors L. Melikian and L. Diab. I am indebted to Professor Michael Suleiman who commented on an earlier version of this paper.

References

1. Al-Salem, F. The role of ideology in the politicization of students of the gulf. Mimeo. Kuwait University, 1978.
2. Farah, T. Group affiliations of Palestinian students in Kuwait. Mimeo. Kuwait University, 1979.
3. ———. Aspects of Consociationalism and Modernization: Lebanon as an Exploratory Test Case. Lincoln, Nebraska: Middle East Research Group, 1975.
4. Farah, T., and Al-Salem, F. The traditionalism and modernization dichotomy: The cases of Lebanon and Kuwait. *J. Soc. Sci.,* 1976, **4,** 38–52.
5. ———. Alienation among Kuwaiti and non-Kuwaiti university students. *J. Gulf & Arab Peninsula Stud.,* 1976, **2,** 243–248.
6. ———. Political efficacy, political trust, and the action orientations of university students in Kuwait. *Internat. J. Middle East Stud.,* 1977, **8,** 317–328.
7. Melikian, L. H., and Diab, L. N. Group affiliations of university students in the Arab Middle East. *J. Soc. Psychol.,* 1959, **49,** 145–159.
8. ———. Stability and change in group affiliations of university students in the Arab Middle East. *J. Soc. Psychol.,* 1974, **93,** 13–21.

4
Group Affiliations of Arab University Students in the United States

Tawfic E. Farah

Summary

Family, national (ethnic) origin, and citizenship have been found to form the hierarchy of group affiliations among undergraduate students attending the American University of Beirut (AUB). Interestingly no significant differences were found between the results of the studies conducted in 1957 and in 1971. A study conducted in October 1977 among a random sample consisting of 420 Arab undergraduate men and women at Kuwait University (KU) indicates that Arab undergraduates representing thirteen Arab states in addition to Palestinians ranked religion first in their hierarchy of group affiliations. They ranked family second, followed by citizenship, national origin, and political ideology (regardless of the respondent's sex).

A 36-item forced choice questionnaire was administered in September 1981 to a random sample of 100 Arab undergraduate men and women attending California State University, Fresno (CSUF), who had spent at least two years in the United States. Mean age of the respondents was 21.68. Ninety-seven percent were Moslems and 15 percent were women.

The results indicate that these Arab undergraduates representing six states in addition to Palestine ranked religion first in their hierarchy of group affiliations, followed by political ideology, citizenship, national origin, and family.

It is, however, understood that our findings cannot be generalized to other populations.

A. Introduction

A study published by Melikian and Diab in 1959 sought to determine the hierarchy of group affiliations of Arab university students at AUB. The authors also assessed whether such a hierarchy is affected differentially by sex, religion, or political interest of the *S*s. They found that "family ranked first with ethnic group, religion, citizenship, and political party in order of rank. No relationship was found between the order of hierarchy and the variables of sex, religion, and political orientation. A strong culture core was suggested as determining the hierarchy" (4, p. 159).

Fourteen years later the same investigators sought to determine *(a)* the persistence and/or change in the hierarchy of Arab university students' group affiliations from 1957-58 to 1970-71, *(b)* whether this hierarchy is affected by the sex, religion, or political orientations of the *S*s, and *(c)* possible differences in group affiliations between Palestinian Arabs and other Arabs in view of the drastic developments in the Palestinian community since the Arab-Israeli war of June 1967 (5).

These two studies were replicated in a different cultural milieu, Kuwait (2).

This study attempts to replicate the previous studies in a different setting—the United States. Attention was focused on the undergraduate student who has spent a minimum of two years in the United States. It was suspected that some of the values, i.e. group loyalties, of these students would begin to change as a result of their stay in a Western urbanized environment.

B. Method

1. Subjects

Every attempt was made to replicate the three previous studies, and the samples are comparable to a large degree. A random sample consisted of 100 Arab undergraduate students attending CSUF. The sample was made up of male students from Lebanon, Kuwait, Saudi Arabia, Egypt, Jordan, Syria, and Palestine. They were all Moslems. The ages of the *S*s ranged from 18.5 to 25 years, with a mean age of 21.68 years and a standard deviation of 2.08.

2. Procedure

The questionnaire consisted of 36 items in addition to the usual questions that seek background information about the *S*s' sex, age, citizenship, religious affiliation, and national (ethnic) origin. Respondents were not asked to indicate if they belonged to a political party. However, they were asked to indicate on the forms if they subscribed to a particular political ideology or not. Since no names were required on the forms, we are fairly confident that most of those who subscribed to a particular ideology did so indicate. *S*s answering in the affirmative are classified as "politically oriented"; the others are "nonpolitically oriented." Group affiliations were determined by a scale developed by Melikian and Diab (4, p. 149). Two items listed here are illustrative:

1. If to show your loyalty to your nation *(a)* You were forced to

give up your religion permanently, both in private and in public, or *(b)* You were forced to give up your family and never see them again. Which would you choose?

2. If in order to subscribe to a political ideology *(a)* You were forced to give up your religion permanently, both in private and in public, or *(b)* You were forced to become a permanent exile from the country to which you belonged. Which would you choose?

A choice of an alternative in a question meant a greater preference for the other alternative. In the first question, for example, a respondent choosing *(a)* gets a score of 1 for *(b),* i.e., for family. The total number of scores gives the respondents' preference scores.

C. Results

Most *S*s ranked their religion, Islam, first in their hiearchy of group affiliations, followed by political ideology, citizenship (Kuwaiti, Palestinian, Syrian, etc.), national origin (Arab), and family (regardless of the nationality of the respondent).

Islam, the religion of most of these students, permeates their lives. It was ranked higher than family ($\chi^2 = 8.17$, $p < .01$). Family, in contrast to its standing in the 1977 responses of KU students, was ranked last. Political ideology was ranked a clear second to religion, followed by citizenship and national origin, by the politically oriented respondent. Among those who are not politically oriented, religion was ranked first, followed by citizenship, national origin, family, and political ideology.

D. Discussion

After a minimum of two years in the United States, the vast majority of Arab undergraduates attending CSUF still consider Islam paramount in their lives. Some tell us that they have become more devout Moslems in the United States than they were in their own home countries. Regularly they go to the mosque in the city of Fresno, California, socialize with other Moslems, and read Moslem periodicals. Their social lives revolve around the mosque, picnics, dinners, trips, and conventions. A word of caution is in order. Islam as these students practice it is not necessarily a reaction against modernity as it is at times described. On the contrary, being a good Moslem does not run contrary to one's desire for scientific and technical education (3, 6). This holds true for both politically oriented and nonpolitically oriented students. In the sixties and early seventies the politically oriented Arab students in the United States were followers of secular political ideologies, i.e., the Arab Nationalist movement, Baath Party, supporters of the different Palestinian guerrilla groups. This is not the case among the Arab undergraduates attending CSUF in 1981. Political orientation probably means that the student subscribes to a conservative Moslem ideology. He is a sympathizer or a member of one of many "Islamic political organizations." In Egypt, for example, we know of five such organizations: Moslem Brothers Association, Jamat al-Tafkir w'al-Hijra, Shabab Muhamad, Jund Allah, and al-Jama al-Islamiya. Moslem activism has appeared in Tunisia, Algeria, Syria, Kuwait, and Saudi Arabia as well as in the Gaza Strip. It does not seem to make any difference whether the student was from Saudi Arabia or Tunisia. This finding holds true for Palestinians too.

Very few among the *S*s consider themselves Arabs first. In fact they mentioned being Moslem first followed by a political ideology. Citizenship was third, followed by loyalty to one's national origin and family.

Of course, Islam is not experiencing a revival among these students because it really was never moribund. However, there seems to be politization of these students along Islamic lines. In addition, their language of politics is increasingly peppered with religious symbolism. Some of the *S*s resort to religious symbols as well. Many young men grow their beards in a supposedly traditional Islamic manner and many college-bound young women cover their heads and wear long dresses.

Finally, a word of caution: These findings should not be generalized to Arab students in the United States in general or Arab-American elites.

References

1. Dessouki, A. *Islamic Resurgence in the Arab World.* New York: Praeger Publishers, 1982.
2. Farah, T. Group affiliations of university students in the Arab Middle East (Kuwait). *J. Soc. Psychol.,* 1978, **106,** 161–165.
3. Ibrahim, Saad. Anatomy of Egypt's militant Islamic groups. *Internat. J. Middle East Stud.,* 1980, **12,** 423–453.
4. Melikian, L. H., and Diab, L. N. Group affiliations of university students in the Arab Middle East. *J. Soc. Psychol.,* 1959, **49,** 145–159.
5. ———. Stability and change in group affiliations of university students in the Arab Middle East. *J. Soc. Psychol.,* 1974, **93,** 13–21.
6. Stevens, R. Sudan's republic brothers and Islamic reform. *J. Arab Affairs,* 1981, **1,** 135–145.

5
Group Affiliations of Children in the Arab Middle East (Kuwait)

Tawfic E. Farah and Faisal Al-Salem

In 1959 and again in 1971, Melikian and Diab sought to determine the hierarchy of group affiliations of Arab students at the American University of Beirut. In the first study, they found that students ranked family first, followed by ethnic group, religion, citizenship, and political part in order of preference (3). No relationship was found between the order of hierarchy and the variables of sex, religion, and political orientation. In the second study, they found no major change in the order of preference for the group as a whole, although they did find some differences in ranking by sex and political affiliation of the students (4). In 1977 these two studies were replicated in a different cultural milieu, Kuwait, where university students ranked religion first, followed by family, citizenship, and national origin (1). On the basis of other studies in Kuwait, however, it was suspected that some group affiliations may be changing among younger students (2), and the present study was conducted in 1976-77 to determine the hierarchy of group affiliations in junior high school students in Kuwait.

A list of all 123 intermediate junior high schools in Kuwait was first drawn up. A stratified random sample of five girls' schools and five boys' schools was chosen. Master lists of all Kuwaiti boys and girls attending these schools were obtained, and a random sample of 500 boys and girls was isolated. *S*s were all Moslems, 11 to 16 years of age (mean age 13.8). Each *S* was interviewed individually in Arabic by a Kuwaiti during the academic year 1976-1977. The survey instrument was a mixture of open-ended and close-ended questions, story completions, and standard questions about the *S*s' sex, age, citizenship, and religious affiliations. Group affiliations were determined by a scale adopted from Melikian and Diab (3, p. 149).

Most *S*s regardless of sex ranked religion first in their hierarchy of group affiliations followed by citizenship (Kuwaiti), family, and national

Reprinted with permission from *Journal of Social Psychology* 111 (1980):141–142.

origin (Arab). Islam, the religion of most Arabs, seems to permeate the lives of the *S*s. They ranked it even higher than family ($\chi^2 = 8.10$, $p < .01$); in contrast to an earlier study (1, p. 164), family was not ranked second. Family loyalty appears to be declining while loyalty to one's state, Kuwait, appears to be gaining ($\chi^2 = 8.19$, $p < .01$), regardless of sex. Citizenship is gaining in importance at the expense of the family. Loyalty to the state (Kuwait) is gaining at the expense of loyalty to the Arab nation. Most *S*s consider themselves Moslems first, Kuwaitis second, and Arabs fourth. Familial affiliation is in third place.

These results—that group affiliations of Kuwaiti children seem to be changing from those of older university students—are not surprising given the direction and content of the political socialization efforts of the regime in Kuwait over the past 17 years, since the country gained its independence.

References

1. Farah, T. Group affiliations of university students in the Arab Middle East (Kuwait). *J. Soc. Psychol.,* 1978, **106,** 161–165.
2. ———. Political socialization of Kuwaiti children. Mimeo. Kuwait University, 1980.
3. Melikian, L. J. and Diab, L. N. Group affiliations of university students in the Arab Middle East. *J. Soc. Psychol.,* 1959, **49,** 145–159.
4. ———. Stability and change in group affiliations of university students in the Arab Middle East. *J. Soc. Psychol.,* 1974, **93,** 13–21.

Part II

Family, Religion, and Social Class

6

Oil and Social Change in the Gulf

Levon H. Melikian and Juhaina S. Al-Easa

I

The objective of this study is to report the findings of a survey conducted between 1974 and 1978 among Qatari college men and women students. The first part will describe the geographical, demographic, and cultural setting. It will emphasize relevant areas rather than attempt a comprehensive description of the Qatari culture. This will be followed by a description of some of the significant changes that have been observed in the Qatari family in the recent past starting from the year 1949, when the revenues from oil began to markedly accelerate the rate of change. In the third, and main, part of the study, the empirical data will be presented. In this section inter-sex comparisons of present attitudes, as well as comparisons with assumed traditional attitudes, will be made. Even though we cannot be sure that current attitudes held by our subjects will be translated into actual behavior in the future we assume, however, that their presence is an indication of change.

II

Qatar is an independent Moslem Arab state. It gained its independence in 1971 and was first admitted to membership of the Arab League and later the United Nations. Prior to independence a treaty with Britain "protected it" from other powers and took charge of its foreign relations. The country was never occupied in the classical sense. There was no British army of occupation and no British administration to speak of. All local administrative affairs remained in the hands of the ruling Al-Thani family with Britain keeping a low profile. The British were more interested in keeping other foreign powers out than in ruling the country.

The State of Qatar is situated on the west coast of the Arabian Gulf. A peninsula, it is one hundred miles long and ranges in width from thirty to fifty miles. It is four thousand square miles of flat, mostly

Reprinted with permission from *Journal of Arab Affairs* 1, no. 1 (1981):79–98.

arid land. Rainfall is scanty but enough to provide seasonal grazing grounds for the Bedu and their flocks.

The indigenous population is of pure Arab stock. It consists mainly of nomadic tribesmen who, over the years, had slowly become sedentarized and settled along the coast. They became fishermen, pearl divers, or traders—a few raised sheep and camels. There were a few non-Arabs in the country such as Indians and Iranians who were small traders, middlemen, and craftsmen. By 1970 the population had increased to 111,133, which was nearly equally divided between the indigenous population and expatriates. The annual rate in the increase of the indigenous population is estimated at 8 percent. This is attributed to an increase in the birth rate as well as to a liberal policy of naturalization whereby Arabs from the surrounding Gulf areas could take up Qatari citizenship. The increase in the number of expatriates, estimated to be 8.1 percent, was mainly due to the increasing demands for experts, professionals, teachers, laborers, and others who were needed for its development and industrialization programs. Expatriates not only brought their skills and services but also customs that have been copied by the local population. Though Qatar was never isolated from other cultures the present contact with foreigners is higher than at any other period of its history. Over 80 percent of the population is located in the capital, Doha, with the remainder, mainly the nationals, scattered in small towns and villages along the coast.

Although the local population is of pure Arab stock it is divided into two highly differentiated groups: descendants of the Bedouin tribes who still carry the name of their tribe and identify with it and who are known as the *qabail;* and the descendants of Arab tribes who have returned, in relatively recent times, from the west coast of Iran whence their ancestors had immigrated over the past two centuries or more. These had lost contact with their original tribes and are known as the *hawalah.* This phenomenon is not only characteristic of Qatar but also of the Gulf states of Bahrain, Kuwait, and the United Arab Emirates. Even though both the *qabail* and the *hawalah* are Arabs and Moslems they do not intermarry to any appreciable extent as the *qabail* consider themselves to be of a purer, and hence superior stock whose ancestry can be traced to the main tribes of their origin.

Since the early fifties Qatar has been enjoying a boom economy because of the spiraling increase in its oil revenues. These revenues are utilized to provide a free education up to the university level, free medical services, free electricity and water, low-cost housing as well as opportunities for work with a regular income, which their grandfathers never enjoyed. The present industrialization program being implemented is aimed at the diversification of the economy. It includes a gas liquification plant, an oil refinery, cement factory, flour mill, steel processing, plus other plans that provide for a petrochemical complex and the recovery of offshore natural gas. All of these developments have left their mark not only on the structure of society but on its way of life. In one way or other they will influence the structure and function of the family.

III

In Qatar, three levels of family structure exist. The tribe, clan, and family (extended) represent the three levels of the kinship system. Kinship shapes almost all the individual and group patterns of behavior. The net of relationships within this system extends to many generations and connects each tribe with its branches in areas outside of Qatar, mainly in Saudı Arabia, Kuwait, Bahrain, and the United Arab Emirates. The maintenance of these connections has made it possible for many tribal members to acquire Qatari citizenship in spite of their having been born or having resided outside the country. Tribal loyalties, if not family loyalties, however, are on the decline as a result of the demand of the urbanized society and an evolving modern state. People depend for their livelihood upon participation in a "modernized" oil economy rather than upon a pastoral economy of grazing and camel breeding with its jealously guarded tribal territories and rights.

The family, whether extended or conjugal, remains the basic unit in society and has acquired many of its salient features from Islam. Islam permeates almost every phase of life in Qatar. Its tenets govern every aspect of marriage, divorce, custodianship, inheritance, and other matters related to the family and its members. The family in Qatar, as in the other Gulf states, still remains to a very large extent the primary institution for economic and social control as well as for the protection of the rights of its members. It still retains, in varying degrees, the traditional characteristics of being patriarchal, extended, patrilineal, patrilocal, endogamous, and occasionally polygamous.

The large extended family was the dominant type. It consisted of grandfather, grandmother, their married sons with their wives and children, and their unmarried children all living under the same roof. Other relatives such as widowed daughters, unmarried paternal aunts, nephews, or cousins may also have lived in the same household. The running of the day-to-day activities of the house was generally under the direction of the grandmother while the grandfather and his sons were responsible for its economic affairs. The conjugal units living within the extended family were held by close emotional ties which were generally bolstered by mutual economic and social interests. It appeared to be a continuous unity that did not generally disintegrate with the death of the grandfather who was replaced by the eldest son.

Extended families living near each other were, and still are, generally related in that they belong to the same lineage, clan, or tribe. Al-Easa estimated that prior to the oil era, almost 50 percent of the families living close to each other were related. This figure, according to the same study, had dropped to 37 percent by 1975.[1] The tendency for proximal living of relatives is still reflected in the residential areas of the capital which are named after the clans or tribes which originally lived, or still reside, in them. It is more apparent in rural areas where a whole village may be inhabited by one or two clans only. The residential pattern of the extended family has somewhat changed. Whereas previously all members lived under one roof, the grandfather and each of his married sons now live in separate dwellings within one compound. They still share a common kitchen and a common *majlis* or guest room. The classical extended family is, however, on the decline with the nuclear family slowly replacing it as the dominant type.

Role and status are traditionally determined by age and sex. Men are considered to be superior to women and older people command more respect than younger ones. These criteria apply both within and outside the family circle. At the wider social level education and wealth have begun to assume a greater role in determining status. The husband is the provider who is responsible for the economic affairs of the family, while the wife is expected to take care of all domestic affairs. This role differentiation is clearly reflected in the following popular expression, used to congratulate a man on his marriage: "The money is from you and the children from her." Playing these roles not only enhances the status of each but also reinforces the marital bond. Among the more conservative sections of the population all shopping, whether for food or clothing, is made by the husband or an older son. Women are not supposed to go to the marketplace or leave their house unless they are accompanied by their husband or son. The role differentiation is further reinforced by the segregation of the sexes at the age of ten. However, variations from this strict code are slowly becoming more common.

Relationships between husband and wife, parents and children, and between siblings themselves, are characterized by a hierarchical power structure that reflects the role-status pattern described in the previous paragraph. Simply stated the young are expected to obey the old and the females are expected to obey the males. A study conducted by Melikian in Saudi Arabia, a country which is not only adjacent to Qatar but shares the same culture, religion, and oil economy with it, provides us with empirical information about this point. The study was designed to answer the following question: which status category in the family obeys the others more frequently? The respondents were college students in Saudi Arabia who had never left the country. The results showed the following hierarchy from "Obeys others least" to "Obeys others most":

> Father, eldest son, eldest daughter, mother, husband, youngest son, youngest daughter, and wife.

The above represents the ranking of means of each status category. The only significant differences were between the means of the father and all others except the eldest son, and between the eldest son and the other categories. When the same study was conducted on another group of Saudi students at the same university, who had lived outside of Saudi Arabia for a minimum of one year or more, the mother shared the peak of the hierarchy with the father and the eldest son.

These findings seem to indicate very clearly that the concentration of power—power being defined as obeying others least—is in the hands of the father and the eldest son in the traditional families while among the exposed families—those who have resided abroad—the mother's position is equal to that of the father and to that of the eldest son. The position of the eldest son may have been enhanced by his level of education which far exceeds that of his father. In fact most of the fathers in this study did not have more than three years of schooling.[2]

The father's authority extends to many areas. He not only controls the money but decides who his sons and daughters are to marry, who they can mix with, and when to change their place of residence. The authority of the mother is restricted to the house within which a hierarchy of power also exists. The mother exercises her authority over her daughters-in-law, her unmarried daughters, and grandchildren. But most students of the Arab family seem to feel that the wife, in her own way, wields more authority over husband and children than is commonly recognized.

Authority and power patterns are not, however, the only basis for relationships within the family. Respect, love, and mutual understanding between the different members are common. A young married couple is not in love but grows into it over the years. Fathers and sons accept and respect each other. Children accept the authority of the father without perceiving it as a threat to their egos, while the relationship between mothers and sons is an intense and tender one. Sons remember their fathers for their achievements, sacrifice, and courage, while they remember their mothers for their sacrifice, love, and tenderness.

The Qatari family plays a major role in the socialization of its children. It provides them with a social orientation from childhood and throughout their lives. Where the child is raised in an extended family setup, grandparents, uncles, and aunts, as well as his parents, contribute to his socialization. Strong emphasis is placed on training a child to conform to the patterns laid down by his elders. Corporal punishment is employed as well as withdrawal of privilege. Fathers become active in bringing up their sons between the ages of 5 and 7. At that time the father starts taking his son along to the *majlis,* the guestroom, in which the elders and men of the family and their male guests congregate in the evenings. They may discuss family problems, current events, resolve family quarrels, listen to the old men recount their experiences, or discourse upon religion and morals. When ten urban and twenty rural fathers were asked why they took their children to the *majlis* they all answered by saying that "it is the place where he learns our manners and customs and emulates the adults around him and learns from their experiences." The *majlis* is an informal school where the boy child learns how to listen, and how to perform the rituals of hospitality with his father. The father also takes his sons to the mosque to join other men in prayers. Here the child experiences a sense of a community which extends beyond the confines of the family. As the boy grows older he is encouraged to participate in communal activities but mainly with children from the same family and clan. As the boy grows up he may accompany his father to work, or go on errands for him or his mother. These responsibilities increase with age.

The mother in her turn sees to it that her daughter grows up into an adult who can play the role prescribed by society. By the age of seven she is given simple household duties, which progressively become more difficult. She is told that she will have to serve and respect not only her husband, but her in-laws and other kin living in the same house. Her upbringing revolves primarily around preparing her to play the role of wife and mother in accordance with the expectation of the culture.

Even though no definite studies have been made on the socialization of the Qatari child it can be legitimately said that the process instills conformity and docility. In addition religious injunctions teach that obedience to parents and grandparents comes second to obedience towards God and the Prophet.

The school does complement the work of the family in socialization although at times it seems to be in conflict with it. This becomes evident in the wide gap in the level of education between parents and children, and the relative absence of any communication between the two. Mass media, especially television, of which Qatari children are fond, is also diminishing the role of the family as an agent of socialization.

With the growing affluence in the country many parents, not only among the wealthy, are employing foreign women as maids and "nannies" for their children. This new status symbol could, in the long run, have an effect on the raising of Qatari children. The institution of the "nanny" ought to be investigated as another agent of socialization.

IV

Marriage in Qatar, as in other Moslem countries, is perceived to be a religious duty. Parents see to it that their children—sons and daughters—marry early to a spouse of equal descent, and do not feel at ease until they see all their children married. They would also like to live to see their grandchildren and be involved in raising them. They feel more adequate as parents and more esteemed by the community once they have achieved these two goals. Marriages tend to be arranged by the parents rather than the young people and at times it appears as if it is an arrangement between two families rather than an arrangement between the couple. The procedure generally begins when the son is able to support a wife and expresses his desire for marriage. The girl on the other hand does not initiate this procedure but is given a chance to accept or reject her suitor. Early marriages, especially for girls, are common. The average women marry men who are between 5 and 10 years older than they are.

Preference is given first to marriges contracted within the extended family, next to a marriage within the lineage, followed by marriage within the tribe. Exogamous marriages are not particularly favored or condoned. Marrying from within the family insures that the principle or condition of equal descent is fulfilled. Thus a man ought to marry one of equal descent status, but if no such suitable spouse is available he may marry a woman of lower descent. Such a marriage is allowed because the children will take the descent status of their father and not of their mother. A woman, however, is never allowed to marry a man of a lower descent than herself though she may marry someone of a higher status. Descent takes precedence over wealth and an often quoted saying enjoins a woman to marry a man of good descent even though he may be poor. "Take a man of good descent even though you may live on a mat." This condition poses many problems for higher-status families who probably have a higher proportion of unmarried daughters than the general population. This problem becomes more serious when high-status men are better educated than the women. In fact it is believed that one reason for the establishment of girls' schools and colleges in the country was to counteract this problem. The concept of *kafaa* or quality in Islam includes more than descent—it refers to such things as religion, character, wealth, and the permission of the girl's parents or guardian for marriage.

The above principle does not mean that all spouses within the same status are considered equal. Internal divisions within the stratum mean that a man chooses a wife from a series of possible spouses graded in order of preference ranging from his patrilineal parallel cousin, father's brother's daughter to any other woman within the stratum. Preference for marriage from within the descent group is not, however, a religious injunction. It appears to have other roots that may be social or economic in origin.

How widespread is this practice? To answer this question 124 men and women college students were asked to indicate in which of the following ways their parents and grandparents were related: paternal cousin, maternal cousin, same lineage, same tribe, unrelated from another tribe. The results are shown in Table 1.

Assuming that the grandparents got married in the early thirties, it is evident that even before the oil era the pattern of paternal-cousin marriage was not prevalent.

V

How do young Qatari men and women perceive marriage? A filler item was introduced into a Sentence Completion Test designed to study the model personality of the Qatari. The stem of the sentence which the respondents were asked to complete was: "Marriage is _____." Fifty

Incidence of Marriage with the Descent Group

Table 1

	Parents (N = 124)		Grandparents (N = 123)	
	F	%	F	%
Paternal Cousins	13	10.48	16	13.01
Maternal Cousins	12	9.68	2	1.63
Same Lineage	35	28.23	42	34.15
Same Tribe	15	12.10	26	21.14
Another Tribe	49	39.51	37	30.08

men and thirty women responded to this. The results are presented in Table 2.

Qatari college students perceive marriage as inevitable. Most men are practical about it while the women tended to idealize it. More men than women see it as restricting their freedom. More men than women appear to be concerned with its sexual and procreative aspects. Almost all expect to get married and expect to remain monogamous.

The same group was asked to indicate the age at which they expected to get married. The men expect to get married at an average of 25.9 and the women at an age of 23.4 years as shown in Table 3.

How endogamous are they in their preferences and what are the personal attitudes they expect in their future spouse? Sixty-four men and 34 women students were asked to indicate which one of the

Perceptions of Marriage among Qatari College Students

Table 2

	Men (N = 50)		Women (N = 30)	
	F	%	F	%
1. Inevitable	21	42	14	47
2. Positive effect: security, success, bond.	16	32	12	40
3. Negative effect: problems, restrictive.	8	16	2	7
4. Sexual outlet and procreation	5	10	1	3
5. Unnecessary	---	---	1	3

Expected Age of Marriage among Qatari College Students

Table 3

	Average age	Range
Expected age of marriage:		
Women students (N = 38)	23.4	20-27
Men students (N = 73)	25.9	20-35

following they preferred to marry: paternal cousin, a close relative, from the same clan, from Qatar, from the other Gulf states, from other Arab countries, or a non-Arab. Their responses appear in Table 4.

These results show a striking difference between the attitudes of men and women. The first three categories show that 61 percent of the men preferred to marry either a paternal cousin, or someone from the same lineage or clan, while the remaining 39 percent preferred to marry an outsider.

By comparison only 24 percent of the women preferred to marry a relative while the remaining 76 percent opted for an exogamous marriage. The difference between the two groups is significant at the .001 level of confidence (Chi Square 14.2). It seems that the majority of the men are in favor of the traditional pattern of endogamous marriages whereas the women tend to prefer an exogamous one. It is doubtful, however, that these women will have the freedom to marry according to their preference.

Preferred Status of Marriage Partner

Table 4

	Men (N = 64)		Women (N = 34)	
	F	%	F	%
Paternal cousin	14	22	2	6
Close relative (lineage)	17	27	0	0
Same clan or tribe	8	12	6	18
Qatari (unrelated)	12	19	17	50
Gulf States	9	14	6	18
Arab country	4	6	3	8
Non-Arab	0	0	0	0

When a young man or woman expresses a desire to marry an "outsider" his elders generally quote this proverb: "The beauty of a *thaub* ("gown") is enhanced by a patch from the same material." In other words a stranger or a non-relative will not fit into the family and may disrupt its harmony. It is interesting to note that when young men are asked to spontaneously recall some proverbs almost 90 percent of them recall the above proverb first. Another proverb, often quoted by the young men, illustrates the already expressed preference of the women subjects: This proverb says "The female goats of the country prefer the foreign male goats." Folk wisdom, as expressed in this proverb, appears to be conscious of the preferences of the women.

Assuming that the respondents marry the partner of their choice, what are some of the personal qualities which they would like this person to have? To answer this, in a limited way, the same group of men and women were asked to rank three personal qualities in order of preference. The results in Table 5 show the proportion of men and women who ranked each statement first.

Some interesting differences appear. In the first place a larger proportion of women than men preferred the qualities of companionship and a pleasant disposition in their spouses. Secondly, over twice as many men want their future wives to share in their beliefs and opinions. The same proportions of men and women rank intelligence and common sense first. Over half the women emphasized pleasant disposition and companionship in a husband.

These indicators of the traditional attitudes of the men were further confirmed by their reaction to situations suggesting specific relationships between husband and wife. When the subjects were asked to choose one of two alternative questions seen in Table 6, significant differences

Preferred Qualities in Marriage Partner

Table 5

	Proportion ranking each statement	
	Men (N = 98)	Women (N = 100)
a. Shares my beliefs and opinions.	35	15
b. Intelligence and common sense.	29	30
c. Pleasant disposition and a good companion.	35	55

Attitudes toward Husband-Wife Relationship

Table 6

	Men (N = 99)		Women (N = 76)	
	F	%	F	%
1. (a) A man should feel closer to his wife.	44	63	33	87
(b) A man should feel closer to his family (father & mother)	26	37	5	13
2. (a) A wife should be allowed to make decisions on her own even though she disagrees with her husband.	15	21	27	71
(b) A good wife obeys her husband always.	58	79	11	29

were found between the two groups—with the men taking the more traditional position. The difference in both situations was significant at the .001 level of confidence (Chi Square 8.14 and 24.02).

Attitudes towards family size are shown in Table 7. Both men and women wanted fewer children than they expected to have, the difference being significant at the .05 level of confidence for both men and women (t = 2.28 for men and 2.27 for women). Men also appear to want and expect more children than women. Here again the difference is significant

Attitudes toward Family Size

Table 7

	MEN (N = 65)			WOMEN (N = 34)		
	Boys	Girls	Total	Boys	Girls	Total
Expected	2.56	1.92	4.48	1.88	1.68	3.56
Wanted	2.20	1.55	3.75	1.29	1.09	2.38

at the .01 level in the case of expecting ($t = 3.22$) and the .05 level in the case of wanting ($t = 2.33$). Both men and women also appear to expect and want more boys than girls with the trend being more marked in the case of the men. Qatari college students neither expect nor want as many children as their parents had. Seventy-nine percent of the men and 82 percent of the women in this study indicated they favor limiting the number of children. If this finding is valid it means that the number of Qataris would decrease in the future. Such a condition is not in the interest of a country where nationals are already outnumbered by the expatriates.

VI

The findings are summarized as follows:

1. More men than women see marriage as a practical and inevitable event in their lives, an event that restricts their freedom. While women also see the inevitability of marriage, more of them tend to idealize and romanticize it. They visualize it as a mutual bond, a companionship, which contributes to the security of the couple.
2. Men still prefer to marry at the same age as their fathers did. The age of the women they prefer to marry is considerably less than the age at which women themselves prefer to get married.
3. Most of the men prefer to marry a relative, from within the tribe, who shares their opinions and ideas, while most of the women prefer to marry a non-relative, from outside the tribe, who has a "pleasant disposition" and who will be a "good companion."
4. Both men and women expect to have more children than they would like to have. Men seem to want more children than women.
5. Most of the attitudes of the women towards the issues studied are less traditional than those held by the men. College women appear to press for a more egalitarian status with the men—at least within the context of the family.

What does the future hold for the family in Qatar and other Gulf States. Here are some projections:

1. The extended family in its traditional form will be replaced by the nuclear family.
2. As a result of increasing education and consequent economic independence from their fathers, most if not all young men would upon marriage live in separate households. The trend for proximal living will, however, continue for some time.
3. Both young men and women will insist on getting to know each other before getting married. Arranged marriages will not be acceptable to the young couples.
4. Though not widespread at present, polygamous marriages will continue to decrease.
5. College-educated women will try to delay marriage dates until

they graduate. College-educated men who claim that they would prefer to marry a girl with the same education level may come to accept marrying a girl closer to them in age. The age differences between husband and wife will decrease, with women marrying at an older age than their mothers did.

6. Judging by the attitudes of young men, endogamy in a modified form will continue. There will be fewer paternal-cousin marriages and fewer marriages from within the same lineage. The shift will be towards marrying from within one's tribe and one's country.

7. Young married couples will have fewer children than their parents did. The consequences of a reduction in the birth rate among the indigenous population may not be in the interest of the country.

8. Women will strive for a more egalitarian partnership in the family.

The above projections are not necessarily limited to Qatar only. Change in the predicted directions has been documented by Goode,[3] Melikian,[4] and by Prothro and Diab[5] for the modern Arab family, and has been observed among the Rwala Bedouins by Musil[6] as far back as 1928. An intensification and broadening of these changes is apparent. The important question, however, relates to the function of the family. Will the family in Qatar continue to remain a source of security and support to the individual as it changes into the nuclear type? How will loyalty and closeness to family members be demonstrated? Will nepotism, for example, diminish? If it does, will this be due to a change in the family or to an emergence of a modern state? Will endogamy decrease because of changes in attitudes or because segregation will become less strict and the young people from different sectors will have a chance to meet each other? What will happen to all the projections should the oil wells run dry?

The less traditional attitudes which the respondents possess have been triggered by the oil industry (industrialization), sedentarization, urbanization, and by education. They are also being reinforced by the mass media and the increasing contact with foreigners and exposure to different ways of life. Since the holders of these attitudes are the future leaders in the country they will in all probability be emulated and thus become the initiators and carriers of change.

Notes

1. Juhaina S. Al-Easa, "Acculturation and the Changing Family Structure in Qatar," unpublished Masters Degree Thesis (Cairo: Cairo University, 1975).

2. Levon H. Melikian, "Modernization and the Perception of the Power Structure in the Saudi Arab Family," paper presented at the International Congress of Applied Psychology, Munich, 1978.

3. W. J. Goode, *A World Revolution and Family Patterns* (New York: The Free Press, 1970).

4. Levon H. Melikian, "Attitudes of Married Women Towards Marriage

and Children: An Exploratory Study," unpublished manuscript (Doha, Qatar: University of Qatar, 1976).

5. E. T. Prothro and Lutfy Diab, *Changing Family Patterns in the Arab East* (Beirut: American University of Beirut, 1974).

6. Alois Musil, *The Manners and Customs of the Rwala Bedouins* (Prague: Czech Academy of Sciences and Arts, 1928).

7
The Emerging Islamic Order: The Case of Egypt's Contemporary Islamic Movement

Fadwa El Guindi

I

Since the beginning of the nineteenth century, intellectual sociopolitical thought in Egypt and elsewhere in the Islamic East was dominated by the opposition between secularist Egyptian nationalism and Islamism. Controversy between nationalists and Islamists was represented by distinguished leaders of theory whose proponents kept the debate alive long after its inception.[1] With the Egyptian Revolution of 1952, Nasir's Arabist socialism replaced nationalism as the dominant secularist political ideology, which, as it subdued Islamism, gained much appeal in most of the Third World and particularly within the Arab world itself.

The new ideological polarity—Arabist socialism versus Islamism—then became the framework and focus of debate by intellectuals and ideologists. The misleading assumption underlying recognition and acceptance of this polarity is that the two phenomena have equal ontological status. As ideology, therefore, it is believed that there could either be Arabism or Islamism dominating the character of policy and thought; they are mutually exclusive and hence cannot co-exist.

Therefore, according to this viewpoint the two are seen as ideological forces competing with each other. To those favoring secularist ideology the emerging local assertiveness and international visibility of Islam poses a threat. First, they see Arabist ideology as being challenged by Islam's renewed strength and growing appeal. Second, since secularists view Islamism as an ideological obstacle to social change and progress, these recent developments are seen as threatening hopes for, and goals of, modernity.

Analysis of the recently gathered data[2] in Egypt on the contemporary Islamic Movement challenges these assumptions and the prevalent view

Reprinted with permission from *Journal of Arab Affairs* 1, no. 2 (1981):245–261.

that considers Arabism and Islamism as mutually exclusive. It alternatively suggests an orientation which deals with Islam neither in structural opposition to Arabism nor as empirical alternative to it, since the two are not of equal ontological status. It is argued that such presumed equality is inherent to an orientation which focuses on phenomena exclusively as ideology. A significant difference is found to exist between the two phenomena both in terms of ontological status and content, and this difference reveals a complementarity between Islamism and Arabism rather than the commonly assumed polarity.

The case of Egypt will be used to discuss the ways in which the two phenomena differ and clarify the nature of their complementarity. The focus will be on the content of Islamism as revealed in the analysis of the contemporary Islamic Movement, specifically on two fundamental features: the unprecedented active role of women in the movement and the concomitant formation of a Muslim ethic. These will be reviewed in the context of the nature of Islam and its dynamic character, and the role for Muslims in social change in Egypt and in redefining an emerging sociocultural order in the Middle East today.

Although the focus of this analysis is the contemporary movement, the general phenomenon is not a recent and novel development independent of earlier events. The historical dimension is relevant. Islamic movements are rooted in Islamic history and more directly in Egyptian Islam. However, its official birth in Egypt occurred when *Jama'it al-Shubban al-Muslimun* (society for male Muslim youth) was founded in 1927, in which Hassan al-Banna was very active.[3] In 1928 al-Banna founded what became the major society, *Jama'it al-Ikhwan al-Muslimun* (society for Muslim Brothers). Subsequently, other societies and splinter societies were formed.

Although there is affinity between the contemporary movement and earlier developments, it would be an oversimplification to consider the contemporary movement simply as a revival of earlier forms. Features characteristic of the contemporary movement reflect significant change that can be understood adequately only if analyzed in sociocultural context.

To achieve adequate understanding of the Islamic Movement as a unified phenomenon, two levels—formal and informal—must be explored. The informal level is particularly rich in data very relevant for understanding local-level reality. It is unfortunate that generally the local-level reality tends to receive less, if any, systematic attention from scholars of Islam; it is either dismissed as not serious or skipped because of its invisibility and absence of concreteness. It is also quite true that researchers often lack familiarity with the methodology most suitable and productive for the study of informal domains of human experience. As a result data on informal aspects of Islamic movements are scarce.

To bridge this gap, a systematic examination of the informal aspects of the contemporary movement expressed in the form of a community of *al-mitdayyinin* will be attempted.

II

The general topic of Islamic movements is timely and there is an explosion of speculative and scholarly work about it confusing superficially similar phenomena. Accordingly, I must first identify the specific phenomenon of analysis. The empirical and systematic data-gathering base makes it possible to isolate and analytically distinguish three phenomena that are otherwise dealt with as monolithic.

The mainstream core of the movement is to be distinguished from two phenomena commonly blurred with it: (1) the general religious revival which is not Islam-specific occurring in Egypt following the war of 1967; and (2) the later militant outbursts by groups of men and women who are members of specific Islamic societies. This militant component is an aspect within the broader umbrella of alternative Islamic activity but is distinguishable from, and secondary to, the mainstream movement which is the subject of this analysis. To clarify the basis upon which these two phenomena, religious revival and militant component, are separated from the primary unit of analysis, I will first discuss the criteria of differentiation for each, respectively, and subsequently move to the focus of this analysis, namely *al-gama'a* (the community or the society) and *al-mitdayyinin* (the religieux/religieuses).

Whereas the general religious revival can be shown to be a direct response to the 1967 Arab-Israeli war, the Islamic Movement is a separate and more complex development. Major visible manifestations of the movement clearly appeared after the 1973 Ramadan war. Whatever the link, however, according to this analysis the Islamic Movement, unlike the link made between the religious revival and the 1967 war, is not considered to be a direct response to the 1973 Ramadan war.

Religious revival is defined here in terms of four factors. First, the 1967 war was locally acknowledged as a defeat, and reaction to it was general for Muslims and Copts alike. Second, the symbolism in the dramatic event of the public appearance of the image of the Virgin Mary several months after the war was also general.[4] Like the religious revival itself, the symbolism of this event was not confined to one religious group or class. It involved Copts and Muslims from all urban segments of Egypt. Third, the difference between religious revival and the Islamic Movement as two separate phenomena is locally recognized and consciously verbalized. Finally, the religious revival resembles spontaneous mass responses of similar nature under similar widespread and documented circumstances.

III

Since it is misleading to generalize about the Islamic Movement in Egypt on the basis of a few militant outbursts, the differential character of each of the two phenomena upon which the analytic separation is based will be made.

A prime example of the militant component is the widely publicized case of recent violence in Egypt by a group named *Gama'it al-Takfir wal-Higra* (society of repentance and flight).

Information in the media described this group as having lived as a communal cult in which interactional, organizational, and behavioral rules were rigid, standards inflexible, and goals utopian. Marriage occurring during its brief existence was endogamous and according to *'urf* (common law) and polygynous for the leader.

Although this describes a specific Islamic group, undoubtedly its general orientation places it as an alternative movement to the Islam of the *'Ulama,* or Establishment Islam. It is a movement from below, by and for non-elitist elements, building an alternative to elitist Islam.

At this general level of an alternative Islamic ideology the militant component shares with the mainstream Islamic Movement the notion of separateness from Institutional Islam. Otherwise the militant component separates itself from the mainstream alternative Islam on the basis of a distinct social organization, the nature of its leadership, and the goals and tactics for bringing about change in society.

To be specific, whereas the mainstream core of the movement is invisibly bounded via its ideology and conceptual formulation without any physical isolation of its membership, the militant component is concretely bounded by its physical retreat from both mainstream society and the mainstream movement, led by a male leader with a strong charismatic personality, surrounded and followed by devotees, both men and women, who are completely overwhelmed by his ideas.

At the foundation of this communal retreat is an attitude of strong discontent with, and intolerance of, existing political, economic, social, and moral trends. Growing Westernism is seen as leading to moral sexual laxity; increasing materialism to personal and institutional corruption; modernism to decreasing respect for tradition and moral authority. This, coupled with a growing passivity of Establishment Islam and elitism of authority, leads to militancy which becomes a unique and effective method to bring about the desired change. Roger Bastide, in his study of messianic movements, describes similar manifestations as escape into utopia. He sees it as a stage in which it ceases to be a "movement" and becomes a "sect," characterized by rigidity and separation from mainstream society. This observation is applicable to the Egyptian militant component of the Islamic Movement. As it grows more militant, it becomes less and less tolerated by the authorities, its efforts will be aborted, and its goals are not met. Its life-style is considered radical by standards of mainstream society, and it is seen as disrupting traditional life and challenging meaningful values. Ironically, it is neither favorably regarded nor supported by the mainstream movement. Hence, it is the core of the movement, the subject of this analysis, which remains strong and continues to grow, gaining popular appeal at all corners of urban society.

Having distinguished the two phenomena, religious revival and militant component, from the core Islamic Movement, the core needs to be identified and explicated. According to Mahfouz, who has carried out research focussing on the militant "in captivity," one needs to distinguish *al-Jama'a al-Islamiyya* (the Islamic society) from other *jama'at diniyya* (religious societies also for Muslims) and be aware that *al-Jama'a* itself is not one group but many; that is, there are *jama'at Islamiyya* (Islamic societies).[5]

On the other hand, Hanafi views *al-Jama'a al-Islamiyya* as "one umbrella under which all Islamic activities are involved, all Muslim groups. . . ."[6] The difference between the two views is interesting.

What is at issue here is the difference between a literal perspective which considers each concrete grouping as a separate *jama'a* (society), versus an ideational perspective which groups all concrete representations sharing one ideology as one unified conceptual reality. Therefore, even though there appear to be several Islamic societies each with its own name, the difference among them exists only at the literal level. To clarify further the notion of literal (concrete) grouping, it is diagrammatically represented in Figure 1.

If one approaches the phenomenon according to this literal orientation any one or more of the societies can be explored as societies, in which case *al-Jama'a al-Islamiyya* refers to A_3 in Figure 1.

It is justifiable, however, to approach the phenomenon—as done here—as a single conceptual reality represented at its formal level by *al-Gama'a al-Islamiyya* (*al-gama'a* is local Egyptian Arabic for *al-jama'a*) and at its informal level by the "community" of *al-mitdayyinin* (religieux, religieuses).

IV

The term *al-gama'a* itself merits some clarification. It is the spoken Egyptian Arabic equivalent of *al-jama'a,* and it is used in traditional context in reference to wife, family, or home. In Wehr's dictionary *jama'a* means group community. In hadith sources, *jama'a* signifies the whole body of Muslims,[7] in which sense *jama'a* and *umma* become identical in usage. In Islamic political theory the difference between *jama'a* and *umma* is blurred in the context of authority adding to the confusion. However, in some contexts, *jama'a* refers to representations of the *umma,* which is the entire community of believers. This latter conceptualization of *jama'a* as representatives and *umma* as the entire community of believers is similar to the actual structuring of the contemporary Islamic Movement into two layers: a formal one, *al-gama'a,* and the informal community of *al-mitdayyinin.* This structuring is diagrammed in Figure 2.

This term is not based on vernacular usage. That is, no reference is made in the vernacular about "community." However, my data show evidence for the formation of a social cultural collectivity of active Muslim women and men manifesting characteristics of a community

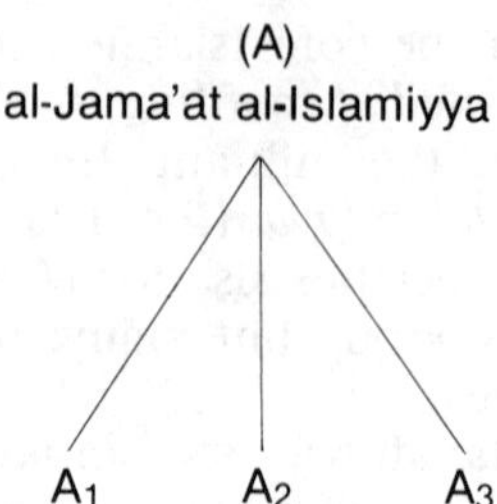

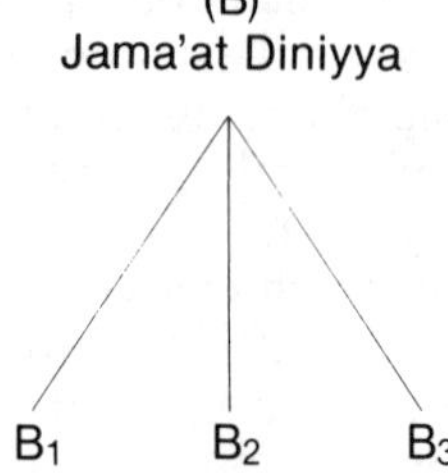

FIGURE 1:
A concrete representation of Islamic Groups divided into two major groupings: *al-jama'at al-Islamiyya* (the Islamic societies) and *jama'at diniyya* (religious societies). These in turn consist of various named societies, represented as A_1, A_2, etc.

within society at large. Whereas there is no single term in the vernacular to refer to this observed phenomenon as community, there is a term locally used in reference to its membership, namely, *al-mitdayyinin.*[8]

One "joins," as it were, via internal transformation which occurs spontaneously to individuals, removing them spiritually, intellectually, and ideologically from mainstream society, even as they remain in it physically. A person continues to live at home with the family but believes "beyond" with other Muslims in the wider community of Islam. Once an individiual, by volition and analytic thought, has reached a state of *iqtina'* (conviction), he/she is then *multazim(a)* (from *iltizam,* adherence), hence a member.

As a member, one adheres to ritual rigidity, behavioral, verbal, and dress prescription, and to the strict avoidance taboo between the sexes. The transformation which has occurred internally within the individual becomes publicly translated into visible symbols and rituals which serve

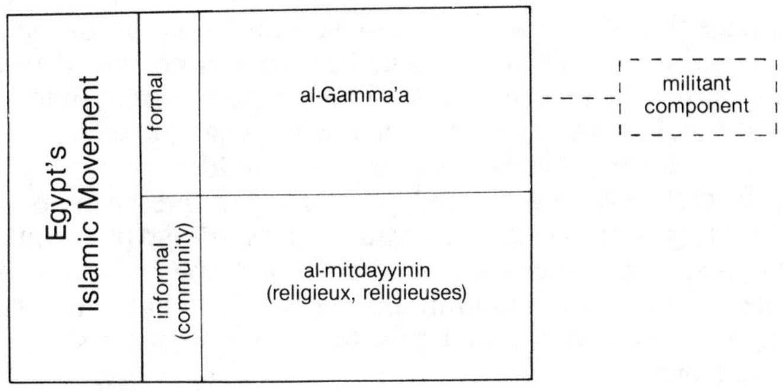

FIGURE 2:
An ideational representation of Egypt's Islamic Movement divided into the formal level, *al-Gama'a,* and the informal collectivity of *al-mitdayyinin* (religieux, religieuses). Militant Component is marked by a broken line indicating conceptual separateness from, despite its ideological relatedness to, the formal aspect of the Islamic Movement.

to define the premises of a movement and outline its boundary. At this point a member lives at home but belongs to a community which is within mainstream society but no more part of it. Mainstream society organization is, therefore, undergoing a process of reordering. Dispersed as students among the various campuses and universities of urban Egypt an ideological unity is emerging that is both apparent and real. At the formal level the unity is observational, at the informal, analytic. Together they represent an Islam in Egypt that is alternative to Institutional Islam, the Islam of the Establishment, the *'Ulama* (savants) of al-Azhar. What is significant about this alternative is that it has emerged from within, that is, it is genuinely indigenous to the Muslim world, and that it comes from below, that is, from the non-elitist (intellectual, political, religious) elements of society, crosscutting socioeconomic strata. In contrast with sociopolitical elitist ideologies, such as socialism, this movement has strong popular youth appeal. More important is the role of women in this movement and the inception of a Muslim ethic, an ethic that is compatible with Arab-Islamic tradition and meaningful to its bearers.

V

Quite conspicuous in urban Egypt of the '70s is the bewildering new Egyptian woman, the young urban college student who is partly or completely veiled in public. The image of this new woman is dramatic and since there is no equally dramatic male counterpart, her image has become the focus of observers' attention. There is an apparent paradox in the image that this new woman evokes, an equation of incongruence as it were, which seems to put together what is perceived to represent being modern and progressive by being active and visible in public, college-educated, and career-oriented with what appears to be fundamentalist, backward, passive, subordinate, hidden.

It is further puzzling to find her strongest presence to be in the professional (practical) colleges and majors of Egyptian universities, such as medicine, veterinary medicine, pharmacy, and engineering. These are the majors demanding the highest national entry score levels and which are considered in Egypt to be the most prestigious majors and professions.

It would be deceptive and misleading if one were to emphasize the quantitative factor alone, since numerically the phenomenon of this new veiled college woman can be shown to be insignificant in terms of total population. Yet it represents a visible collectivity which certainly has such a qualitatively strong, dominant presence in today's urban Egypt that it cannot be dismissed on the basis of statistical distribution. Its meaning and significance, if understood in a sociocultural context, can shed light on the inevitable transformation which Egyptian society has been gradually undergoing during the past two decades and the dynamics within Islam as it attempts to overcome the tension between the two forces, *asala* (authenticity/tradition) and *asriyya* (progress).

The general topic of the nature of change, and how the Islamic Movement functions to overcome the resulting tension between tradition and progress, needs some clarification. The first concerns veiling, a complex institution integrated in modern Middle Eastern society with disproportionate attention from those who treat it as an exotic artifact. The very term "veil" conjures up Hollywood-style images of harems, sensuality, mysteries of the Casbah, and Casablanca.

Other than a few exceptions, the literature on the Middle East is full of references to "the veil" as if such an undifferentiated object really exists. In fact there is not one single word in Arabic that would correspond to the English term veil. Various Arabic terms, such as *burqu', hijab, tarhah, chador, 'abayah,* etc. refer to the variety of "veils" and their multiple usages and rich symbolism. In addition to the exotic image associated with the veil, there is an implicit assumption that creeps frequently into Middle Eastern studies, namely that veiling reflects the low, submissive status of women sharing the culture in which it is institutionalized. Again, this oversimplifies a domain rich in symbolism and meaning.

In the context of the Islamic Movement what is referred to as "veil" is in fact one element, itself complexly differentiated, in a total dress code called *al-ziyy al-Islami* (the Islamic dress). The young Egyptian woman assertively wearing it is part of a larger movement in Egypt and elsewhere in the Islamic East. It is only in this totalistic context that the contemporary "Islamic" veiling can be understood.

The second aspect to be clarified concerns men. Because veiling is so visible and conspicuous, particularly in the case of Egyptian women who have deveiled since 1923, there is disproportionate attention directed at women and at veiling. However, it should be pointed out that *al-ziyy al-Islami* refers to a dress code for both sexes. Men, like women, in this movement must conform to a specific dress code which is distinguishable from secular clothing. The significance lies not in the fact that women are veiling or reveiling, but that women are actively involved in the movement, so visibly, so intensively, and so assertively, that at least one scholar has suggested that women must have begun the movement. In both intensity and form, women's involvement is significant and reflects a new trend. The early Islamic societies of the '20s, the most popular of which is *al-Ikhwan al-Muslimun* (the Muslim Brothers) were male-dominated in congruence with the androcentric names of societies such as *al-Ikhwan* (brothers), *al-Shubban* (male youth), etc. Accordingly, women's involvement, which eventually actualized in the '20s, remained marginal, concerned mainly the wives of "Brothers," and concentrated on activities that are more or less an extension of their maternal, domestic roles.

Conversely, the contemporary movement is referred to at its formal level by the name *al-gama'a,* which in any of its various senses, family, community, or representative society, is a gender-neutral term. Informally, its membership consists of "sisters" and "brothers" forming a sororal/fraternal collectivity, both sexes having equal presence and similar opportunity of involvement and avenues for leadership. Sisters and brothers are involved in activities of similar nature, adhere to a dress-verbal-behavioral code, and collectively support the underlying ideology which separates them from mainstream society and from Establishment Islam.

Unlike women's formal participation in the '20s as a society, women's contemporary involvement is voluntary, informal, and of a non-elitist, popular character.[9] The role of women in this movement entails a strong message: It dispels the stereotypic division of religion into Islam, controlled by men, on the one hand, and the little tradition preoccupying the women in the Muslim world, on the other. The Islamic Movement is their avenue to join the Great Tradition.

Traditional formal Islam in Egypt has gradually become bureaucratized, rigidified, and a domain controlled by *al-'Ulama* (the Savants of al-Azhar), hence elitist. As such, the bulk of the people—the non-elites and women, whose lives are seriously influenced by the doctrine of Islam as it is interpreted by *al-'Ulama*—are not active participants in the Islamic process. This situation is at a time when the rate of education for non-elites in Egypt is accelerating and, further, at a significantly higher rate for women than for men. A grass-roots movement, from below, to reintegrate Islam into culture simultaneously functions to reduce people's detachment from Islam.

Reintegrated, Islam becomes interwoven in people's daily lives, needs, and values. As non-elitist elements of society increasingly share in the definition and interpretation of Islamic rules and traditions, Islamic doctrine is gradually converted into Muslim ethic. The content of this ethic concerns no esoteric matters. Rather it addresses core issues of relevance to the lives of women and men as they interact in sociomoral space of Egypt in the face of change and development. This ethic is being vividly expressed and reinforced via symbol and ritual as manifested in the contemporary movement. Veiling is one example.

Muslim ethic is thus woven in sociomoral terms by the culture bearers, building on a strong intellectual base supplied by leading scholars of the movement such as Qutb and al-Mawdudi among others. Shaped by various dynamic forces, it becomes the fabric which cements Muslims in their movement to overcome imposed barriers and provides content to empty elitist ideology, whether political, or religious.

It is in this sense that Arabist nationalism and Islamism are complementary. While the former supplies a framework, the latter fills it with meaning. What was empty formal ideology from above is emerging from below as a new reality—the Islamic order within which Arabs form a strong core.

Notes

This analysis utilizes my Commentary in the Conference: *Resurgence of Contemporary Islam,* SUNY, Binghamton, March 13–14, 1981, and revisions of my paper "Alternative Islam in Contemporary Egypt: A Re-Ordering from Within and Below" presented in the Ford Foundation Summer Workshop: *Rich and Poor States in the Middle East,* July 2–9, 1980, von Grunebaum Center for Near Eastern Studies, UCLA, Los Angeles.

I thank co–workshop participants, Galal Amin, Nazih Ayubi, Hazem Beblawi, Ali Dessouki, Saad Ibrahim, Malcolm Kerr, Georges Sabbagh, Sayyid Yasin, and Ibrahim Karawan for reading and commenting on an earlier version.

Data upon which this analysis is based were gathered during fieldwork carried out in Egypt between 1976 and 1980. A Faculty Grant from UCLA African Studies Center and Ford Foundation Grant No. 770-0651 provided support for my fieldwork.

1. Rifa'a al-Tahtawi, for example, inflamed Egyptian pride in its pharaonic past through his ideas on patriotism. On the other side, there was Gamal al-Din al-Afghani calling for Pan-Islamism and the Qur'an as sole authority, influencing men of thought like Muhammad Abduh and others.

2. The fieldwork techniques utilized in this research are systematic participant-observation, structured interviewing, in-depth interviewing, natural setting conversation, and gathering the Islamic literature which is read by the members in the movement for the analysis of its formal dogma and ideology. Central to the anthropological method is the use of informants, not subjects or respondents, for interviewing, and observation is in natural setting.

3. As intellectual debate between nationalists and Islamists continued, the throne was weakening, a reconciliatory school of Islamists, the Modernists, was growing, and al-'Ulama were growing more passive and ineffectual. In the meantime, as a power struggle developed between two elites a 'movement' was

developing from below. A new leadership emerged from the masses, among Egyptian youth. Before World War I the seeds of an alternative Islam were being planted, and some societies had already formed even though they remained in the background. Most significant was the dynamic Hassan al-Banna. Unlike elitist institutional Islam, al-Banna was able to reach the discontented masses by interacting directly at the local level. It was in coffee houses in Isma'iliyya that gradually ideas developed and an ideology of an Islam alternative to that of al-Azhar began to take shape. Ironically, many of the youth joining this, then new, movement were themselves from al-Azhar.

4. The reference here is to the image in light of the Virgin Mary appearing publicly in Zeitun, Cairo, several months after the war and continuing to reappear for several months afterward. Thousands of Muslims and Copts—men and women, young and old, from all strata—flocked to the spot where the Virgin Mary is purported to have once sat to rest under a tree and where then her image was appearing in light. People waited hours and days to catch a glimpse of the "miracle."

5. Personal communication. Professor A. Mahfouz teaches Islamic Law at Helwan University, Cairo, Egypt.

6. Interview with Professor Hassan Hanafi, Professor of Islamic Philosophy at Cairo University.

7. Interestingly, the same term *jama'a,* a fundamental Islamic concept, is used as the name of a prophetic-charismatic Christian movement in Katanga, Congo. In Swahili *jama'a* means family.

8. It is specifically used by members with reference to other members, by Muslim and Coptic student nonmembers when referring to members, and formally in the periodical *al-Da'wa* (the Call) as for example in Issue 51, p. 35. As a term of reference *mitdayyinin* allows one to draw a boundary line around this exclusive membership. As for terms of address there are two gender-linked terms: *akh* (brother) and *ukht* (sister) preceding the individual's name. These two are also used internally as reference terms to specific individuals.

9. The usage of elitist/non-elitist here is not equivalent to socioeconomic strata or classes but refers to the possession of exclusive access and/or control.

8
The Economic Basis of Civil Conflict in Lebanon: A Survey Analysis of Sunnite Muslims

Hilal Khashan and Monte Palmer

I

Throughout most of its recorded history, domestic conflict in the Middle East has been essentially communal, with the overwhelming majority of the population organized into ethnic or confessional groups which provided the region's social structure. Loyalty to the communal groups, if not absolute, exceeded loyalty to such a nebulous entity as the state. As various groups vied to maximize their share of meager resources, individual interests and those of the communal groups became virtually inseparable. Class consciousness in the Marxian sense of the word was either nonexistent or was pre-empted by religious and tribal loyalties—Marx's opiate of the masses. Even in periods of social disorganization and grinding poverty, it was a religious saint, a Mahdi, who provided the vehicle for social restructuring. Frustration and desperation found cathartic expression in religious fanaticism, not in class action.

After World War I, the infusion of Western economic, political, and ideological concepts in the Middle East accelerated forcing traditional and communal loyalties to compete with the nascent appeals of nationalism, class, and ideology. This was especially significant in those states which bore the brunt of Western incursion into the parochial pattern of life. In Lebanon, where both trends are typified, communal loyalties continue to enlist the unwavering support of large segments of the population. Yet, by all appearances, sizable strata of the Lebanese population also manifest clear signs of class consciousness and attachment to a variety of Western ideological doctrines. Lebanon, after all, has probably been more intensely exposed to Western economic and ideological concepts than any other Arab state.

Reprinted with permission from *Journal of Arab Affairs* 1, no. 1 (1981):113–132.

While most observers acknowledge that communal and economic variables are the primary social forces structuring the Lebanese environment, the absence of empirical data has made it difficult to assess the extent to which class or economic variables do, indeed, compete with communal loyalties in shaping the political outlook of Lebanon's citizenry. It is the objective of this study to report the results of a survey of 415 Lebanese Sunnite Muslims residing in Sidon. It is believed this study will shed some very interesting light on the influence of economic variables which affect the conflictual behavior of Lebanon's Sunnite community. The data, as presented, will examine the impact of economic and class variables on three types of Sunnite political behavior as follows:

1. Economic variables and Sunnite perceptions of Maronites and Palestinians.
2. Economic variables and political participation.
3. Economic variables and preferred outcomes of the conflict.

II

To examine the role of these variables upon the social and political behavior of a Lebanese Sunnite community a questionnaire of 191 items was administered to a random sample of 415 Sunnite Muslims of Lebanese origin residing in Sidon. Sidon was chosen as a location for three reasons. First, despite its mixed population, Sidon remains a predominantly Sunnite area; second, it is large enough to ensure a sizable random sample, yet small enough to allow for effective manageability and inclusion of its various sectors; third, it is not a combat zone. By Lebanese standards, it is relatively safe, and probably the only Sunnite area of Lebanon in which a survey of this nature was feasible. However, selecting a random sample of Lebanese Sunnites in the Sidon area proved to be a formidable task. The population of Sidon is mixed, with thousands of urban Palestinian refugees scattered throughout the city. Moreover, thousands of rural Shiite Muslims were resettled in Sidon in the wake of the 1978 Israeli invasion of South Lebanon. The first problem, accordingly, was to separate Lebanese Sunnites from members of other religious and confessional groups.

Second, reliable statistics for Sidon's population and its distribution were unavailable, but unofficial estimates placed it at 100,000 inhabitants. With more than twenty residential quarters, it was virtually impossible to ascertain the population of each quarter. Thus, random drawing of residential quarters for the selection of respondents and assigning a number of cases to each in proportion to their population was not a viable option.

Third, in the 1960s and 1970s, many of the more affluent Sidonians had moved out of the city limits into the suburbs, which presented the field researcher with yet another problem.

Fourth, the urban development of Sidon has been neither even nor methodical. Residential units have no consistent pattern with high-rise apartments existing side by side with older, single-occupancy houses. Neither streets nor residential units are numbered and streets are laid out erratically. No distinct boundaries exist between one section of town and another, such that citrus groves abound within the city limits, and many residential units are camouflaged within their confines. Hundreds of two-story buildings in the old sector are interconnected; shops, houses, schools, militia depots and headquarters, mosques, and convict hideouts compose one inseparable and highly unidentifiable conglomeration.

To overcome these problems, Sidon was divided into fifteen sampling sectors. The city is rectangular in shape with one major highway cutting through the entire length. A map was sketched to show all avenues intersecting the main highway and the city was then divided into fifteen imaginary rectangles. Eventually 69 respondents were interviewed in each of six rectangles selected by lot. This process continued until all rectangles were sampled with a total of 415 respondents being interviewed.

Given the precarious nature of survey research in a conflictual environment, four reliability test measures were imposed upon the data: (1) internal consistency; (2) response bias; (3) congruence with reality; and (4) analysis of variance.

The test for internal consistency compared the percentage distributions of several pairs of similar items. In this regard, all respondents who claimed to belong to the upper class also stated that their income was above average. Examination of upper-middle-class respondents showed that 81 percent were above average incomes while 19 percent reported an average income. Only 1.5 percent of middle-class respondents mentioned a below-average income. Among the working-class respondents 10.5 percent reported an average income, while the majority (89.5 percent) admitted that their income was below average. In another example, none who claimed to be close to a certain group in one item reported hostility toward it when responding to related items.

For the problem of response bias, three sets of similar items, presented in reverse order, were examined to determine if any tendency occurred for respondents to answer either first or last responses with greater frequencies. No such tendencies occurred. Third, as to congruence with reality, response patterns derived from the survey were evaluated by a panel of experts drawn from two universities in Beirut, and the results were found to be consistent by all members of the panel. Also, in order to ascertain content validity, four of the panelists were presented with two lists, one for the variables, the other with the scale names, and were requested to regroup the individual variables under the proper scale headings. This was followed by a discussion between the panelists and the field investigator in which inconsistencies of scale-variable matching were resolved. The panel members also suggested modifications on items they felt to be ambiguous.

Fourth, as the survey was conducted by three interviewers, it was deemed advisable to test for reliability of the subpopulations. The one-way analysis of variance test was applied to eight scales in the three subsamples and no significant difference emerged between response patterns of the three subsamples across all eight scales examined.

III

The concept of social class, while poignant in emotional terms, submits to a variety of definitions and interpretations. This is particularly true in the case of Lebanon and the rest of the Middle East, as the region lacks the strong industrial traditions generally associated with the emergence of class consciousness in Western societies.

To overcome ambiguities of definition a variety of economic indicators were employed ranging from income through occupation to self-perceived social status. The test and percentage distributions for the class indicators appear in Table 1, as do the percentage distributions for a social-class summary scale combining the three social-class items.

It should be noted that some variation existed in the class lines derived from the three items but that factor analysis indicated that the social-class items used in the scale were unidimensional and were roughly equal in their ability to measure class consciousness among respondents. All correlations used in the analysis are based on the combined SES scale to avoid bias resulting from a single indicator.

IV

Examination of Sunnite political behavior involves Sunnite perceptions of the two main protagonists in the civil conflict, the Maronites and the Palestinians.

According to a purely communal model of group relations one would expect the Lebanese Sunnites to be uniformly hostile to the Maronites. In this regard, one might recall that the Sunnites and the Maronites have coexisted in a state of tension for generations, a state of conflict that was clearly exacerbated by the French Mandate and the inauguration of a new political structure which relegated the Sunnites to a secondary position in Lebanon's political and economic hierarchy.

On the other hand, one might anticipate that Lebanon's Sunnites would manifest considerable warmth toward the Palestinians residing in the Sidon area. This is especially true since the Palestinians entered Lebanon's civil conflict in response to appeals for help made by the leaders of the Muslim-Leftist alliance.

This study, however, was undertaken five years after the start of the civil war and at a point in time at which the Palestinians had effectively replaced the central government as the dominant military force in the Sidon area. The dominant position of the Palestinians, while not

Table 1

SOCIO-ECONOMIC STATUS
N = 415

What is your occupation?

		Cases	Percent
High Status Occupation		107	25.8
Medium Status Occupation		154	37.1
Low Status Occupation		154	37.1
	Total	415	100.0

In the Context of Lebanon's Current Economy Do You Consider Your Income To Be:

		Cases	Percent
Above Average		87	21.0
Average		155	37.3
Below Average		173	41.7
	Total	415	100.0

In Terms of General Social Classes, Would You Consider Yourself to Be a Member of the:

		Cases	Percent
Upper Class		39	9.4
Middle Class		185	44.6
Working Class		191	46.0
	Total	415	100.0

Combined SES Scale

	Code	Cases	Percent
Highest	1.	34	8.2
	2.	48	11.6
	3.	32	7.7
	4.	79	19.0
	5.	36	8.7
	6.	79	19.0
Lowest	7.	107	25.8
	Total	415	100.0

vociferously opposed by the Sunnites, was complicated by the fact that Lebanese Sunnites generally accorded the Palestinian refugees an inferior social status. A possibility thus existed for Palestinian–Lebanese Sunnite affinity to be eroded by both the military dominance of the Palestinians and by the reversal of status roles. The Palestinians, being sensitive to this problem, have gone to great lengths to avoid open confrontation with the Sunnite Lebanese by offering them preferential treatment in the allocation of social services provided by the administrative and welfare apparatus of the PLO.

How did the respondents perceive Maronites and Palestinians, and how were attitudes influenced by the respective socioeconomic positions? The results are shown in Table 2 which provides the text and percentage distributions for a variety of items designed to measure levels of warmth or hostility toward each of Lebanon's major communal groups. The percentages indicate in striking fashion that the Sunnites are sharply divided in their attitudes toward Maronites and Palestinians and that there appears to be limited support for both. Indeed, of all groups, Sunnites accord their warmth primarily to the Greek Orthodox, a finding that gives clear lie to the notion that the civil war is simply a religious confrontation between Christians and Muslims. Feelings toward the Shia, Druze, and Armenians are neutral and appear to be irrelevant from a political perspective.

The operationalization of communal closeness or hostility was based upon three items requesting respondents to list the sect they felt "closest to," "second closest to," or "least close to." This procedure clearly reflected the use of a "thermometer" to indicate party or ideological preference in Western voting studies. The responses thus acquired were recorded to provide an interval closeness-versus-hostility scale for both the Maronites and Catholics on one hand, and the Palestinians on the other. In somewhat simplified terms, the scaling procedure involved assigning each sect two points for each "closest" response, one point for each "second closest" response, zero points for "neutral" or "not mentioned" responses, and minus one point for each "least close" response. The test and marginal distributions for the scale items appear in Table 3.

To arrive at any clear variation in Sunnite attitudes toward Maronites and Palestinians as shaped by economic variables, the items and scales relating to communal perceptions (Table 2) were cross-tabulated with the social-class items and scale appearing in Table 1. The resulting coefficients are presented in Table 4.

If the variation in attitudes toward Palestinians and Maronites was striking, the influence of economic variables upon those perceptions was more so. The data have graphically demonstrated the strong relationship between SES variables and favorable perceptions of Maronites. The findings were consistent for all variables, and were equally reflected in the summary SES scale (see Table 4).

When SES and perceptions of Maronites were positively correlated,

Table 2

COMMUNAL CLOSENESS

Closest Group to You:

	Cases	Percent
Maronites/Catholics	33	8.7
Shia	21	5.5
Greek Orthodox	160	42.1
Palestinians	49	12.9
Syrian Muslims	93	24.5
Druze	24	6.3
Total	380	100.0

Second Closest Group to You:

	Cases	Percent
Maronites/Catholics	25	8.2
Shia	39	12.8
Greek Orthodox	94	30.8
Palestinians	51	16.7
Syrian Muslims	48	15.7
Druze	48	15.7
Total	305	100.0

Group Least Close to You:

	Cases	Percent
Maronites/Catholics	133	32.0
Shia	11	2.7
Greek Orthodox	--	--
Palestinians	266	64.1
Syrian Muslims	--	--
Druze	5	1.2
Total	415	100.0

the results showed an inverse relationship between SES variables and perceptions of Palestinians, but the relationship, it should be noted, is moderate. It indicates that while most Sunnites perceive Palestinians negatively, this tendency is stronger among wealthy Sunnites than among their poorer counterparts (see Table 4).

V

Having found that economic class does, indeed, have a profound impact upon confessional perceptions, the next area of inquiry was the

Table 3

MARONITES and CATHOLICS CLOSENESS SCALE		
	Cases	Percent
Closest	27	8.9
Second Closest	25	8.2
Neutral	147	48.2
Least Close	106	34.8
Total	305	100.0

PALESTINIANS CLOSENESS SCALE		
	Cases	Percent
Closest	45	14.8
Second Closest	51	16.7
Neutral	23	7.5
Least Close	106	61.0
Total	305	100.0

Table 4

COEFFICIENTS FOR
COMMUNAL PERCEPTIONS
WITH SOCIO-ECONOMIC STATUS (SES)
N = 304

	Dependent Variable	
	Palestinians	Maronites
Class	g = -.25, r = -.15	g = .56, r = .46
Income	g = -.24, r = -.17	g = .57, r = .53
Occupation	g = -.32, r = -.22	g = .58, r = .47
SES Scale	g = -.24, r = -.20	g = .52, r = .54

Significant at .05 level or better.

Table 5

POLITICAL INTEREST
N = 415

Do You Follow Political Press Reports Avidly?

		Cases	Percent
Yes		215	51.8
No		200	48.2
	Total	415	100.0

How Often Do You Follow Political Events?

		Cases	Percent
Daily		143	34.5
Several Times a Week		118	28.4
Weekly		93	22.4
Less		61	14.7
	Total	415	100.0

extent to which class differences shape Sunnite political behavior, particularly overt Sunnite participation in the civil conflict.

In examining the political behavior of Lebanese Sunnites, three varieties of behavior were considered: (1) non-specific political interest, (2) partisan activity, and (3) overt conflictual participation. Two non-specific indicators of general political interest requested respondents to indicate the general intensity of their political involvement, the text and percentage distributions for which appear in Table 5.

As the percentage distribution in Table 4 indicates, approximately 50 percent of the respondents considered themselves to possess an avid interest in the political process. When the subject was narrowed to actual membership in a political party, the number of participants dropped to approximately one-fourth, with a similar number (114) acknowledging regular participation in demonstrations or riots (Table 5).

Finally, when the questions were specifically directed to actual participation via a militia or in a war-related experience, the number of participants dropped further to 32 respondents or approximately 8 percent of the total sample. There was, however, one stark exception to the pattern: when asked if financial contribution had been made to a paramilitary organization, all but 48 respondents answered in the affirmative. Similarly, when asked if contributions had been voluntary or motivated by expedience, more than two-thirds of those donating to a paramilitary organization indicated they had done so out of expediency rather than conviction. The latter results are explained by the fact that it was dangerous not to contribute to a paramilitary organization. As a friend expressed this sentiment, "it is truly difficult to resist a magazine salesman wearing a submachine gun."

Questions relating to participation raise the question of reliability under the best circumstances. This is particularly true in a strife-torn state such as Lebanon, and more so in the case of questions relating to conflictual behavior. To what extent, then, is it reasonable to assume the veracity of response patterns which indicate that only one-fourth of the sample's respondents were members of political parties and only 8 percent reported membership in paramilitary organizations? In assessing this question confidence in the reliability of the responses was reinforced by two important considerations. First, informal interviews with a large number of Lebanese politicians and scholars intimately familiar with participation patterns among the Lebanese Sunnites in Sidon indicated that the reported response patterns were generally congruent with their personal estimates of participation patterns of the Sunnite community. In this regard, it was generally observed that Sidon was not a main theatre of the war and that the Sunnites had generally manifested greater tendencies toward withdrawal and self-preservation than toward open involvement.

Second, in responding to the participation items, the respondents manifested little hesitancy in expressing their positions or in refusing to answer questions. It should be noted that, after five years of war, those individuals who had played an active role in the conflict were reasonably well known and had little to lose by disclosing their involvement. In fact, active participants were more likely to wear their involvement as a badge of honor. It should also be noted that not only did virtually all interviewees respond to the question on monetary support of a paramilitary organization, but well over half of the respondents indicated making a contribution under duress, a position they might logically be avoiding given that the paramilitary organizations are highly visible in the streets of Sidon. Similarly, there was the willingness of a sizable percentage of the respondents to indicate "warmth" toward the Maronites.

An examination of the impact of social class upon the various types of political behavior, outlined in Table 5, shows that, in the case of attitudes toward Maronites and Palestinians, the influence of class variables on political participation was often dramatic. Correlations between social class and general political awareness, for example, indicate clearly that political interest and political awareness are far higher among the more prosperous and better-educated members of Sidon's Sunnite community (see Table 6). These results were expected and are fully congruent with participation studies throughout the world.

Table 6

COEFFICIENTS FOR PARTICIPATION WITH INCOME AND EDUCATION
N = 406

Independent Variable	**Dependent Variable**	
	Membership in Militia	Demonstration
Education	g = -.71, r = -.18	g = -.25, r = -.13
Income	g = -.80, r = -.24	g = -.56, r = -.31

Independent Variable	**Dependent Variable**		
	Political Interest	Frequency of Paper Reading	Leadership
Education	g = .71, r = .45	g = .67, r = .51	g = .65, r = .26
Income	g = .40, r = .24	g = .39, r = .30	g = .38, r = .12

Significant at .05 level or better

When the level of participation shifted to membership in political parties, the data revealed little difference in participation on the basis of class or level of education. The exception to this was a slight tendency for members of lower-income groups to be more active in political parties than their more prosperous counterparts. This result was undoubtedly shaped by the fact that the pre-war political alignments were shattered by the protracted conflict. This gave rise to the dominance of the Leftist-oriented political parties in Sidon. Conservatism, the logical mode of political expression for the more prosperous members of the sample, was ebbing at the time of the survey. This situation, coupled with the inconclusiveness of the civil war, also explains the relatively low level of partisan activity in a highly politicized state.

If party membership was relatively constant across social classes, this was clearly not the case for leadership positions in political parties and organization. The higher-income groups, and particularly the more educated members of the sample, dominated political leadership positions. The gamma coefficients presented in Table 6, for example, suggest that the probability of leaders coming from high-income or

Table 7

INCOME WITH RIOTING AND MILITIA MEMBERSHIP

Income and Membership in Militia

Income		Belong to a Militia
Above Average		---
Average		15.6 percent
Below Average		84.4 percent
N = 32	Total	100.0

Income and Rioting

Income		Do You Demonstrate
Above Average		2.6 percent
Average		36.8 percent
Below Average		60.7 percent
N = 117	Total	100.0

highly educated segments of the Sunnite community was 38 percent and 65 percent better than chance, respectively.

If the poor constitute the rank and file of Sidon's political partisans, they also are the foot soldiers of its militias. It is the poor that do most of the rioting and demonstrating (g = .56) and it is the poor who also belong to the militias (g = .80). In this instance, the coefficients suggest that the probability of rioters coming from low-income groups was 56 percent better than chance. The probability that militia members were from low income groups was 80 percent better than chance. The results, it must be stressed, do not suggest that all poor Sunnites demonstrate or belong to a militia, but merely that Sunnites who did riot or belonged to a militia are drawn primarily from the ranks of the poor. This relationship is depicted clearly in Table 7, displaying the cross-tabulations between income and rioting and income and militia membership, respectively.

The finding that the poorer Sunnites are far more involved in conflictual participation is, of course, fully congruent with the earlier finding that the lower classes feel the most intense animosity toward the Maronites.

It it also interesting to note that those individuals who belong to a militia were more likely to perceive the war as a sectarian conflict rather than as a class conflict, indicating that the lines between sect and class among the foot soldiers are not clearly defined.

Table 8

PREFERRED OUTCOME OF CONFLICT
N = 415

Preferred Outcome of Conflict	Cases	Percent
Independent State	334	80.5
Reunion with Syria	70	16.9
Partition: Christian/Muslim	11	2.7
Total	415	100.0
What Kind of Political Arrangement Do you Prefer for Post-Civil War Lebanon?		
New Formula	380	91.6
Pre-war status	19	4.6
Partition: Christian/Muslim	16	3.9
Total	415	100.0

VI

Thus far the evidence shows that economic differences have exerted a profound influence on both the communal perceptions and political behavior of Lebanon's Sunnite community. How, then, do these differences in communal perceptions and political behavior influence desired outcomes for the civil conflict?

Preferred outcomes for the civil conflict were ascertained by two questions, the test and percentage distributions for which appear in Table 8.

Quite surprisingly, and most important from the study perspective, the overwhelming majority of respondents preferred the maintenance of an independent Lebanese state, albeit a state under a revised formula for the distribution of power and resources among Lebanon's communal groups.

In spite of the strong support for an independent Lebanon among all social classes, the influence of economic difference was clearly present. No member of the upper-income group, for example, desired the partition of Lebanon into Christian and Muslim states or the merging of Muslim Lebanon with a larger Arab state. The latter alternative, however, was found desirable by approximately 18 percent of the lower-income group.

Similarly, 20 percent of the upper-income group expressed a preference for a return to the pre-war national pact, an option found acceptable by only one member of both the average- and lower-income categories.

Table 9

WORKING WITH MARONITES AND SES
N = 415

	Highest SES						Lowest SES	Total
	1.	2.	3.	4.	5.	6.	7.	
yes	8.2	11.3	7.5	18.6	7.5	17.6	18.3	88.9
no	---	.2	.2	.5	1.2	1.4	7.5	11.6
					Grand Total Percent			100.0

g = .69, r = .29
Significant at .001 level

The most dramatic differences, however, occurred in reference to the preferred restructuring of Lebanon, with 34 percent of the lower-income respondents demanding Maronite subservience as opposed to only 2 percent of the upper-income group.

The lower-income group, then, is likely to remain available for mobilization in future confrontations, an interpretation further supported by a question asking respondents if they felt they could more or less forgive and work with the Maronites once the war was over (see Table 9).

VII

The objective has been to examine the influence of economic variables upon historical patterns of communal hostility in Lebanon. Specifically, the study examined the extent to which Sunnite Muslim perceptions of Maronites and Palestinians, the two major protagonists in the Lebanese civil war, varied upon the basis of economic social status.

The traditional/historical model of communal conflict in Lebanon led to a hypothesis that Sunnite Muslims should manifest hostility toward the Maronite community regardless of the economic or status position of its numbers. Similarly, it was hypothesized that religious affinity between the Lebanese Sunnites and the Palestinians in the Sidon area would result in high level of Sunnite support for the Palestinian presence, a support augmented by presumed Sunnite hostility toward the Maronites. This was also hypothesized to be constant across class lines.

The study results indicate in striking fashion that Sunnite attitudes toward the Maronites were sharply divided along class lines. The more prosperous members of the Sunnite community expressed considerable support for the Maronites, while lower-class members of our sample registered intense hostility toward them.

The data also revealed that the politically mobilized members of the population were drawn primarily from less advantaged socioeconomic strata, since they expressed the most intense hostility against the Maronites. Respondents showing hostility for the Maronites consistently registered closeness for Palestinians; the reverse however, was not always true. Attitudes toward the Palestinians were less influenced by economic considerations, but the data shattered any notion of strong Lebanese Sunnite support for the Palestinian presence.

Caution is needed, however, in weighing the apparent lack of support for Palestinians among the respondents, for the survey was taken at a moment of disenchantment among respondents as a result of political events since 1975. Before the war started, Sunnites appeared to believe that the PLO was their strategic reserve. They also assumed that, in case of a military confrontation with the Maronites, the PLO would tip the balance of fighting in favor of the Muslim-Leftist alliance. This apparent vision of the Sunnis did not materialize. It appears that Sunnite support for the Palestinians fluctuates on a need basis. Whenever the Sunnis feel directly threatened by Maronites their level of support for Palestinians increases. When the perceived Maronite threat diminishes, support for Palestinians uniformly declines and, at the time of the survey, it was low indeed.

Part III

Socialization and Alienation

9
Patterns in Child-Rearing Practices

Edwin T. Prothro

Lebanese Norms

Let us begin with the questions of greatest interest to the area scholar: "How do Lebanese mothers treat their children? Are there national norms, by which Lebanese mothers of all groups could be differentiated from mothers of such a country as the United States?"

To the extent that the six communities studied are typical of Lebanon as a whole, it can be stated with assurance that there are indeed patterns of child rearing which are widespread in Lebanon and that many of them can be differentiated readily from patterns in such countries as the United States.

Lebanese parents, mothers and fathers alike, profess themselves eager to have children and pleased at every pregnancy. The delight is particularly great when the couple is childless or when they have no sons. A few lower-class mothers, and mothers of large families, may doubt the suitability of a pregnancy, but they are in a minority and are rarer than American mothers with ambivalent feelings on becoming pregnant.

The newborn child is received with warmth and treated with indulgence. He is breast fed from birth, usually on demand, and picked up whenever he cries. He is swaddled for several months, which usually makes it possible for his mother to keep him at her side day and night. Most mothers spend much time with the infant, fondling him and playing with him, though one in four report themselves as too busy for such activities.

Indulgence for most infants begins to decrease as they approach the first birthday. Weaning takes place abruptly, either late in the first year or early in the second, and is accompanied about half the time by emotional upset. Toilet training usually begins before the first birthday, and training techniques are severe. Nevertheless, training is not usually completed until late in the second year.

Mothers oppose all manifestations of aggressive impulses by children. Most of them do not want a child to fight, even in self-defense. Aggression against parents is most severely frowned upon. The good child is thought of as one who is obedient and polite, though this ideal seems to be achieved only rarely. There is little permissiveness for making noise, fighting, or even playing in the home, but neither is there much expectation that the child of five will carry out constructive household tasks. The mothers seem to aim at coping, or enduring, rather than at molding. Corporal punishment and threats of punishment, rather than praise or reward, seem to be the chief techniques of control. Furthermore, mothers often report evidence for the operation of conscience as a control, and this is particularly true of mothers who rely less on physical punishment. Mothers who wish to reward their children often give them something to eat, and food occupies an important place in the thoughts of the children. Perhaps because of this, feeding problems are not common.

The attitude toward sex is generally repressive. Nudity is tabooed from infancy. Children receive no sex instruction. Masturbation in children is denied by most mothers, and any occurrence punished promptly on discovery.

Evidence for training in sex roles from birth is found in the slightly greater permissiveness for nudity in males. By age five there is a tendency for a child to identify to some degree with the like-sexed parent, thus demonstrating that the role is being learned. In describing their hopes for the future of their children, mothers speak more of marriage for the girls and of education and employment for boys. Parental roles seem well defined, with responsibility for the child and household resting on the mother. The mothers ordinarily discipline the children, and they are more likely to approve of the fathers' disciplinary actions if they judge them to be severe.

Arab mothers are permissive of dependency in children and sometimes even encourage it, but Armenian mothers look upon it as a nuisance. For neither group, however, is dependency as serious a problem as in America. Lebanese mothers generally expect the child to behave independently at a fairly early age. This expectation may be an outgrowth of the mothers' tendency to focus attention on infants and to expect siblings to care for the younger children. If the psychological explanation of an "achieving society" were granted, we might then explain the enterprising, achieving nature of the Lebanese, as shown in such matters as their rapidly developing economy, as an outgrowth of this early training in independence.

A majority of the mothers believe that their child-rearing practices differ from those of the generation in which they grew up, and that current practices are superior. Not only do they perceive cultural change, they look upon it as a net gain.

Group Differences within Lebanon

From this brief summary it can be seen that there are many child-rearing practices typical of all of the groups studied, so that they seem to be characteristic of the Lebanese generally. In spite of the variety of religious and ethnic groups in the nation, there is a certain homogeneity in this aspect of the culture. Many child-rearing practices cut across the lines of religion, class, and language.

Let us next examine the . . . subject of group differences: "Are there differences between Christian and Moslem mothers, or between Aab and Armenian mothers? Are mothers in the Beqaa Valley similar to those of the coastal capital city? Do the lower-class peasants differ from middle-class mothers?"

There are few practices in which city mothers differ from those of the valley. *Urban-rural differences are rare,* as might have been expected from the close village ties of city Lebanese. . . . City mothers had to keep closer watch on children, particularly regarding playing in the street, than did valley mothers, but this is a fairly obvious aspect of city life. City mothers were also rated as warmer in general than were valley mothers. The modernization factor, to be discussed shortly, probably accounts for most of this difference.

Class differences in child rearing were also few in number, and this was particularly true of mothers in the valley. Middle-class mothers were rated warmer on the average than were lower-class mothers, and they reported some scheduling of nursing more often than did lower-class mothers. Lower-class mothers had more reservations about pregnancy than did other mothers, swaddled infants a little longer, and were a little more likely to punish frequently. The middle-class children did better on the "intelligence test" than did the lower-class children. In all of these respects, except for swaddling, the class differences obtaining in Lebanon were identical with those obtaining in America. Many other class differences in child rearing found in American studies were not found in Lebanon. In child rearing, then, some class differences resembling those in the United States may be discerned, but class similarities are often found in Lebanon where class differences obtain in America. So far as this aspect of the culture is concerned, class seems less important in Lebanon than in the United States.

Within the general pattern of Lebanese practices *there was some variation from one religious sect to another.* Gregorian mothers seemed on the whole to be more dominant and demanding, less permissive and less warm, than were Arab mothers. They had more often held employment prior to marriage, and they, rather than the Gregorian fathers, dominated in making decisions in the home, on discipline and other matters, to a greater degree than did other mothers. They kept closer tab on the child and expected more of him in the performance of tasks around the house. They were more likely than were others to rely on beating and scolding as a disciplinary technique, and had more faith in the efficacy of physical punishment. They more often described their husbands as severe disciplinarians than did other mothers. Their children, finally, were more likely than others to score above average on the "intelligence test."

The Orthodox mothers as a group differed from the Lebanese norms in only a few items. They were on the average warmer than other mothers, and they relied more than the others on discussion and reasoning as a disciplinary technique.

Sunni mothers had more children, on the average, than did the Christian mothers. In their disciplinary techniques they differed from others in placing less responsibility on the child, in less frequently rewarding good behavior, and in relying more on empty threats. They reported more separation of father and child, and less severity of the father as disciplinarian. More than other groups, they opposed all fighting, even in self-defense. Their descriptions of a good child included "clever" more frequently than did those of other mothers. Nevertheless, a higher proportion of their children scored below average on the "intelligence test" than did the children in other groups.

Students of Lebanese society have often mentioned that the Christians of Beirut, and especially those of the middle class, are the most modern of the people to be found there, and that the rural Moslems, particularly those who are peasants, are the most traditional in their outlook and behavior. In the analysis of the answers given by these mothers to our many questions, it was noted that *child-rearing practices often reflected the differences between modern and traditional mothers.* On many variables, the mothers expected to be more modern were at one extreme, those considered traditional at the other extreme, and the other mothers at some intermediate point. On a few items, the "modern" mothers and the "traditional" mothers were similar to each other and different from the other mothers.

The following characteristics were more likely to be found among "modern" mothers and less likely to be found among "traditional" mothers than among Lebanese mothers generally:

1. Higher education, even when the effect of social class is excluded.
2. Warmer treatment of the five-year-old child.
3. Shorter duration of breast feeding, with more scheduling of feeding.
4. Belief that a child should learn how to fight when necessary.
5. Use of the withholding of favors as a disciplinary technique.
6. Greater emphasis on mothers' decisions in domestic affairs.
7. More reported dependency of the children.
8. Demands and expectations of the sort which in American studies had typified mothers of high achievement need.

Both "modern" and "traditional" mothers found more time to spend with the infant than did other mothers. Both also reported more often than others that their children knew something about how babies were born, but this similarity was only apparent. Children of the Beirut Orthodox group had received some instruction from the mother, and children of the Baalbek Sunni group had been at home when the process of birth occurred. Both groups of children also received earlier independence training than did others, but here, too, the similarity was superficial. The "traditional" mothers began earlier than others to leave the child to his own devices, while the "modern" mothers began earlier to train the child in independent accomplishment.

The term "transitional" is sometimes applied to groups showing evidence of modernization. The implication of such a term seems to be that more modern groups are at an intermediate point between wholly traditional and wholly modern practices, and hence necessarily in a stage of transition. Such reasoning is not compelling, however. It is quite possible that the more modern group has already undergone some change, and reached a relatively stable point, while the more traditional group is now in a state of transition. The "modern" mothers in our samples, for example, reported that they were acting as their mothers had, while the "traditional" mothers reported that they were following practices quite different from those they had experienced as a child. If these perceptions are accurate, then it is the more traditional mothers of Lebanon who are "transitional."

In general it might be said that the similarities in child-rearing practices among the different groups of Lebanese mothers outweigh the differences. Class differences and city-valley differences are few. The greatest differences are those associated with religious sect, and those between the mothers in groups which are more "modern" and those more "traditional."

Cross-Cultural Patterns of Child Rearing

Next let us consider questions of primary interest to the behavioral scientist. Are there relationships among child-rearing practices and child behavior in Lebanon? Do these relationships hold in Western and Middle Eastern cultures alike?

In many American studies of child rearing, it has been found that the two factors of warmth vs. coldness and autonomy vs. control run through many aspects of mothers' behavior with their children. Both of these factors seem to be of significance in the behavior of Arab and Armenian mothers. At the same time, however, the relation in Lebanon between each of these factors and other variables was often different from the relation that had been found in America.

Warmth

In Lebanon as in the United States middle-class mothers were more often rated warm than were those of the lower class. In each of the countries mothers rated low in warmth produced more emotional upset in their children in the process of toilet training than did mothers rated high in warmth, and this difference was particularly noticeable in both cultures when the mother used severe training techniques. In both countries, too, the mothers rated higher in warmth had children rated higher in conscience. In Lebanon five-year-old children were more likely to be dependent on their mothers if their mothers were high in warmth.

In America this relation did not hold for warmth generally, but only for overtly demonstrative warmth.

Lebanese mothers were more often rated warm in their treatment of boys than in their treatment of girls. Warmer mothers reported more feeding problems than did other mothers. Neither of these relationships obtained in America. On the other hand, in the United States a slight correlation was found between feelings about becoming pregnant and warmth toward the child. In the same study it was also found that spanking by a warm mother was more likely to be reported as effective than was spanking administered by cold mothers. Neither of these relationships obtained in Lebanon. Some of the concomitants of warmth apparently vary with the culture.

Independence and Dependency

The autonomy vs. control dimension, or independence and dependence factors, have been linked in America to strong achievement need, and to high degrees of achievement. Among the Lebanese families studied, it was found that in the middle class, and in the groups noted currently for eminence in economic achievement, there was greater than average expectation and demand, as well as reward, for independent accomplishments, and for assumption of responsibility. In a general way, our results on achievement seem compatible with those of Western studies.

The only child was found in the Massachusetts study to be more dependent than other children. There were few only children in our samples, but these, together with children having only one sibling, were found to be more dependent on the average than were children in larger families. In neither country was sex, ordinal position, or degree of infant indulgence of the children related to dependency at age five.

Lebanese children weaned after eleven months were generally less dependent than children weaned earlier. This relationship could not be checked against American findings because so few American children were nursed longer than a year. The attitude of Arab and Armenian mothers toward dependency was likewise related to the degree of dependency manifested. The greatest amount of dependency was reported by mothers who approved of dependency, somewhat less was reported by mothers who disapproved, and the least amount was reported by mothers who were neutral or ambivalent toward dependency. This curvilinear relationship was not found in the Massachusetts study because few mothers approved of dependency, but it was found there that neutral mothers reported less dependency than disapproving mothers.

Other Interrelations

Having considered the variables relating to warmth and to independence and dependency, we now list briefly some of the other relationships among variables found in our investigation.

1. Although happiness on becoming pregnant was reported by most

mothers, more lower-class than middle-class mothers had some reservations on the subject. Mothers were more often delighted when the pregnancy was their first, or when there were no male children in the existing family. Feelings about pregnancy were not linked to warmth shown the five-year-old. In all of these results, our findings agree with those of the Harvard study. In only one aspect was there disagreement in results. New England mothers who had worked before marriage were more often delighted over pregnancy than were those who had never worked, but in Lebanon the opposite was true. This difference may perhaps be attributed to the fact that employment for unmarried girls is not a traditional activity in Lebanon, as in America, whereas in both cultures motherhood is a traditional part of the wife's role.

2. Weaning produced less emotional upset when it occurred early and when it was decisive than when it occurred later or was indecisive. Feeding problems at age five were not related to emotional upset at weaning or toilet training. All of these observations are congruent with those of the Massachusetts study.

3. The use of reasoning rather than punishment as a disciplinary device was associated with a high degree of conscience, just as it was in America. In Lebanon, unlike America, girls showed no more evidence of conscience than did boys. One reason for this difference may be that Lebanese girls are treated less warmly than are boys, and warmth of mothers' behavior is related to amount of conscience. Thus the tendency of girls to identify more easily with the mother than boys do, and thereby acquire conscience more readily, is offset in Lebanon by the greater coolness with which girls are treated. . . .

Toward Future Research

The insights which this investigation has provided into family life in Lebanon and into some of the patterns of child rearing and child behavior found there would appear to justify the belief that the research techniques of child psychology can be applied profitably to cross-cultural research. Not only have we learned something about Lebanese mothers and children, we have also learned much about mother and child behavior in general. This study is only a first step, however, and points to the need for more research with other groups. Only after the accumulation of far more data will we be able to make with any confidence the generalizations and predictions so sorely needed by those offering counsel on child care. In view of the certainty that counsel will be called for, and given, on a basis of the fragmentary knowledge now available, the demand for further research appears acute.

In calling for further cross-cultural research, recognition must be given also to the importance of initial analyses of behavior made in one culture. The studies of significant elements of child rearing in America provided the model for this investigation in Lebanon. In order to build up a general picture of behavior, it is first necessary to analyze the elements and dimensions of behavior, and to devise instruments for assessing such behavior. As such analyses move forward, additional cross-cultural studies become possible. These studies can in turn provide clues for further analysis. Through such an interplay between intensive analysis and extensive cross-validation may arise generalizations worthy of a science of behavior which attempts to embrace mankind.

10
Values and Societal Development: Education and Change in Nasser's Egypt

Michael W. Suleiman

There has been much discussion among social scientists as well as policymakers concerning the role of values in the process of development. One can find no unanimity, however, as to which aspects of "development" are the most important and which should, therefore, receive the greatest attention.[1] According to one view, basic structural and performance changes in the society (the objective environment) must take place before any effective and/or permanent changes in the attitudes and values of the people are effected. Others argue, however, that changes in the realm of the subjective (attitudes and values) are basic for any successful attempt at development. The proponents of this view argue that modernization is a state of mind and that, if a nation wants to develop, then it must change the attitudes and values of its people. In general, the former point of view has been advocated by economists and Marxists, whereas the latter position has been advanced by sociologists, anthropologists, psychologists, and leftist reformers or Western liberals. In *practical* terms, however, David McClelland claims that the reverse situation has obtained.[2]

Even when the importance and centrality of values are recognized, however, scholars need to determine what specific values are associated with traditional or underdeveloped societies and which ones are found in the so-called developed countries. Thus, it is generally agreed that in the traditional and underdeveloped countries, people perceive the world as full of uncontrollable forces that restrict and dominate their lives and, further, that they are *helpless* to change the situation. Consequently, the reaction is either to utilize spiritual or magical powers to propitiate and appease the forces of nature and thus secure "protection" from them or to "accept" nature and live in harmony with the universe. Furthermore, traditional societies have and encourage hierarchical social structures in which one small group is dominant and one large group is submissive, and where the social position is inherited, not achieved. In such societies, behavior is usually unchanging or slow to change and is governed by custom, rather than by law. Social relations are usually restricted to family members, including the extended family, with corruption and nepotism as concomitant attributes. In such situations, there is an absence of creative activity, and economic productivity is low. Development, on the other hand, requires that the world be perceived as somewhat threatening and that, therefore, one must constantly strive to harness the forces of nature. Not only that, but in harnessing the forces of nature, the individual must be guided by the view that order and rationality are possible once the basic rules or laws are discovered. The individual is brought up to internalize a sense of duty to achieve. This, as well as the personal responsibility to transform the world, transcends any concern with the profit motive.[3]

Method

As the building block of the political system, the individual provides much information for social scientists interested in the process of the inculcation of values and the ramifications of early orientations upon the development of nations and countries. It is generally assumed that children learn certain concepts and acquire particular attitudes from the material they use at school, even if that material is ostensibly used to teach them how to read or is provided merely for entertainment. Hence my interest in studying elementary school primers, even though values are also acquired through child-rearing practices within the family, from contact with peer groups, from the media of communication (radio, television, cinema, magazines, newspapers), and from books, games, etc. Other studies have shown the usefulness of concentrating on elementary school readers for a study of preferred values in a particular country.[4]

The readers used in the third, fourth, fifth, and sixth grades in Egypt prior to the 1952 revolution as well as those in use in 1972-1973 have been selected for our study.[5] These textbooks were and are used in all public schools throughout Egypt. In other words, they are read by almost all school children in that country. Furthermore, these texts or some modifications of them are extensively used in several other Arab countries. Hence, whatever impact such texts have extends throughout much of the Arab world. Since the study covers the period preceding the revolution as well as another period when the revolutionary regime was long in control, it will enable us to detect the changes, if any, which have been introduced with the arrival of a new and more activist regime.

Not every item in these texts was read and evaluated. In fact, pieces containing descriptions of historical events or geographical regions, essays, religious texts, and poems were eliminated from our study.[6] In total, 131 stories from the 1952-1953 period and 77 stories from the 1972-1973 period were read and analyzed, a total of 208 stories. Much time was spent adapting and refining some content-analytical methods for the study of textbooks. In the end, I employed an anthropological framework, a psychological one, and a sociological orientation as well as my own schema. In this paper, however, it is primarily the sociological and anthropological frameworks that are developed and discussed. All stories were read twice, once by a graduate assistant and once by me.[7] A conference session then ironed out any differences in the scoring.

The Results

Though several complex schemes for identifying and rating values in elementary school primers have been devised, J. Lawrence Wiberg and Gaston E. Blom of the University of Colorado set up an "attitude scale" and a manual for instruction in its use that are quite simple and straightforward.[8] Thirty-eight attitudinal sets were identified. "Attitude" is defined as "an attribute or characteristic, either personal or impersonal, to which value, such as good-bad, superior-inferior, desirable-undesirable, useful–not useful, wanted-unwanted, important-unimportant, could be affixed."[9] In this paper, value and attitude will be used interchangeably. For each story, a decision was made as to whether each of the thirty-eight attitudes was "present" or "absent." Each attitude, if present, was scored only once, regardless of how often it appeared in the story.

It is clear from Table 1 that by far the most important attitude of all is the great Egyptian passion for helping people, caring for others, offering protection and nurturance to fellow human beings as well as to animals and all living things. This attitude was present in 138 of the 208 stories or in 66.3 percent of the total. We also find that the stories are replete (51 percent) with references to death and dying, the portrayal of realistic danger, and different forms of illness or injury. Such situations, as well as those depicting scenes of cruelty, tormenting, meanness, ruthlessness or maliciousness (27.4 percent), were often presented with a view to illustrating the concern and caring of others, obviously teaching the young students to be kind and considerate toward those in need.

Another highly prized attitude is one that glorifies alertness, attentiveness, capability, intelligence, and cleverness (47.6 percent). In one story, for instance, two boys were out in the fields for a picnic when they spotted through their binoculars a gang robbing a house. Though they were too young to stop the robbers themselves, they showed much intelligence by having one of them run to the nearest town and call the police for help while the other remained in his place watching through his binoculars the path taken by the robbers, which he then reported to the police when they arrived. The police were then able to follow and catch the robbers.[10]

The above story gave a good example of alertness and intelligent behavior. At times, however, the examples provided instances of "clev-

Table 1

Values in Egyptian Elementary School Readers, 1952-53 and 1972-73

Value	Number of Times Expressed	%	Value	Number of Times Expressed	%
Caring, helping	138	66.3	Cleanliness, neatness	29	13.9
Death, illness	106	51.0	Physical weakness	28	13.5
Intelligence, alertness	99	47.6	Nonconforming	28	13.5
Food and drink	97	46.6	Social regulations and social rules	28	13.5
Working, toiling	88	42.3	Uncaring	27	13.0
Play, sport	80	38.5	Role playing, imitating	18	8.7
Courage, valor	77	37.0	Dirtiness	16	7.7
Obedience to authority	60	28.8	Nationalism, patriotism	15	7.2
Cruelty, meanness	57	27.4	Exploring, discovering	14	6.7
Economic transactions	53	25.5	Ignorance, inalertness	14	6.7
Conforming	52	25.0	Selfishness	9	4.3
Religiousness	50	24.0	Lassitude, laziness	9	4.3
Ambition, persistence	49	23.6	Physical strength	4	1.9
Recognition of other countries	49	23.6	Peace, pacifism	4	1.9
Education in schools	45	21.6	Cowardice	3	1.4
War, weaponry	43	20.7	Interactional physical passivity	2	0.96
Oldness	39	18.8	Motor competence, dexterity	2	0.96
Interactional physical aggressiveness	38	18.3	Motor incompetence, clumsiness	1	0.48
Competitiveness, rivalry	36	17.3			
Family togetherness	33	15.9			

erness," or one person getting the better of another through trickery. In "The Donkey and the Bull," for instance, the donkey advises the bull to pretend that he is sick and thus avoid work. When the owner finds that the bull is "sick," he uses the donkey in its place, leaving the bull to eat aplenty and relax all day. That evening the donkey returns and tells the bull that it had better show signs of health and vigor if it is to avoid the butcher's knife. Though it was a lie, this trick worked and the bull was back on the job, as the donkey sat there laughing and enjoying his "cleverness" and success.[11]

Table 1 also shows that food or drink are mentioned in almost half of the stories in these texts (46.6 percent). Thus the Egyptian concern about and interest in food or food items are clearly demonstrated. It is also worth noting that references to work, toil, or labor are only slightly more frequent than references to play, sports, or recreational activity (42.3 percent vs. 38.5 percent).

Knowing the traditional Egyptian and Arab emphasis on courage, fortitude, and daring, it is not surprising to find that this attitude is found in a relatively large number of the stories in these texts (37 percent).

The results in Table 1 also indicate that these textbooks tend to emphasize deference and obedience to authority (28.8 percent) as well as the more general attitude of conforming to the demands of others (25 percent). This attitude is presented in various forms, most often perhaps in an almost blind obedience to the authority of the parents or older people in general. Also, a general lack of initiative was often "encouraged" through examples showing a child adapting his behavior to facilitate harmonious interaction with other children.

Ambition, persistence, striving for advancement, power, or honor appeared fairly frequently in these stories (23.6 percent).

Among the least emphasized attitudes, one is surprised to find nationalism or patriotism. Thus, very few stories (15, or 7.2 percent) depicted an awareness of the country of the primer, much less presented a discussion of national heroes, national holidays, loyalty to the country, or such pictures as school children saluting the flag. It is possible that the writers of these stories were not certain which "nationalism" to emphasize, Egyptian, Arab, or Moslem. Confusion or ambivalence on this issue could have produced the low number of references. The alternative explanation is that the writers deliberately avoided nationalist or patriotic themes.

The stories, apparently reflecting the sentiments and views of the writers and policymakers, showed little or no interest in developing in the young motor competence, dexterity, or physical strength.

Finally, exploration, curiosity, and discovery and learning through role-playing and imitation are two attitudes that are not often present in Egyptian stories (6.7 percent and 8.7 percent respectively).

The textbooks were also analyzed using an anthropological framework. Dr. Florence Kluckhohn has suggested that there are five basic problems which all social organizations face and to which they devise some response by way of "solution."[12] The answers to these problems can and do provide social scientists with a means to studying the value orientation of the societies concerned. We shall discuss four of these problems and how they were "resolved" in the stories under study, as illustrative of the general Egyptian policymakers' view of these matters.[13]

The Egyptian response to the question of man's relation to nature is to present a harmonious relationship that exists (or should exist) between man and nature. This was found to be the theme in 124 of the stories (60 percent) as opposed to only 44 stories (21 percent) emphasizing the idea of working to overcome difficulties presented by natural forces (such as poor weather, high mountains, flooding rivers, etc.). In the remaining 40 stories (19 percent), the theme was one of people being subjugated to nature, giving in and/or merely attributing their defeat or failure to "Fate," "God's will," or "bad luck."

The attitude toward time expressed in the stories was characterized by an emphasis on the present (76 percent) and to some extent on the past (23 percent), but hardly any stories (2, or 1 percent) stressed the future and the idea of working hard now and planning and sacrificing so that a brighter future can be built.

The personality type most favored in the Egyptian stories is one that glorifies spontaneity and what the person *is* rather than what he can do (47 percent). The next most popular personality type is that classified as "doing," i.e., one which emphasizes accomplishment or getting things done (31 percent). Themes emphasizing self-realization or developmental aspects (being-in-becoming) were found in 46 stories (22 percent).

Finally, in treating a person's relationship with others, textbook writers de-emphasized familial ties (found in only 21 percent of the stories) and encouraged individualism (39 percent) or collateral, i.e., egalitarian and cooperative, ties (40 percent).

We are now in a position to review the values found in Egyptian readers to determine their applicability to developmental themes. Our conclusions are as follows:

1. There appears to be no definite plan by textbook writers to emphasize development above other objectives.

2. The most important value by far is a major concern for the welfare and well-being of others. This does not, incidentally, refer to public or governmental assistance or welfare programs. Rather, it is people expressing their concern for other people—and not necessarily their own families or relatives.

3. Among the emphasized values associated with development are the following: intelligence; alertness; working; toiling; ambition; persistence; individualism or a cooperative relationship with others; some emphasis on a personality type that favors "doing" or getting things done.

4. Some of the preferred values do not contribute to development and could, in fact, detract from it. Among these are some that reflect

Egyptian and general Arab traditional values, such as courage or daring as well as the almost ubiquitous presence of food and drink. We shall return to the question of food later when we talk about consumerist attitudes.

5. The preferred attitude toward nature in these texts is one of subjugation to it or of man's being in harmony with it. The former attitude in particular does not aid the developmental effort. In fact, it hinders it.

6. Emphasis on the present rather than on future gratification is also detrimental to development and will be discussed later. The same is true of the fascination with "being" as a personality type.

The Effect of the Egyptian "Revolution" on Values

The importance of values in the development or retardation of any society becomes evident when we observe that all major revolutions have been accompanied with a substantial change in the value system of the society involved.[14] In fact, I would argue that a good measure of how "revolutionary" a movement is can be determined by the extent of value and attitude change it has effected among the people being "revolutionized." Using this yardstick, then, let us examine how revolutionary the Egyptian coup of July 23, 1952, has been.

A quick look at Table 2 shows us that the top nine values or attitudes advocated during the Egyptian monarchy remained unchanged (except for minor shifts in ranking) some twenty years after the "revolution." Only two relatively important changes may be noted. First, the emphasis on helping others and caring for them became even more pronounced after the military coup, increasing in frequency of occurrence from about 57 percent to 83 percent. Though in both cases it remained the most important value or attitude, the increase in emphasis is statistically significant, as Table 3 demonstrates. In other words, the change was probably not a mere chance happening.

Second, situations depicting attitudes of conforming, conceding, or acquiescing became more frequent in the newer texts (32.5 percent vs. 20.6 percent) and this attitude moved up in rank from fifteenth to tenth. Here again, as is seen in Table 4, the change is probably not by chance but may be inferred to reflect a tendency to encourage conformity and discourage nonconforming.

The third, and by far the most important, change occurred in the attitude toward the favored personality type. Thus, as Table 5 clearly shows, since the "revolution" there has been a definite drop in the number and percentage of stories depicting the personality type that is concerned only with describing what the individual is like and what his emotions and desires are. Simultaneously, we observe a greater emphasis on the personality type that is concerned with self-development or with getting things done.

Very few other changes took place.[15] It might be noted that attitudes

Table 2

Top Ten Values in Egyptian Elementary School Stories

Values in 1952-53 Stories	**N**	%	**Values in 1972-73 Stories**	**N**	%
Caring, helping	74	56.5	Caring, helping	64	83.1
Death, infirmity, illness	70	53.4	Food, drink	44	57.1
Intelligence, alertness, cleverness	64	48.9	Working, toiling	37	48.1
Food, drink	53	40.5	Death, infirmity, illness	36	46.8
Working, toiling	51	38.9	Intelligence, alertness	35	45.5
Courage, daring, fearlessness	46	35.1	Play, sport, recreation	35	45.5
Play, sport, recreation	45	34.4	Courage, daring, etc.	29	37.7
Obedience or deference to authority	35	26.7	Cruelty, tormenting, meanness	26	33.8
Cruelty, tormenting, meanness	31	23.7	Obedience or deference to authority	25	32.5
Recognition of other countries, nationalities or ethnic groups	31	23.7	Conforming, conceding, acquiescing	25	32.5

Table 3

Caring and Helping as a Value in Egyptian Elementary School Stories		
	1952-53 Stories	**1972-73 Stories**
	(N = 95)	(N = 70)
Caring	78%	91%
Uncaring	22	9
	100%	100%

$x^2 = 5.4 : P < .05$

Table 4

Conforming and Non-Conforming as a Value in Egyptian Elementary School Stories		
	1952-53 Stories	**1972-73 Stories**
	(N = 41)	(N = 29)
Conforming	66%	86%
Non-Conforming	34	14
	100%	100%

$x^2 = 3.7 : P < .10$

Table 5

Personality Type as a Value in Egyptian Elementary School Stories		
	1952-53 Stories	**1972-73 Stories**
	(N = '131)	(N = 77)
Being	56%	31%
Being-in-becoming	17	31
Doing	27	38
	100%	100%

$x^2 = 13.0 : P < .01$

toward women showed little change. In general, the main characters in the stories continued to be predominantly male. Also, sisters usually deferred to their brothers and girls were generally presented as less active and more docile than boys.[16]

In summary, then, it can be confidently stated that no sweeping revolutionary change in the realm of values took place in Egypt after 1952.[17] It is not for lack of trying, however. It is true, of course, and well known that Gamal Abdel-Nasser and his military junta did not have much of a plan or an ideology to guide their actions when they first came to power. Nasser himself realized this and stated it publicly.[18] A few years later, however, and especially after the 1956 Suez invasion and, more importantly, after the breakup of the United Arab Republic in 1961, a certain brand of socialist ideology was beginning to be formulated.[19] The question of attitudes and values was also raised. Nasser himself recognized the enormity of the task when he stated: "To build factories is easy, to build hospitals and schools is possible, but to build a nation of men is a hard and difficult task."[20]

The task of "building a nation of men" is much harder for any developing country today than it was for the Western countries when they were in the earlier stages of development. A major difference can be seen in the realm of values.[21] During their period of major economic advancement, the Western countries had a value system that encouraged hard work, personal sacrifice, and investment (the so-called Protestant ethic), and at the same time the elite were little hampered by concern for the poor or the fear of popular rebellion. In any case, these countries had predominantly "producer" attitudes, i.e., "work and productivity drives in the individual that are geared to basic sectors of the economy."[22] In recent times, however, Westerners have acquired primarily "consumer" attitudes, i.e., "consumption drives shaped by the continually changing standards of rich countries."[23] Unfortunately, these are the attitudes held by most people in the poor or underdeveloped countries also—at the very time when the leadership is allegedly anxious to "modernize" or "develop" the country. The consequence of these "low producerist–high consumerist" attitudes is stagnation, if not decline, which characterizes much of the Third World today. The "modernity" that one sees in certain sectors of a developing country (mainly the capital city) is merely a manifestation and product of these consumerist attitudes which motivate those economically able to buy the flashy cars, refrigerators, air conditioners or airplanes—most or all of which were made in the industrialized or developed countries. In fact, these "modern" sectors act as a parasite that retards rather than advances economic development.[24] This "modern" sector is usually composed of the urban middle and upper classes in the Third World.[25]

In the case of Egypt we saw that, though some of the favored attitudes and values encouraged development, several others encouraged consumerism. Included among the latter are the emphasis on (1) food and eating, and (2) present rather than future gratification.

The conclusion that we reach, then, is that the 1952 coup has not been revolutionary in the realm of values and attitudes. The dominant values in Egypt before and since the coup are more typical of a traditional than a development-oriented society. The most important concerns of the policymakers and textbook writers appear to be reflective of urban middle-class concerns and attitudes. These attitudes tend to be consumerist in nature but they also reflect a very strong element of caring for and helping others who are in need.[26]

This is *not* to say that these are the only changes in attitude brought about by the new Egyptian regime. There is no question, for instance, that one major change, not reflected in our study, pertains to the pride and dignity the "new Egyptian" feels now that his country has been liberated from its colonial masters and especially since the Nasser regime was able to deal some major blows to the imperialist powers.[27] This *is* to say, however, that one important agency for value change, the school textbook, has been underutilized or ignored for these purposes. As a matter of fact, a cursory and casual look at the movies, television, newspapers, books, magazines, the family, and the armed forces leads us to believe that the new regime did not invest much time, money, or effort in the difficult task of setting up a modern society. Hence the ease with which Nasser's successor, Anwar Sadat, was able to steer the country toward more "moderate" policies and behavior, both domestically and internationally.

Notes

1. In fact, development theorists often find it difficult to include values in their models, except as a by-product of change. For a critique and exposition of this view, see Ratna Dutta, *Values in Models of Modernization* (Delhi, India: Vikas Publications, 1971). For a good summary, critique, and bibliography on values and development, see Everett E. Hagen, *On the Theory of Social Change* (Homewood, Ill.: The Dorsey Press, 1962). For a stimulating discussion, see Jean-Yves Calvez, *Politics and Society in the Third World,* trans. M. J. O'Connell (Maryknoll, N.Y.: Orbis Books, 1973).

2. David C. McClelland, "Motivational Patterns in Southeast Asia with Special Reference to the Chinese Case," *Journal of Social Issues* Vol. 29, No. 1 (1963), pp. 6–19.

3. For a detailed discussion of these issues, see Hagen, *On the Theory of Social Change,* especially Part II.

4. See, for instance, Richard deCharms and Gerald H. Moeller, "Values Expressed in American Children's Readers: 1800–1950," *Journal of Abnormal and Social Psychology* Vol. 64, No. 2 (1962), pp. 136–142; and I. L. Child et al., "Children's Textbooks and Personality Development," *Psychological Monographs* 60 (1946).

5. While in other countries analysis of first-grade readers was possible and useful, I found that the first- and second-grade readers in Egypt merely contained material for teaching the children how to spell and had no "values" that one could study. The textbooks examined in this study have all been printed by the Egyptian Ministry of Education (Wazaret al-Ma'aref, later changed to Wazaret al-Tarbiya wal-Ta'lim). Also, because of changes in the educational system, the designated grade-levels on some of the readers are corrected to correspond with the present system. The textbooks examined for the earlier period in this study are: Ibrahim Mustafa et al., *al-Mutala'a al-Arabiyya,* Part I, Year 1 (3rd grade), 1951; Part II, Year 4 (4th grade), 1953; Part III, Year 5 and 1st preparatory (5th grade), 1954; and *al-Mutala'a al-Arabiyya: Qisas,* Year 3 (5th grade), 1949; *al-Mutala'a al-Arabiyya: Qisas,* Part IV, Year 4 (6th grade), 1948. The books used in 1972-1973 were: Mohammed Ahmed al-Murshidi et al., *al-Qira'a wal-Mahfuzat,* 3rd grade (1972), 4th grade (1970), 5th grade (1971), 6th grade (1971); and Mahmud Rushdi Khater et al., *Nahnu Naqra',* 3rd grade (1968), 4th grade (1971), and 5th grade (1972). There was no second reader for the 6th grade.

6. The other items could, of course, be analyzed for value orientation. However, the approach of this and similar studies concentrates on the stories as the units of analysis.

7. This was done to check the reliability of the scoring technique, i.e., the rate of agreement between the two scorers. Reliability was high, at 91 percent agreement considering all decisions on "attitude present" or "attitude absent."

8. See J. Lawrence Wiberg and Gaston E. Blom, "A Cross-National Study of Attitude Content in Reading Primers," *International Journal of Psychology* Vol. 5, No. 2 (1970), pp. 109–122; and their "Cross-National Attitude Rating Manual—1970 Version" (mimeographed).

9. Wiberg and Blom, "A Cross-National Study," p. 110.

10. The story was entitled "*Batalan Saghiran*" [Two young heroes] and is found in *al-Qira'a wal-Mahfuzat,* 4th grade (1972-1973 period), pp. 140–144.

11. "*Al-Himar wal-Thawr*" [The donkey and the bull], ibid., pp. 179–184.

12. F. R. Kluckhohn, "Dominant and Substitute Profiles of Cultural Orientations," *Social Forces* Vol. 28, No. 4 (May 1950), pp. 376–393. See also

F. R. Kluckhohn and Fred L. Strodtbeck, *Variations in Value Orientations* (Evanston, Ill.: Row, Peterson and Co., 1961).

13. The four problems and the suggested solutions as conceived by Dr. Kluckhohn are as follows: (1) Man's relation to nature: man subjugated, man in nature, and man over nature; (2) Time dimension: past, present, and future; (3) Valued personality type: being, being-in-becoming, and doing; and (4) Modality of relationship: lineal, collateral, and individualistic. The fifth problem relates to "innate predispositions," with the three likely answers being that man is basically good, basically bad, and neither good nor bad. An attempt was made to determine the orientation of the textbook writers on this issue. However, the attempt was abandoned because it was not possible to detect the authors' views on this question.

A similar, though not identical, discussion may be found in Jean-Yves Calvez, *Politics and Society in the Third World,* especially ch. 11. See also Joseph W. Elder's research in India on a similar topic, "National Loyalties in a Newly Independent Nation," in David E. Apter (ed.), *Ideology and Discontent* (New York: The Free Press, 1964), pp. 77–92.

14. For a discussion of revolutions and the importance of value change, see Nadim el-Bitar, *al-Idyulujiyya al-Inqilabiyya* [Revolutionary ideology] (Beirut: Al-Mu'assassa al-Ahliyya lil-Tiba'a wal-Nashr, 1964).

15. For a blistering attack on the low literary quality of the post-1952 texts and the poverty of information in these texts, see the following series of articles by Lewis Awad, all in *Al-Ahram,* "*Dimoqratiyyet al-Ta'lim*" [The democracy of education], 19 February 1971, p. 7; "*Al-Thawra al-Mudadda wal-Ta'lim al-Misri*" [The counterrevolution and Egyptian education], 26 February 1971, p. 6; "*Ahzan Ibn-Batuta fi Diar misr*" [The tribulations of Ibn Batuta in Egypt], 12 March 1971, p. 6; "*Maneton Abusan*" [Manethon frowning], 19 March 1971, p. 7; and "*Jalsa Ma' U aba' al-Aryaf*" [A meeting with the literati of the countryside], 26 March 1971, p. 6.

16. Similar findings were obtained from a study of popular fiction among elementary school students in Egypt. See Huda Barada, el-Sayed el-Azzawi, and Jaber Abdel-Hamid, "Dirasa Tahlilieh li-Qisas al-Atfal" [An analytical study of children's stories], in Huda Barada and el-Sayed Al-Azzawi (eds.), *al-Atfal Yaqra'un* [Children read] (Cairo: Al-Hai'a al-Misriyya al-Aamma lil-Kitab, 1974), pp. 177–235, 208–209.

17. The same argument has, of course, been made by dissident Egyptian leftists. See, for instance, Anouar Abdel-Malek, *Egypt: Military Society* (New York: Random House, 1968). A similar conclusion, based on different data, may be found in Jack Crabbs, Jr., "Politics, History, and Culture in Nasser's Egypt," *International Journal of Middle East Studies* Vol. 6, No. 4 (October 1975), pp. 386–420.

18. See, for instance, Gamal Abdel-Nasser, *The Philosophy of the Revolution* (Buffalo, N.Y.: Economica Books, 1959).

19. In particular, see *Mithaq al-Amal al-Watani* [The charter of national action] (Cairo, 1962).

20. These remarks were part of President Nasser's speech at the opening of the National Assembly in 1957, as quoted in Peter Mansfield, *Nasser's Egypt,* rev. ed. (Baltimore, Md.: Penguin Books, 1969), p. 246.

21. The remarks about "building a nation of men" are, of course, sexist. However, perhaps neither Nasser nor his audience were aware of this bias—as aspect that compounds further the problem of value change.

22. Alan Wells, "Toward an Empirically Grounded Theory of Development,"

The British Journal of Sociology Vol. 23, No. 3 (September 1972), pp. 312–328.

23. Ibid., p. 323.

24. It has also been argued that the modern "center" sectors of the developing countries, rather than contribute to true development, help to maintain the dependence of such polities on the industrialized and developed countries. See Johan Galtung, "A Structural Theory of Imperialism," *Journal of Peace Research,* No. 2 (1971), pp. 83–84.

25. It is worth noting that the educated, including those with advanced degrees, within the Arab world are generally part of the middle class and often share the high consumerist attitudes of that class. The same is true of the educated Arabs who emigrated to Western countries—except that the latter generally have high producerist attitudes as well. In fact, often it is their *frustration* with the lack of concern for high achievement in their home country that drove them to emigrate and/or keeps them from returning.

26. This is a wonderful trait that Arabs should be proud to have. It is interesting that the Menninger Foundation sponsored a week-long seminar in early November, 1975, in New York City to discuss the theme of "Caring" and how to motivate Americans to care about others.

27. On this point, see Wilton Wynn, *Nasser of Egypt: The Search for Dignity* (Cambridge, Mass.: Arlington Books, 1959).

11
Political Socialization in Kuwait: Survey Findings

Tawfic E. Farah

This paper reports the findings of two separate studies that sought to examine the political socialization processes in Kuwait. The first, conducted among Palestinian youths in Kuwait, examines their acquisition of values supportive of the Palestine Liberation Organization (PLO). The second examines the political socialization of Kuwaiti youths.

Three areas were investigated:

First, to what extent do these youths view their respective leaders (Yasir Arafat and Sheikh Salim Al-Sabah) as benevolent? It is theorized that youths learn to support a political system in two stages. Initially children support specific authority figures; later they transfer this support from individual leaders to political institutions. As J. Massey stated: "This image of benevolent leader dominates the cognitive and effective dimensions of the child's political world. Moreover, it . . . serves as a major enduring source of support for the political system on which its effect overflows."[1]

This thesis, known as the "benevolent leader thesis," has some obvious flaws, i.e., not all the governed perceive their leaders as benevolent. It is true that some children in the United States, Britain, and the Netherlands have been found to idealize their heads of state. But Chicano and Black children, for example, have less support for political leaders than do white children. In Canada and Australia, to cite another example, children's images of leadership are not personalized. Children in these countries were found to be more supportive of institutions than of individual leaders.[2]

Second, what are the sources of support for these leaders?

Finally, how is support for these leaders related to a more general attitude of trust in the PLO on the one hand and the Kuwaiti government on the other?

The Setting: Politics in Kuwait

Politics in Kuwait is not unlike politics in many Gulf states. Kuwait is a small country of 6,880 square miles tucked away in the upper Gulf between Iraq and Saudi Arabia. It is a very rich country with annual revenues from the sale of its oil of 21 billion dollars a year. Its per capita income is about U.S. $16,600. Obviously the revenues are not divided equally among its population, half of which are expatriates. Some of this wealth filters down to Kuwaitis—albeit in different degrees—through a comprehensive womb-to-tomb welfare program provided by the state, i.e., the ruling Al-Sabah family. Some of these benefits are enjoyed by the expatriates as in free medical care. The Al-Sabahs have continuously ruled Kuwait since 1756, a total of two hundred and twenty-five years—a fact often ignored by many students of politics in that mini-state.

A Kuwaiti, when compared with an expatriate, is indeed a member of a privileged and affluent group. He is relatively well-to-do and enjoys one of the highest per capita incomes in the world. (Some pockets of poverty also exist in Kuwait.) He is entitled to free medical care, free schooling (including a university education), and a constitutionally guaranteed right to a job.

The Al-Sabahs have been responsive in the political arena as well as in the economic sector. In a region of the world where political freedoms are not the norm, thirty-five thousand Kuwaiti men have recently elected a *consultative body,* a parliament. Neither Kuwaiti women nor expatriates (men and women) are entitled to vote. Kuwaitis are "relatively" free to express their political views. The Al-Sabahs have generally been tolerant rulers. Yet the decision-making process is reserved for an informal coalition of the ruling family and approximately twenty leading merchant families. The coalition is dominated by the Amir (the ruler), who is the first among equals. He is the Patriarch of the whole tribe or the extended Kuwaiti family. (Kuwaiti society is often referred to in official government pronouncements as "a family," "one family." The ruler is referred to as "the father.") The Amir is the final arbiter of all political, economic, and social issues.

But access to this small political system is not blocked. It is often gained through personal and informal channels. The functions of interest articulation and interest aggregation in this political system are performed by the extended family. An individual is apt to go through a relative or a friend to reach a decision maker. The function performed by the friend or the relative is referred to as *wasta.* The decision maker can also be reached directly or through *wasta* at the *diwaniya,* or *majlis* (as it is referred to in other states of the Gulf and in Saudi Arabia).

The Palestinians constitute the largest single expatriate community in Kuwait. They came to the country in two waves: directly following the establishment of the State of Israel in 1948 and following the Arab defeat in 1967. While many of them are well educated and are well-to-do, the majority of them belong to the low end of the socioeconomic status scale. The PLO along with al-Fatah commando group have their own offices in the country. They are generally free to mobilize and agitate in the Palestinian community, but they do not operate any training camps in the country.

The Sample

Palestinian Subsample

Data are derived from responses of a Palestinian subsample (N = 240) to a questionnaire administered to Palestinian youths in Kuwait during the academic year 1975-1976. The students were enrolled in the first, second, third, and fourth intermediate grades. Their ages ranged from 10 to 16 years. The sample was limited to this age group to enhance comparison with similar studies.

The subsample was broken down as follows:

1. Fifty Palestinian boys and fifty Palestinian girls enrolled in the public schools were chosen at random. Class lists were obtained from the administration of each public school. Random numbers were assigned to each boy and each girl. Using a table of random numbers, a sample of fifty boys and fifty girls was isolated, making a subsample of 100. It should be pointed out that these schools were administered by the PLO in the academic year 1975-1976, yet the curriculum was the official Kuwaiti Ministry of Education curriculum. There is no evidence that these students were exposed to special courses in the history, geography, and culture of Palestine. However, individual teachers could have used some periods of instruction to discuss the cause of Palestine. It is generally assumed that Palestinian children who attend public school come from lower-income groups. Socioeconomic data generally confirm this statement. Social class and family income among Palestinians in Kuwait can generally be determined when the father's occupation is known. Most students in this sample were from lower- and lower-middle-class families. In 96 percent of the cases the mother did not work.

2. Another fifty Palestinian boys and fifty Palestinian girls were chosen in the same manner from private schools in Kuwait for a subsample of 100. These students generally came from better economic backgrounds than those attending public schools. In 93 percent of the cases the father was the only working member of the family.

3. A purposive sample of forty *Fatah's Ashbal* ("tiger cubs") attending PLO schools was further isolated. The Ashbal are given paramilitary training and political indoctrination besides the regular course of study. All *Ashbal* in the subsample came from lower- and lower-middle-class families.

Kuwaiti Subsample

The Kuwaiti subsample (N = 500) was isolated a year later. A list of all 123 intermediate junior high schools in Kuwait was drawn up. A stratified random sample of five girls' schools and five boys' schools was chosen. Master lists of all Kuwaiti boys and girls attending these schools were obtained and a random sample of 500 boys and girls was chosen. The respondents were all Muslims, 11 to 16 years of age (mean age 13.8). Each respondent was interviewed individually in Arabic by a fellow Kuwaiti during the academic year 1976-1977.

Hypotheses and Measurement

Support for Arafat

Yasir Arafat, or Abu Ammar as he is popularly known, is chairman of the PLO and leader of al-Fatah organization. He was identified as the benevolent leader by the Palestinian students whose support for him is extensive. He is the most powerful and prestigious political figure to Palestinian youth. In addition, Yasir Arafat has become a symbol of Palestinian armed resistance. His *kaffiya* ("headdress") and his battle fatigues are the same attire worn by all Palestinian guerrillas. In that sense he is also a *fedayi* ("one who is willing to die for a cause"). He is perceived as a military and a political figure; he addresses the United Nations and is a military commander in the battlefield.

Three questions were used to operationalize support for Arafat:

1. Is Abu Ammar hardworking?
2. Does Abu Ammar do good work?
3. Does Abu Ammar help the Palestinian people?

Support for the Amir

Three items were used to operationalize support for the Amir.

1. Is the Amir hardworking?
2. Does the Amir do good work?
3. Does the Amir help the people?

Each question could be answered "always," "sometimes," "never," or "don't know."

Sources of Support

To probe for the sources of support for Arafat and the Amir a set of hypotheses was proposed:

H_1 Support for both leaders is independent of political indoctrination.

The Palestinian leadership has recognized the importance of teaching young Palestinians, often referred to as the "generation of liberation," to support the Palestinian revolution's goals. The maximum goal is a democratic nonsectarian state in Palestine; the minimum goal, an independent state on the West Bank and Gaza. Young Palestinians often join paramilitary groups known as *Ashbal,* where they are exposed to such political instruction. Hence, it is hypothesized that the *Ashbal* are more supportive of the chairman than non-*Ashbal.*

However, the Kuwaitis do not have the equivalent of the *Ashbal.* Are we then to expect their level of support of the Amir to be less than the *Ashbal*'s level of support of Arafat?

H_2 Peer group influence is more important in encouraging support for both leaders than classroom instruction.

Schools do have an obvious impact upon childhood socialization. Civics courses are offered in the intermediate schools in Kuwait. However, it is significant that the courses included in the Kuwaiti curriculum encourage supportive attitudes toward the Kuwaiti political system and its leaders, not toward the PLO and its leaders.

Although civics courses *per se* are not media of Palestinian political socialization, informal meetings of students outside the classroom foster this socialization. Palestinian students converse about the revolution and its exploits with their friends and peers. In answer to the question, "What do you talk to your friends about?" the majority replied that they talked about *fedayi* exploits and Palestine. Of course, children converse about other things as well, but apparently Palestine dominates their conversations. This aspect of the socialization process appears more important in encouraging support for Arafat and the PLO than classroom instruction. Hence, the number of years spent in the classroom is expected to be independent of the Palestinians' level of support for Arafat. Does this hold true for the Kuwaitis?

H_3 Palestinian children learn to support their leaders from their parents.

Families in nonindustrial societies are closely knit. Loyalty and obedience to family decisions in all areas of life rank high in the value hierarchy of members of society. Family obligations are less binding and less salient in industrial societies.

An Arab youth learns respect, reverence, and, above all, loyalty to his family. But despite Palestinian and Kuwaiti youths' loyalty to family, loyalty to one's country is expected to be stronger.

H_4 Poor Palestinians and poor Kuwaitis will be less likely to support their respective leaders.

Specific survey items were used to construct an index of socioeconomic status: (a) What is your father's job? (b) Where do you live? (c) What school do you go to? (d) Did you take a vacation this summer? (e)

Table 1
Support for the Chairman (in Percentages)
by Age and Grade in School

	Grades		
	1st (N = 82)	2nd-3rd (N = 155)	4th (N = 73)
	%	%	%
I. Is the chairman of PLO hard working?			
Always	89	91	95
Sometimes	5	6	5
Never	3	3	—
Don't know	3	1	—
II. Does the chairman of PLO do good work?			
Always	90	90	95
Sometimes	8	8	—
Never	2	—	5
Don't know	—	2	—
III. Does the chairman of PLO help the people?			
Always	85	91	93
Sometimes	10	8	3
Never	5	1	4
Don't know	—	—	—

NOTE: For all three questions the model response of each group is "always." Conversely, the proportion of "never" response is extremely low.

Where did you spend your vacation? All items were coded high, middle, or low.

Data Analysis and Findings

Support for Arafat

Yasir Arafat is very visible to Palestinian children in Kuwait. Respondents were asked, "Who is the most important person in the Palestinian revolution?" The overwhelming majority named Yasir Arafat. The students were also asked to identify the chairman of the PLO and 100 percent were able to do so.

The distribution of responses to the support questions are shown in Table 1. No relationship between year in school (age) and the level of support for the chairman is shown. A possible explanation for this finding is that support for the chairman reflects a Palestinian child's reverence for authority figures in general, and *fedayeen* in particular. To disentangle support for the chairman of the PLO from reverence for authority in general, one must examine support for other well-known authority figures. Thus the instrument included questions about other *fedayi* leaders, parents, movie stars, and soccer stars. Indices of support were formed by adding responses to the component items. The mean support scores for each authority figure are presented in Figure 1. The high level of support for Yasir Arafat is clearly not a particular manifestation of general childhood deference for authority figures but a specific indication of support for the chairman.

Support for the Amir

The distribution of responses to the support questions is shown in Table 2. As with Arafat, no relationship is ascertained between year in school (age) and the level of support for the Amir who was correctly identified by all respondents.

The high level of support for the Amir is not a manifestation of childhood deference for authority figures in general but a specific indication of support for the Amir as indicated in Figure 2. Yet among the Kuwaiti responses we detected a great admiration for soccer stars. Jassim Yacoub, a prominent soccer star, was mentioned often as a man the youths wanted to emulate.

Having provided some perspective with which to evaluate the support for the chairman and the Amir, the analysis will now identify its sources.

Sources of Support

Because Yasir Arafat is a leader of al-Fatah besides his other roles, it is surprising that political indoctrination does not have any impact on support. *Fatah Ashbal* are not significantly more supportive of the chairman than the others. The mean support score is 7.9 for the non-

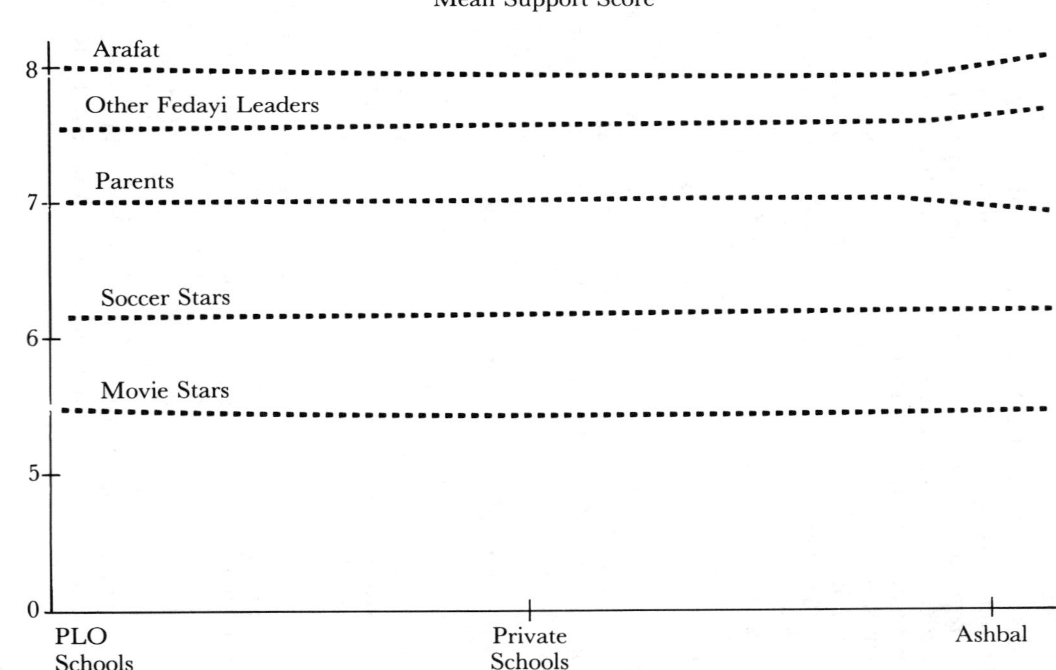

Figure 1 Mean Support Scores for the Chairman and Five Other Authority Figures

Table 2
Support for the Amir (in Percentages)
by Age and Grade in Junior High School

	Grades		
	6th (N = 152)	7th-8th (N = 200)	9th (N = 148)
	%	%	%
I. Is the Amir hard working?			
Always	82	81	84
Sometimes	—	9	6
Never	—	—	—
Don't know	18	10	9
II. Does the Amir do good work?			
Always	90	90	93
Sometimes	10	10	—
Never	—	—	—
Don't know	—	—	—
III. Does the Amir help the people?			
Always	90	93	93
Sometimes	10	7	7
Never	—	—	—
Don't know	—	—	—

NOTE: For all three questions the model response of each group is "always." Conversely, the proportion of "never" response is extremely low.

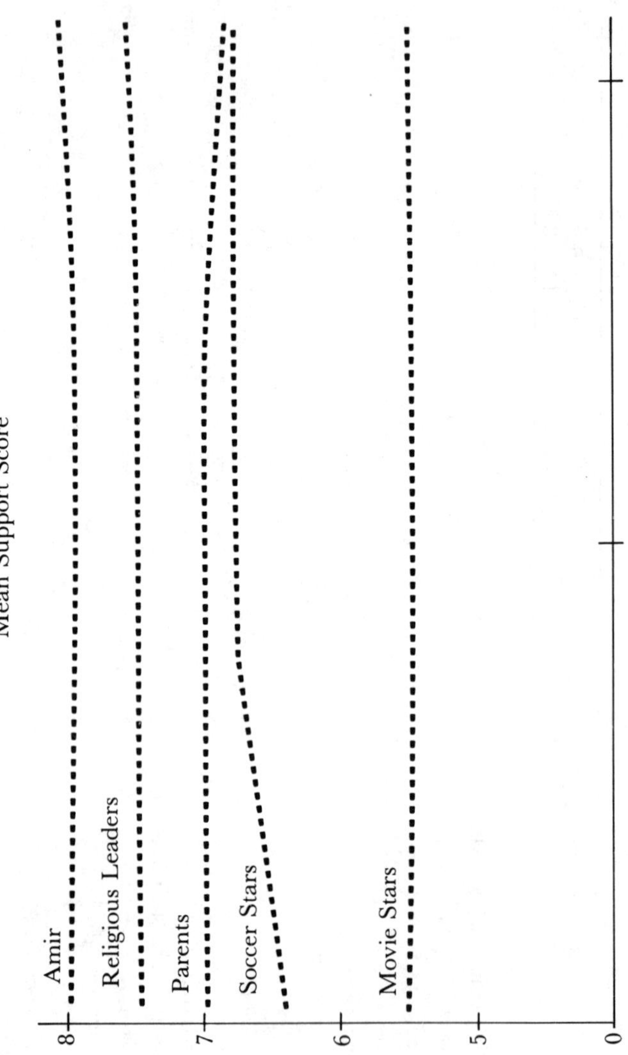

Figure 2 Mean Support Scores for the Amir and Five Other Authority Figures

Ashbal and 8.1 for *Ashbal.* The chairman's support is not confined to the *Ashbal,* and exposure to political indoctrination barely affects support for the chairman. Political indoctrination, however, seems to have a significant impact on other aspects of the political learning process. For example, the *Ashbal* were better able to differentiate between a Zionist and a Jew; the *Ashbal* were less likely to dislike Jews than the other children and more willing to live with Jews in Palestine than the other children.

Among Kuwaiti students, support for the Amir is independent of formal schooling defined by years spent in school, as shown in Table 2.

To explore the role of the family in generalizing support for both leaders, a set of questions was asked. First, the students were asked whether they agreed with this statement: "There is nothing lower than the person who does not feel deep love, respect, and concern for his parents." Seventy-eight percent of the PLO subsample, 76 percent of the private schools subsample, and 64 percent of the *Ashbal* agreed. Ninety-eight percent of the Kuwaiti sample agreed with the same statement. A similar distribution occurred when students were asked whether they agreed or disagreed with the statement: "When I face a problem, I first of all seek a solution or an answer to my problem from either my mother or father."

These findings underscore the family's importance in the respondents' life. Interestingly, however, if the Palestinian youths had to make a choice between loyalty to their family and loyalty to their country "Palestine" (in terms of whom to obey, or whom to defend, or whom to devote yourself to), they invariably chose loyalty to their country over loyalty to their family.

The Kuwaiti respondents made the same choice. As reported elsewhere and in contrast to findings reported in an earlier study conducted among university students, loyalty to one's family appears to be declining while loyalty to one's country, Kuwait, appears to be gaining ($\chi^2 = 8.10$, $p < .01$).

Citizenship is gaining in importance, among respondents of both sexes, at the expense of the family. This is an interesting finding given the existence of sex differences frequently cited in the literature of political socialization, voting behavior, and political participation. Socioeconomic standing is also independent of the support index. Both leaders are equally esteemed by youths of high, middle, and low socioeconomic groups.

Among the Kuwaiti respondents, regardless of the respondent's sex, religion (Islam) was ranked first in their hierarchy of group affiliations ($\chi^2 = 8.10$, $p < .01$), followed by loyalty to one's country and loyalty to one's family.

The relationship between support for Arafat and trust in the PLO and support for the Amir and trust in the Kuwaiti system of government is difficult to analyze vigorously because of the lack of longitudinal data. However, the relationship appears to be positive and quasilinear:

A unit increase in support for Arafat results in an increase of .41 on the index of trust in the PLO; a unit increase in support for the Amir results in an increase of .42 on the index of trust in the Kuwaiti government.

Conclusions

Placed in the context of comparative socialization research, the cases of Palestinian and Kuwaiti youths seem to support the "benevolent leader thesis." Support for both leaders is extensive. It is more extensive than support for various authority figures. Support for the leader leads to trust in the system that this leader represents. Arafat appears to be a crucial link between the Palestinian youths and the PLO. Similarly, the Amir is a critical link between the Kuwaiti youths and their government.

Given the comparative newness of both political systems (the PLO and the independent state of Kuwait), the growth and intensity of support for the leaders and their political systems are impressive. Both leaders seem to be agents of legitimization for both political systems. The importance of this role cannot be overemphasized in any political system but it is especially significant in a region where, as Michael Hudson suggests, the central problem of government is the problem of political legitimacy.

Support for the leaders seems to be learned in one's family and among one's peer group; formal school and formal political indoctrination (as in the *Ashbal*) do not seem to play a significant role in inculcating support. Neither socioeconomic status nor the respondent's sex seems to play a significant role in the level of support.

Notes

1. J. Massey, "The Missing Leader: Japanese Youths' Views of Political Authority," *American Political Science Review* Vol. 69 (March 1975), pp. 31–48.
2. For a review of the socialization literature and a detailed description of the methodology employed in both surveys, see T. E. Farah, "Learning to Support the PLO: Political Socialization of Palestinian Children in Kuwait," *Comparative Political Studies* Vol. 12 (January 1980), pp. 470–484.

12
Gender and Participant Citizenship: Evidence from Tunisia

Mark A. Tessler and Jean F. O'Barr

Theoretical Issues

Introduction

This paper considers an important syndrome of political attitude and behavior patterns associated with development and asks about the degree to which its constituent orientations and their determinants vary as a function of gender. The collection of political orientations in question is participant citizenship, a fundamental dimension of political culture, and individual-level variations in participant citizenship constitute the dependent variable in the analysis to follow. The initial section of this paper provides a brief introduction to the concept of participant citizenship, identifying its major defining components, discussing its relevance and limitations for understanding political development, and setting forth the goals of this investigation of its gender-linked determinants. The focus throughout the paper is on general issues associated with gender and political development. Although the data to be presented are from selected social milieux in Tunisia, variable relationships of potentially general application are examined.

Social scientists rarely employ terms like political development and political modernization in a consistent fashion.[1] Nevertheless, commonalities exist in the scholarly literature on the subject, and one is the view that appropriate citizen orientations are essential for a society to develop politically. Whatever the form of its government, a country cannot be considered politically developed if its population possesses little information about or attachment to the national system, if the bulk of its citizens neither consider themselves united in a political community nor tied in any meaningful way to national institutions. This view is found in the classical literature,[2] that on democratic systems,[3] and that on developing countries.[4] The particular individual orientations usually emphasized in this context are political interest and information, participation in civic affairs, and identification with the national community and its political institutions. As indicated above, these orientations tend to covary and constitute a syndrome which is often referred to as participant citizenship.[5]

It should be pointed out that a focus on participant citizenship does not presume the equation of development with Westernization. Attitudes and behavior patterns derived from a people's own traditions may be no less conducive to political development than social codes imported from the West or elsewhere. Thus participant citizenship should not be viewed as a syndrome of personal political orientations whose content is defined in terms of Western notions of civic-mindedness and political modernity. It is rather defined in terms of generic elements, like political knowledge, involvement, and identity, with no presumption that the particular form or content of these elements is unchanging from one society to another.

Participant citizenship is not a sufficient condition for political development. More than appropriate citizen orientations is required. Essential too is the capacity of political institutions to respond to demands and changing conditions, a capacity usually associated with structural differentiation and complexity. It also appears that political development requires a kind of equilibrium in the growth of participant citizenship and institutional strength. Disproportionate rises in the former may be destabilizing. The opposite imbalance tends to breed authoritarianism. Participant citizenship then is not independent of other aspects of political development, although this makes it no less central an ingredient in the quest for modernization.

Factors that account for variations in development, including political development, are not limited to such within-system attributes as political culture and a polity's institutions. Also relevant are international political and economic arrangements, from which may derive aspects of underdevelopment. Restructuring international relationships in order to increase equity and enhance the autonomy of a developing country parallels domestic needs as an arena for development efforts, and thus internal considerations should not be reified in the study of development. Just as participant citizenship is a necessary but not a sufficient condition for political development, so too with internal political modernization generally.

Though participant citizenship is only one among a number of critical factors, it must be present in the political culture of a society at reasonably high levels if that society is to become politically developed. Yet, despite its centrality, comparatively little is known about the conditions under which participant citizenship tends to emerge in developing countries. Most of the relatively few systematic and empirical studies that have been carried out have been concerned with assessing the impact of standard modernization variables on political orientations, not with accounting for variance on dependent variables as completely as possible. Thus almost nothing is known about the relationship between participant citizenship and a wide range of individual and system-level attributes that may be of considerable theoretical significance and that are certainly highly relevant to the experience of nation building. One such attribute is gender, and a principal objective of this paper is the consideration of this variable in the explanation and prediction of individual participant citizenship levels.

In considering gender-linked determinants of participant citizenship, this paper seeks to contribute to two areas of inquiry. The first concern is a fuller understanding of the political significance of women in developing societies. Toward this end, the paper examines empirical data from one developing country in order to determine whether and how the participant citizenship levels of women and men differ and then discusses the broader implications of the observed relationship(s) between gender and participant citizenship. The second concern is to contribute to the development of social theory that accounts for variance with respect to political attitude and behavior patterns in developing countries. Toward this end, our focus on gender will include its consideration as a specification variable in propositions about other determinants of participant citizenship and an attempt to identify other variables that may in turn specify variations in the relation between gender and individual political orientations. Each of these considerations will be briefly discussed prior to offering a focused problem statement and presenting and analyzing our data.

Women and Political Development

There is a paucity of information about the political behavior of women in the Third World. Not only are we ignorant about whether and how women differ from men on standard indices of political ideas and activities, we also know very little about how women act in the political arena. The literature on women in developing countries may be divided into three general categories, and a brief review of this literature readily demonstrates the limits of present knowledge. First, leaders of Third World women's organizations and the personnel of international agencies approach the topic of women in politics by exhorting women to enter public life in order to improve the quality of their lives and to change conditions which restrict them.[6] Their writings often contain statistical descriptions of women's patterns of voting and officeholding but rarely supply information on women's attitudes toward the changes being urged on them. A second group of writers considers how and why it is culturally normative to exclude women from various forms of political participation in many societies.[7] But many of these same authors also note that even when women are politically involved their activities are usually left out of scholarly analyses.[8] Finally, a third approach does ask how women act politically, but this work is primarily speculative and lacks any empirical base for most of its assertions—simply because until the last few years virtually no empirical work was done on the nature of women's political participation. The present work, done from a dependency perspective, emphasizes the broader social roles women had prior to colonialism and documents how women have a restricted social access to modernization. None of this work, however, relates structural changes to present political behavior. In all reports on Third World politics, then, there are few data on women's political behavior or on the attitudes of women toward political issues.[9]

Despite the absence of firm evidence on the subject, it is reasonable to suggest that in developing countries the political behavior patterns of women and men may differ in significant ways, even when persons of each sex are in comparable circumstances. Indeed, as mentioned above, the widespread assumption that women and men react in a similar fashion to common life-experiences and situations has been specifically challenged by a number of scholars. Boserup was the first to point out that colonialism and subsequently modernization have had a differential structural impact on women and men.[10] She demonstrated with careful economic data how the introduction of mechanization and industrialization dramatically changed participation of women in the labor force in both the agricultural and the nonagricultural sectors of the economies of Third World countries. Those who have followed Boserup have suggested that not only are women "structurally displaced" by modernization but that they react to this change with increasingly negative attitudes toward social life in general.[11] Jacquette, in a review of the literature on Latin American women, cites several case studies showing that the psychological orientations of modern women reflect frustration at the hands of economic and educational forces which exclude them.[12] Pellow, reporting on urban women in Ghana, presents similar findings. Women are caught between two social systems in conflict and express a fatalistic attitude toward modernization because of the plight with which it confronts them.[13] Several recent studies based on the Arab world also report that social mobilization produces among women social attitudes that are different and less positive than those reported in earlier studies based upon men.[14]

The possibility of sex-linked differences in political attitude and behavior is not only of theoretical interest. The particular political orientations of women are of practical significance to those concerned with nation building. First, most developing societies are characterized by a heavy reliance on human resource capital; whatever the particulars of their developmental goals or the specifics of the political structures and political formulae they establish to reach those goals, these countries rely heavily on people to attain their objectives. Women constitute at least one-half of the population, however, and unless these human resources are effectively mobilized and employed, the potential for development would seem to be severely limited. Second, women are sufficiently numerous for their attitudes and values to constitute a major component of the national political culture. As such, the weight of their political views influences the overall political psychology of the nation and contributes in a significant way to the normative climate that shapes the political behavior of all citizens. Finally, and perhaps most important in the long run, women have direct responsibility for rearing the new generation that politicians exhort to new ideas and activities. As socializers of the young in a rapidly changing society, women play a crucial role in the transmission and development of political attitudes. For all these reasons, it is essential to understand more about the political orientations of women and to discover how they might differ from those of men.

Explaining Participant Citizenship

By enhancing our understanding of factors that promote and retard the emergence of participant citizenship, a focus on gender can contribute to more elaborate theoretical formulations aimed at explaining variations in political development. It has been demonstrated frequently that education, urbanization, media consumption, socioeconomic status, and other similar social change variables are associated with political participation and participant citizenship in developing countries,[15] as they are in developed countries.[16] But while social mobilization and greater involvement in the modernization process may increase an individual's level of participant citizenship, major questions need to be raised about this relationship. One reservation stems from a general failure to examine sex, age, and other demographic variables for the possibility of specification effects in the relationship between social change and individual political attitudes. The case of gender is particularly compelling. Inkeles and his associates write, for example, that "we are quite certain that the same forces which make men modern—such as education, work in complex organizations, and mass-media exposure—also serve to make women more modern. . . . We believe the pattern which will eventually emerge for women will be broadly similar to that we observed in the case of men."[17] Yet Inkeles studied only men, and indeed the authors know of no systematic comparison of men's and women's attitudinal responses to social change. Further, a number of feminist authors specifically argue that modernization has a differential impact upon the sexes, tending to generate more negative attitudes toward social life among women.[18] While the case of gender is particularly clear, similar questions should also be raised about age, class, and other personal-status attributes; and as a matter of fact there is already preliminary evidence that the impact of social change on political attitudes is not always the same among young and old,[19] advantaged and disadvantaged,[20] majority and minority.[21] Thus, while life-style variations associated with social change may increase participant citizenship on some occasions, they may be irrelevant or even produce negative political attitudes on others. Future studies must attempt to discover and specify in conceptual terms the locus of applicability of several different relationships between social change processes and participant citizenship, and gender appears to be one especially appropriate focus for such studies.

Beyond refining existing theories concerned with the development of participant citizenship, it is essential to broaden the range of factors that are considered as determinants and/or specification variables in attempts to account for variance along this important conceptual dimension. One category of such variables includes system-level properties having to do with the structure, orientation, and effectiveness of the political system, especially as they relate to the deliberate efforts of Third World leaders to shape popular political attitudes. Indeed a number of scholars have lamented the absence of studies assessing the impact of political institutions and regime policies on individual political attitude and behavior patterns.[22] A factor that may be particularly salient in this regard is the presence or absence of an explicit regime orientation stressing political mobilization and political socialization. Regimes with this kind of mobilization orientation commonly carry out activities aimed at inculcating deliberately chosen national values among the populace, and they usually find it most appropriate to pursue political education and adult resocialization through centralized political institutions, like a single mass-oriented political party.[23] The ability of political leaders to modify individual political attitudes is poorly understood, however, despite the fact that mobilization regimes concerned with social engineering are common among Third World politics;[24] and this suggests that the relationship between regime policies and orientations on the one hand and individual political attitudes on the other is an important area for future research.

It is reasonable to assume that the role of government in modifying political orientations is more critical among some segments of the population than others and that the relationship between regime orientation and participant citizenship is thus itself a variable. Therefore, as with hypotheses involving social mobilization generally, propositions about the relationship between participant citizenship and political system properties like regime orientation should also be tested under conditions specified by gender and other personal attribute variables. In addition, however, these individual-level attributes must not be examined only as specification variables in theories concerned with social mobilization or the character and performance of the political system; they must also be treated as independent variables. The salience of gender in this regard has already been discussed, it having been argued that to be a woman in a developing country is to have certain unique life experiences that well may affect political attitudes. Finally, as with other important independent variables, the relationship between gender and participant citizenship may also vary as a function of other individual-level attributes or of system-level properties. Thus, in sum, the pursuit of a fuller explanation of participant citizenship requires the delineation of a broad range of nondependent variables and the examination of plausible relationships involving each as an independent and/or a specification variable.

Problem and Method

The Problem

The present analysis undertakes to examine with longitudinal data from one developing country the interrelationship between some of the variables that the preceding discussion has identified as relevant to the study of participant citizenship. In so doing, it aspires to provide a firm empirical foundation for assessing the nature and significance of gender-linked determinants of participant citizenship and for incorporating gender into theoretical formulations that shed light more generally on the origins of participant citizenship in developing societies. The particular country from which data for the present study are drawn is Tunisia.

Three nondependent variables will be of specific concern in the analysis to follow. First, a measure of socioeconomic status and class, reflecting levels of individual involvement in the modernization process, will be developed and employed to investigate the consequences of variations in exposure to agents of social change. This will permit an evaluation under varying conditions of some of the propositions about the impact of modernization on political orientations that have been reported elsewhere. It will also permit the introduction of class as a specification variable in relationships involving gender. Second, gender will be employed as both an independent variable and a specification variable. Moreover, to assure that sex is considered independently of other related personal-status variables, comparable subsamples of women and men will be identified for analysis. Third, variations in the political and ideological orientation of the government will be considered. These differences will be measured with longitudinal data collected over a period of time during which the country under study moved from governance by a regime with a mobilization orientation to one without such an orientation. The presence or absence of a mobilization orientation is of interest as a specification variable in relationships involving gender, or gender and class taken together, and as an independent variable whose impact upon participant citizenship may be sex-linked. Before examining the relationships among these variables, however, it is necessary to say something about the relevance of the Tunisian case for a study of this sort and about methodological considerations pertaining to the analysis generally.

The Tunisian Case

While no single country can provide a base for more than tentative generalizations, Tunisia is a highly appropriate setting for an examination of the variable relationships outlined above. Following its independence in 1956, the country was characterized by both high levels of unplanned social change and vigorous regime efforts at modernization.[25] Urbanization increased dramatically, as did literacy rates and school enrollments at all levels. Major legal reforms were enacted and a national public information campaign was launched in an effort to effect a "psychological revolution." A national agricultural and commercial cooperative scheme was also initiated. And the country's ruling single party established itself as an effective instrument of mobilization and political education. This was the situation in 1967, the first year in which data for the present study were collected. It reflected an official and explicit recognition of the relationship between individual attitudes and political development, the presence of many programs accordingly designed to promote attitude change, and a special commitment to women's liberation, including an effort to increase feminine participation in public life.

In 1968 the character of the Tunisian political system began to change, losing much of its ideological zeal and institutional effectiveness.[26] The reasons for this change need not be discussed here. Suffice it to say that struggles for power within the government and other internal and external pressures resulted in the emergence of a new regime, one displaying little concern for planned political and cultural change and emphasizing instead economic policies designed to maximize investment and entrepreneurial activity. Further, not only had the regime's philosophy changed, but party machinery had atrophied at the local level, making it a less effective vehicle for inculcating deliberately chosen national values. Unplanned social change on the other hand remained intense during this period and the economy performed particularly well, intensifying the effects of modernization. Thus in 1973, the second year in which data for the present study were collected, official efforts to promote attitude change were largely absent, as was government concern about feminine emancipation. The overall social context remained dynamic, however, and there were intense debates about the reasons for recent economic gains and the social costs of laissez-faire economic policies.

The Data Base

Data for this analysis are from surveys conducted in Tunisia in 1967 and 1973. Information about the 1967 survey, as well as the principal findings derived from the research, are described elsewhere in detail.[27] Briefly, stratified quota samples of literate and regularly employed adults were drawn in Tunis and three smaller towns. Variables of sample stratification were education, income, and place of residence; and quotas were established to assure that all empirically existing combinations of these variables were included in the sample. A total of 283 persons were interviewed. In 1973, a similar sample was selected, using education and place of residence as variables of sample stratification and substituting occupation for income to control for inflation between 1967 and 1973. A total of 349 persons were interviewed, using the same survey instrument employed in 1967. Table 1 presents the distribution of respondents in each sample across categories of education, income, and

Table 1

DISTRIBUTION OF 1967 (N = 283) AND 1973 (N = 349) RESPONDENTS ALONG DIMENSIONS OF SAMPLE STRATIFICATION

	RESIDENTS OF TUNIS				RESIDENTS OF SMALLER TOWNS			
Level of Education	University	High School	Inter-mediate	Primary	University	High School	Inter-mediate	Primary
1967 Sample								
Income:								
30 dinars	0	0	13	17	—	—	7	17
30-49 dinars	0	17	30	17	—	4	13	5
50-59 dinars	6	18	9	7	—	11	6	1
70-99 dinars	9	6	7	7	—	1	—	1
100 dinars	23	18	13	0	—	—	—	—
1973 Sample								
Income:								
30 dinars	1	6	10	20	—	—	4	12
30-49 dinars	3	8	40	24	—	—	12	14
50-69 dinars	5	10	35	12	—	1	7	1
70-99 dinars	21	10	20	7	—	2	4	5
100 dinars	29	6	6	14	—	1	1	—

In 1967, interviewing was done in Grombalia, Mahdia, and Nefta. In 1973 it was done in Nabeul, Ksar Hillal, and Houmt Souk. All six towns had a population of less than 15,000 when surveyed. In each year, one town selected was from the northern part of the country near Tunis, one was from the Sahel, and one was from the southern part of the country.

place of residence. The table shows that respondents in each year are drawn from a wide range of social categories and, collectively, reflect much of the diversity of the Tunisian middle class and working class.

Measuring Participant Citizenship

The six items listed below are employed as indicators of participant citizenship and constitute the dependent variables in our analysis. Face validity may be claimed for the items, most being similar to items routinely used in political attitude studies. These items also formed acceptable Gutmann scales with data from 1967 and data from 1973. Because more information is derived by considering the items separately, the indicators are not analyzed as a single cumulative index of participant citizenship. Nevertheless, the scalability of the items offers evidence of their reliability and provides an additional basis for inferring validity. Details on our approach to measurement are available elsewhere,[28] as are general works by the authors on the problems of measuring individual political orientations in a developing nation.[29]

Item	Response indicating participant citizenship
1. What are the groups of which you are a member? Do you have any responsibilities in these groups?	Active member of at least one political group.
2. Identify the following political figures.	All four persons named correctly identified.
3. Government and political affairs are often so complicated that persons like yourself cannot understand what is happening.	Disagree.
4. The government does not care much about people like yourself.	Disagree.
5. A village official visited a man who had saved some money and asked him to help finance the construction of a local school. The man replied that he was saving his money for his family and could not give it to the village. Was he right?	No.
6. Rank the following ten professions according to their importance in society.	Profession of government minister did not rank last.

Independent and Specification Variables

Respondents in each year are divided into three categories reflecting socioeconomic status and class. Operationally, respondents are divided on a basis of education and occupational status taken together, as shown in Figure 1. A few respondents are high in one respect and low in the other and these are excluded from the present analysis since their ratings are inconsistent. In general, however, there is a strong association between education and occupational status and most respondents accordingly are classified as either high, medium, or low with respect to both, the cutting points being shown in the figure and designated as upper, middle, and working class respectively. Further, these ratings strongly covary with income, residence, media consumption, foreign travel, and many other routine indicators of social change, suggesting that levels of education and occupational status together constitute a valid operational definition of involvement in the modernization process.

Respondents are next divided according to gender. In both years the

Figure 1

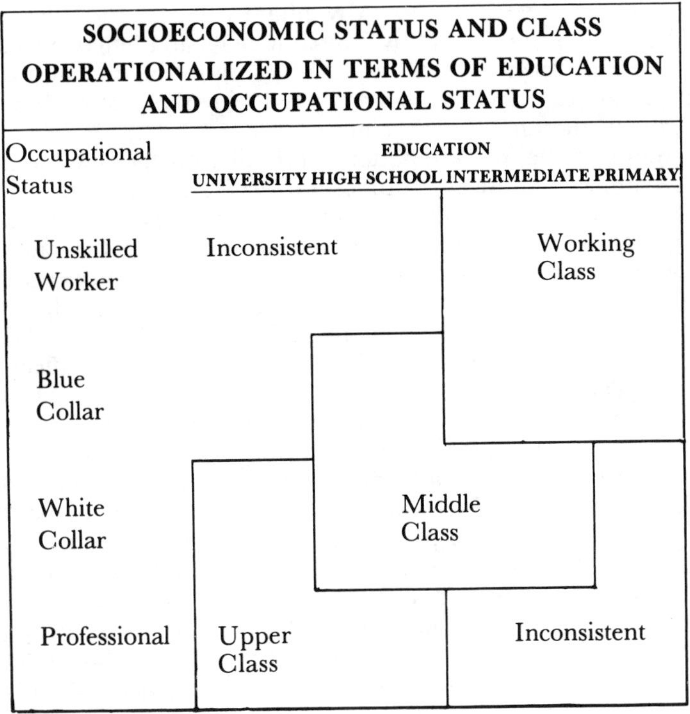

number of women surveyed was relatively small. The study focused on employed individuals and comparatively few women have regular jobs. Also, the ability to interview women outside the capital was severely limited by traditional social codes governing the behavior of women. Finally, although some issues pertaining to women were central to the study as originally conceived, a systematic comparison of the attitudes of women and men was not among its principal preoccupations. Thus, forty-three women were interviewed in 1967, and fifty-nine were surveyed in 1973. To assure comparability in contrasting the views of women and men, each woman was matched with respect to age, education, income level, and place of residence to a male respondent from the larger pool of men interviewed. Male respondents not matched to a female respondent are not considered further in the present analysis, and the exclusion of so many men reduces that data base considerably. Specifically, the total N drops to 204. Nevertheless, rigor and control in the assessment of sex-linked differences is more important than the utilization of all data, all the more so since a separate analysis of men's political attitudes is anticipated. In presenting data, sex is cross-tabulated with class, and aggregate ratings on the dependent variables are given for respondents in each of the six resultant categories for each year. It should be borne in mind that by matching male and female respondents it has been possible to hold constant a number of important but extraneous sources of variance, greatly reducing the possibility of multicolinearity in the analysis of gender.

Variations in regime orientation are built into the analysis by contrasting Tunisian political attitudes in 1967 and 1973. In presenting data from these two points in time, our principal objective is not replication. It is rather the incorporation of an important spatiotemporal variable into the analysis, focusing on conceptual properties which differentiate two otherwise highly comparable situations. The Tunisian regime was characterized by a mobilization orientation in 1967 and a more pluralist and laissez-faire orientation in 1973. The effect of this difference generally may be assessed by contrasting political attitudes at the two points in time. Its relative impact on population categories defined in terms of gender and socioeconomic status change may be assessed similarly. Finally, a comparison of the distribution of political attitudes in 1967 and 1973 will suggest conclusions about specification effects associated with the presence of mobilization efforts. In making these comparisons, not all possible sources of extraneous variance are held constant. Nevertheless, a high degree of control is again present since aggregate levels of unplanned social change are roughly comparable in 1967 and 1973 and since comparisons involve the same social and cultural system and individuals from identical population categories within that system.

The limitations of these data are apparent. The number of respondents is small, only selected population categories are represented, and the entire study is based on a single country. Nevertheless, we believe that the questions to be addressed demand an incremental approach to research, one wherein evidence is assembled by scholars working in different locations and from a variety of intellectual perspectives. Only the cumulative insights to which such studies can collectively give rise will inspire a high degree of confidence, making expectations about work that is definitive or unassailably objective somewhat naive.

We would also offer several observations about the strengths of our study. First, in constructing and administering the survey instrument and in measuring abstracts, rigorous standards have consistently been maintained. The study has a high degree of internal validity. Second, there are comparatively few literate and regularly employed women in most developing countries, necessarily limiting studies of this population category. Nevertheless, information about such women is essential to an understanding of social change and must be collected and analyzed to whatever degree possible. Third, Tunisia is an excellent location in which to explore questions relating to women and modernization. The country has done more to promote women's emancipation than almost any other Arab country. In addition, variations in government policy between 1967 and 1973, the years of our study, permit the inclusion of regime orientation as a variable in the analysis, making the Tunisian case particularly useful.

There is one final consideration that should be mentioned, relating to our belief that it is extremely valuable to reanalyze existing social science data as new insights emerge and new questions about the phenomena under study develop. The study of women in developing societies emerged in the early 1970s as some scholars interested in policymaking sought information about women's exclusion from modernization projects. While these inquiries stimulated the gathering of new data with which to study women in developing countries, they also led some scholars to reexamine existing data sets originally collected for other purposes. Such reanalyses can be highly productive, but obviously they will not be as "neat" as those in which the questions under investigation guide the research from the outset.

Findings and Discussion

Table 2 presents the percentage of men and women responding to each item in a manner indicative of participant citizenship, giving figures for 1967 and 1973 as well as the difference between the percentage for each year. The table will show whether there tend to be sex-linked differences in participant citizenship and, if so, whether these differences vary as a function of the political changes that took place in Tunisia between 1967 and 1973.

In 1967, men had substantially higher levels of participant citizenship than women on four of the items considered, there being no appreciable difference in the other two instances. Specifically, men were most likely to belong to political organizations, to possess political information, to believe that the government cares about them, and to believe that a person's resources should be shared with the state. The situation in 1973 was different. Differences between the sexes were very small in every instance. The only exception is that women were somewhat more likely than men to believe that the government cares about them, a difference which nonetheless is not statistically significant. Table 2 also shows the differences between men in 1967 and 1973 and between women in 1967 and 1973 and, consistent with findings described above, the table indicates that levels of participant citizenship declined substantially more among men than women in every case where there were important sex-linked variations in the earlier year. The conclusions to which Table 2 leads are (1) sex is associated with differences in participant citizenship in the mobilization-oriented political environment that characterized Tunisia in 1967 but not in the more laissez-faire political situation to which the country had turned by 1973 and (2) despite the fact that Tunisia placed greater emphasis on women's liberation in 1967 than in 1973, the sex-linked differences of the former year involve more positive and participatory political orientations among men.

Table 2

PERCENTAGE OF MATCHED MEN AND WOMEN GIVING RESPONSE INDICATIVE OF PARTICIPANT CITIZENSHIP

Item		1967 (N = 86)	1973 (N = 118)	Difference
1. What are the groups of which you are a member?	M	22 *	1	-21**
	W	7	0	- 7
2. Identify the following individuals.	M	52**	18	-34**
	W	19	15	- 4
3. Government and politics are not too complicated to understand.	M	67	53	-14
	W	69	50	-19*
4. The government cares about people like me.	M	78*	40	-38**
	W	57*	56	- 1
5. A man should share his money with his village.	M	78*	62	-16*
	W	61	54	- 7
6. The profession of minister is very important.	M	82	94	+ 12
	W	83	93	+ 10

Probability assessments are based on a non-parametric statistical analysis of raw frequencies:

**Differences between women and men in a single year or between 1967 and 1973 for the same sex are significant at the .01 level;

*Differences between women and men in a single year or between 1967 and 1973 for the same sex are significant at the .05 level.

Table 3 introduces class as an additional nondependent variable, showing the distribution of political orientations across categories of sex and class in 1967 and 1973. Figures in the cells are the percentage of persons responding to an item in a manner indicating participant citizenship in each year and the difference between the 1967 and 1973 percentages. The table follows the logic of factorial analysis. All combinations of nondependent variables taken together constitute the parameters of the table, and ratings on the dependent variable are given for each cell defined by these parameters. By selectively examining the data thus assembled, interaction among the nondependent variables may be assessed. Each may be considered as an independent variable under conditions specified by the others, and each may be treated as a specification variable to determine its impact on the relationship

Table 3

PERCENTAGE OF MATCHED MEN AND WOMEN CATEGORIZED BY CLASS GIVING RESPONSES INDICATIVE OF PARTICIPANT CITIZENSHIP[a]

Item	Class:	1967			1973			Difference		
		W	M	U	W	M	U	W	M	U
		(n = 20)	(n = 40)	(n = 24)	(n = 38)	(n = 26)	(n = 40)			
1. What are the groups of which you are a member?	M	14	22	31	0	0	1	– 14	– 22	– 30
	W	0	6	15	0	0	0	0	– 6	– 15
2. Identify the following individuals.	M	20	56	80	14	0	44	– 6	– 56	– 36
	W	8	15	33	11	13	28	+ 2	– 2	– 5
3. Government and politics are not too complicated to understand.	M	70	52	80	38	50	69	– 32	– 2	– 11
	W	67	60	80	35	54	59	– 32	– 6	– 21
4. The government cares about people like me.	M	90	44	100	25	38	50	– 65	– 6	– 50
	W	50	55	66	60	55	53	+ 10	0	– 13
5. A man should share his money with his village.	M	100	75	60	59	62	65	– 41	– 13	+ 5
	W	83	55	44	65	57	39	– 18	+ 2	– 5
6. The profession of minister is very important.	M	90	96	60	90	94	100	0	– 2	+ 40
	W	83	100	67	100	92	83	+ 17	– 8	+ 16

[a] Due to status inconsistency (i.e., highly divergent levels of education and professional status), one matched pair from the 1967 sample and seven matched pairs from the 1973 sample have not been classified with respect to SES and class and are excluded from that part of the analysis involving this variable.

between the others and the dependent variable. We are of course principally concerned with the role of gender as an independent and a specification variable.

Table 2 suggests that sex-linked differences in participant citizenship depend on the character and orientation of the political environment. Table 3 suggests that these differences also vary as a function of class and, moreover, that specification effects associated with class are not the same in 1967 and 1973. In 1967, sex-linked differences in participant citizenship were not tied to variations in class in any systematic fashion. There was a slight tendency for women to be higher in participant citizenship in the middle-class category, and this may be of some interest since the general pattern in 1967 was for men to have more civic political orientations. More generally, however, differences between men and women were about the same for each class category and the few deviations from this pattern appear to be random. The situation in 1973 was reversed. Unlike 1967, when there were differences associated with sex in the aggregate but not in subcategories based on class, sex-linked differences are discernible with class considered as a specification variable even though these differences do not show up in aggregate comparisons. In the working- and middle-class categories, women had higher levels of participant citizenship on fully half the items. Differences between the sexes were small on the remaining items, but this is significant too because in 1967 men were substantially higher in participant citizenship in most of these instances. In the upper-class category, on the other hand, men remain higher than women in participant citizenship on four of the six items, the difference having in fact increased in most cases.

Differences between responses in 1967 and 1973 are also shown in Table 3. The table shows that among men participant citizenship rarely increased and frequently declined. Moreover, the pattern among male respondents is similar in all three categories of class. Among women, however, changes in participant citizenship are related to class. For working-class women, levels of participant citizenship increased on three items and declined substantially less than those of men on all but one of the remaining items. The pattern is similar for middle-class women. Although participant citizenship rarely increased in absolute terms, relative to men it declined far less. For upper-class women the pattern is different. Women's levels of participant citizenship declined relative to those of men in half the instances considered. In sum, considering sex as an independent variable and class and regime-related differences as specification variables, the conclusions to be drawn from Table 3 are (1) sex-linked differences in participant citizenship do not vary as a function of class in the mobilization-oriented political environment that characterized Tunisia in 1967, but they do vary as a function of class in the more laissez-faire political situation that characterized Tunisia in 1973 and (2) in the latter year participant citizenship levels of women tended to be as high as or higher than those of men in the working class and the middle class, and they tended to be lower than those of men in the upper class.

Table 3 also permits consideration of sex as a specification variable. It reveals that the impact of class on participant citizenship is sometimes but not always affected by sex and that the nature of these specification effects is itself affected by variations in political environment. In 1967, the relationship between class and participant citizenship is sometimes positive, sometimes negative, and sometimes curvilinear. But the important point, so far as the present analysis is concerned, is that these relationships are almost always identical for male and female respondents. In 1973, on the other hand, class does not always relate to participant citizenship in the same way among men and women. Among men the association between the two concepts is consistently positive, the only exception being the item on participation for which there is no variance at all in 1973. Among women, however, the pattern is dissimilar in a number of instances. Moreover, these instances involve items with conceptual similarities. Unlike the pattern observed among men, class and participant citizenship are negatively related among women on items pertaining to the *regime,* items that ask whether the government is worthy of trust and respect. The last three items in the table illustrate this tendency. On items pertaining to *individual* political attributes, however, those asking about participation, information, and efficacy, the relationship between class and participant citizenship is generally positive, and it is consistently similar for men and women in 1973. Thus, in conclusion, (1) sex is not important in determining how class and participant citizenship are related in the kind of mobilization-oriented political environment that characterized Tunisia in 1967, but it does specify differences in this relationship in the more laissez-faire political situation of 1973 and (2) in the latter situation it specifies the direction of the relationship between class and those aspects of participant citizenship having to do with regime evaluation, this relationship being positive among men and negative among women.

Discussion and Conclusion

It is possible to derive from our findings certain potentially generalizable variable relationships and a number of related insights. These relationships and insights pertain in particular to gender, the variable whose practical and theoretical significance concerns us most in this study. But for the most part they focus on gender in combination with socioeconomic status and/or regime orientation as well. In discussing these patterns by way of conclusion, we seek to contribute to a fuller understanding of the ways that women influence and are affected by development processes and also of the conditions under which participant citizenship does or does not tend to emerge in developing countries. Given the previously acknowledged limitations of our data, propositions should naturally be regarded as subjects for additional empirical investigation.

1. The assertion that men and women in comparable circumstances hold similar political attitudes surely needs to be modified. Yet it is also clear that the nature of gender-linked differences in political orientations itself varies as a function of social and political conditions. In the kind of mobilization-oriented political environment that characterized Tunisia in 1967, men were substantially higher in participant citizenship than women. Moreover, this tended to be the case among women and men of comparable socioeconomic status. The reason for this is probably that Tunisian men saw themselves as benefiting substantially from the accelerated pace of development and the greater opportunities for political involvement while women did not see official efforts at political mobilization as enhancing their life chances to the same degree. In other words, the opportunities provided by government mobilization activities were not distributed evenly throughout society and gender was a relevant variable in identifying population categories that saw themselves as having substantially different prospects for seizing these opportunities and improving their personal and social status. In

1973, when the government was less concerned with mobilization and when individuals competed for resources in a more laissez-faire economic and political climate, women and men also had substantially different levels of participant citizenship, but only among upper-class individuals. This is probably because upper-class men benefited most from the situation that prevailed in 1973. They had more wealth and influence to employ in a setting permitting high levels of individual competition and, further, they found their privileged position enhanced by a reduction in government programs aimed at redistributing political and economic power. Middle- and working-class men, on the other hand, faced with growing disparities in the distribution of wealth and privilege and with reduced governmental activity aimed at bringing non-elites into the political process, experienced a decline in participant citizenship that made their levels much more comparable to those of women than had been the case in 1967. The general conclusions to which these findings point are (1) under a wide range of conditions the political orientations of women and men tend to be different, (2) these conditions involve the presence of opportunities for social mobility, among privileged categories when the government does not actively pursue political mobilization and among the populace more broadly when it does, and (3) in such instances the political orientations of women tend to be less positive and participatory than those of men.

2. An extension of the preceding conclusion concerns the relative importance of gender and class in accounting for variations in political orientations. Some scholars argue that class is more important than sex in determining political outlook.[30] These observers suggest that social class (defined in ways similar to those of the present study) overrides gender and that upper-class men and women accordingly have highly similar political orientations, even if this is not the case among lower-class men and women. Our Tunisian data enable us to evaluate this argument and to refine our understanding of the relative utility of class and sex as explanatory variables.

Class does not override sex as an explanatory variable under the conditions that prevailed in Tunisia in 1967. In other words, contrary to the expectation of some authors, sex-linked political attitude differences do not disappear, or even diminish appreciably, as life-style changes associated with modernization take place. Indeed, with respect to political participation and political information, there is a tendency for the degree to which men have higher participant citizenship levels than women to increase as a function of class, suggesting that a deepening immersion in the modernization process presents opportunities for political involvement for men far more than for women. This makes sense generally given that opportunities for participation are expanding in the wake of government mobilization programs. But the important point is that these opportunities are seized more frequently by upper-class individuals than others and, among the upper class, by men to a disproportionate degree. In 1973, the data contradict even more clearly the proposition that class overrides gender. On items pertaining to individual political activity, like participation and information, the pattern is similar to that observed in 1967. On items pertaining to regime evaluation, however, increased socioeconomic status is associated with absolute rather than relative declines in participant citizenship among women and differences between the sexes increase dramatically. Put differently, involvement in the modernization process gave rise to positive political orientations only among men in the competitive political climate that prevailed in 1973. Women, on the other hand, responded differently, apparently believing that their high socioeconomic status would not be sufficient to enable them to improve their life circumstances. In sum, based on our data from Tunisia, there is little evidence that sex-linked differences in political orientations disappear as socioeconomic status and involvement in the modernization process increase.

3. The preceding conclusions are of interest not only to students of women in development but also to those concerned with political culture in developing countries. Since our Tunisian data reveal that increased socioeconomic status and involvement in the modernization process do not necessarily lead to more positive and participatory political orientations, as is hypothesized to be the case in much of the scholarly literature on modernization, these data support the contention that theories of social change will provide useful models only if they are reformulated to incorporate a broad range of individual and situational attributes as independent and specification variables. The individual attribute examined in the present study is gender, and the system-level property considered is regime orientation. It is probable that other variables are relevant as well, however, and thus our analysis not only delineates a number of specific variable relationships but also, hopefully, offers an example of the kind of theoretical elaboration that is needed if political attitude change in developing countries is to be adequately understood.

Only among men from the 1973 sample does our data give evidence of the kind of consistent and positive association between participant citizenship and socioeconomic status that is widely reported in the modernization literature. In 1967, when the government was attempting to increase popular involvement in political life and to effect a more egalitarian distribution of wealth, this pattern was observed with respect to political participation and information, suggesting that upper-class individuals do take greater advantage than others of increased opportunities for individual political activity. But differences associated with class were not consistent for the other items, indicating that the government's reformist policies were generating political satisfaction and support among the lower classes as much or more than among the upper class. So far as gender is concerned, sex-linked differences in participant citizenship did increase as a function of socioeconomic status on items pertaining to participation and information, suggesting again that it is the most privileged population categories, upper-class men, who became most personally involved in the political process. But, more generally, the direction of the relationship between class and participant citizenship was the same for men and women in 1967, and in most instances the magnitude of sex-linked differences also did not vary as a function of class. In 1973, as reported, there was a direct and positive association between socioeconomic status and participant citizenship among men. Among women, on the other hand, this relationship occurred for only a minority of items and, more particularly, it occurred when an evaluation of the regime was not involved. The general conclusions to be drawn are (1) social mobilization does not necessarily increase participant citizenship; (2) this occurs in some but by no means all instances, and more specifically it appears to occur principally among individuals in privileged population categories and when official policies tolerate greater disparities of wealth and privilege; (3) when a government pursues policies of political mobilization, this relationship also occurs with respect to those aspects of participant citizenship involving individual political participation and knowledge; and (4) positive evaluations of the government are negatively related to socioeconomic status among population categories who believe their situation is made worse by modernization, such as women governed by a regime with a laissez-faire political orientation.

4. The proposition that social change has an adverse economic impact on women has become commonplace, and our Tunisian data suggest that there is an adverse political impact as well. The idea that many women had an important economic stake in society which colonialism and then modernization have tended to undermine is well documented. The relevant literature argues that modernization schemes are generally based on conscious or unconscious notions of male dominance, sometimes borrowed, as a matter of fact, from the Western experience, and cites as illustrations of this the fact that men receive technical education which allows them to take jobs while women often learn only domestic skills, that only about 20 percent as many women as men attend school at all, that agricultural development schemes often teach farming skills to men who are engaged in cash cropping but rarely to women who are involved in the subsistence sphere, and that mainline political activity is often reserved almost exclusively for men. In view of this situation, it is not surprising that social mobilization produces less positive political orientations among women than among men and that it often produces negative political attitudes in absolute terms among women.

As reported, our data show that in 1967 the attitudes of women involving an evaluation of the regime did not become more positive as a function of social mobilization and in 1973 there was a strong negative correlation between these attitudes and socioeconomic status among women. It is to be expected that deteriorating conditions and/ or unfulfilled expectations create political alienation among women, though this of course does not reduce the unfortunate implications of this fact for nation building. With respect to attitudes pertaining to individual political attributes, like participation, information, and political efficacy, it may be noted that there was a positive association between class and participant citizenship in both years, albeit a weaker one than that observed among men. The main significance of the latter findings, however, is that women's levels of political competence and sophistication do increase with modernization, making their inferior social and political position that much less justified and undoubtedly increasing further their frustration and anger.

Several of the mechanisms by which upper-class women are put in situations which reduce their levels of participant citizenship can be mentioned. In some cases, women and women's groups seeking to enter politics find themselves victims of the "star" system, in which a few prominent women are invited into the decision-making process while the broader participation of women remains restricted. In other cases, detrimental treatment follows the importation of Western ideas of romance, which place women on an ideological pedestal, away from the sordid affairs of politics. These and other mechanisms work against the full participation of women in political life, portending deleterious consequences for political development. Low levels of participant citizenship among women cannot but hinder the creation of a positive and civic-oriented national political culture, and should women inculcate their political orientations among their offspring, as seems likely, the job of nation building will be set back even further.

5. The mobilization orientation that characterized Tunisian politics in 1967 was more likely than the laissez-faire policies of 1973 to produce participant citizenship among women; but variations in regime orientation in Tunisia are much less strongly associated with political orientations among women than among men, leading to the conclusion that official programs of political mobilization and political education by themselves are insufficient to increase participant citizenship significantly among women. This is somewhat surprising since Tunisian policies up to and during 1967 included programs specifically aimed at women's emancipation. Indeed, during this period Tunisia had by far the most revolutionary approach to women's issues of any country in the Arab world. Nevertheless, it is clear from our data that the expanded opportunities for political participation that are present in a mobilization-oriented regime disproportionately fall into the hands of men and that, in the short run at least, even an explicit official commitment to women's liberation does not lead to social structural change in areas of special concern to women rapidly enough to alter very much women's evaluation of their political and social fortunes.

Several factors help to explain this apparent anomaly with respect to women in mobilizing societies. Policies of mobilization and reform create opportunities for lower-class individuals to improve their station; but, if modernization proceeds so as to make these opportunities available to men to a disproportionate degree, the situation of women is likely to deteriorate. Upper-class women will find their position threatened as conditions of access to high social status broaden. Upper-class men will similarly have their influence and privilege diluted, but they are less vulnerable than women and better able to take advantage of the new opportunities opening up. At lower socioeconomic levels the situation of women is even worse. With social mobilization occurring in the aggregate, individuals who do not find opportunities to improve their situation, those who, in other words, remain in the lower classes at a time when the upper ranks of society are growing, will be worse off relative to society as a whole and thus more politically alienated. It appears that this situation occurs to a disproportionate degree among women, helping to explain why government mobilization efforts do not raise participant citizenship levels as much among women as they do among men. Relative deprivation is also experienced by some men living under a mobilization regime, but this too can compound the problems of women. It is probable that rapid social change enhances opposition to women's emancipation among men who do not have the educational or professional qualifications necessary to take advantage of new opportunities. As we have argued elsewhere, like women generally, these categories of men find themselves disadvantaged by modernization, and their opposition to women's rights increases both for reasons of personal self-interest and because women's emancipation is a symbol of the broader social revolution which they see as responsible for their marginality. All of these factors help to explain why official efforts at political mobilization increase participant citizenship less among women than among men.

None of this is to say that governments might just as well abandon their efforts to change the status of women. It is to argue, however, that such changes cannot be the result of legislation and policy alone. Government attempts at political mobilization must be coupled with far-reaching efforts to effect broad social structural changes which, on the one hand, will assure that women have equal access to whatever opportunities for social mobility are created and, on the other, will reduce the kind of marginality that breeds opposition to women's emancipation. In sum, we have shown that government policy must be of long and persistent duration if fundamental social change is to occur, because the results of programs take time to manifest themselves.

Notes

1. See, for example, Lucian Pye, *Aspects of Political Development* (Boston: Little, Brown, 1966), pp. 31–48, and James Bill and Robert Hardgrave, Jr., *Comparative Politics: The Quest for Theory* (Columbus, Ohio: Merrill, 1973), pp. 66–83.

2. See, for example, Robert MacIver, *The Web of Government* (N.Y.: Macmillan Co., 1947), and Gaetano Mosca, *The Ruling Class,* trans. Hannah

D. Kahn (New York: McGraw Hill, 1939).

3. See, for example, Gabriel A. Almond and G. Bingham Powell, Jr., *Comparative Politics: A Developmental Approach* (Boston: Little, Brown, 1966); Gabriel A. Almond and Sidney Verba, *The Civic Culture* (Princeton, N.J.: Princeton University Press, 1963); and Kenneth Sherrill, "The Attitudes of Modernity," *Comparative Politics* Vol. 2 (January 1969), pp. 184–210.

4. See, for example, Gabriel Ben Dor, "Political Culture Approach to Middle East Politics," *International Journal of Middle East Studies* Vol. 8 (January 1977), pp. 43–63; Samuel Huntington, "The Change to Change," in Roy C. Macridis and Bernard B. Brown (eds.), *Comparative Politics* (Homewood, Ill.: Dorsey Press, 1972); Alex Inkeles, "Participant Citizenship in Six Developing Countries," *American Political Science Review* Vol. 63 (December 1969), pp. 1129–1141; Dankwart Rustow and Robert E. Ward, "Introduction," in D. Rustow and R. Ward (eds.), *Political Modernization in Japan and Turkey* (Princeton, N.J.: Princeton University Press, 1964); Samuel P. Huntington and Joan Nelson, *No Easy Choice: Political Participation in Developing Countries* (Cambridge, Mass.: Harvard University Press, 1976); Donald Rothchild and Robert Curry, Jr., *Scarcity, Choice and Public Policy in Middle Africa* (Berkeley, 1978); Leonard Binder et al., *Crises and Sequences of Political Development* (Princeton, N.J.: Princeton University Press, 1971).

5. Although all of the references cited in the preceding note are relevant, the best definitional statement is provided by Inkeles, "Participant Citizenship." For a recent discussion and summary, see Mark A. Tessler and Patricia Freeman, "Regime Orientation and Participant Citizenship in Developing Countries: Hypotheses and a Test with Longitudinal Data from Tunisia," *Western Political Quarterly* (December 1981).

6. See, for example, Ester Boserup and Christina Liljencrantz, *The Integration of Women in Development* (New York: United Nations Development Programme, 1975).

7. See, for example, Lynne B. Iglitzin and Ruth Ross (eds.), *Women in the World* (Santa Barbara, Calif.: Clio Books, 1976); Jane Jaquette (ed.), *Women in Politics* (New York, 1974); and Michelle Rosaldo and Louise Lamphere, *Women, Culture and Society* (Stanford, Calif.: Stanford University Press, 1974).

8. See, for example, Kay Boals, "The Politics of Cultural Liberation," in Jaquette, *Women in Politics;* Jane Collier, "Women in Politics," in Rosaldo and Lamphere, *Women, Culture and Society;* Jean O'Barr, "Making the Invisible Visible: African Women in Politics and Policy," *African Studies Review* Vol. 18 (December 1975), pp. 19–27; Jean O'Barr, "Pare Women: A Case of Political Involvement," *Rural Africana* Vol. 29 (Winter 1975-1976), pp. 121–134; and Judith Van Allen, "Sitting on a Man," *Canadian Journal of African Studies* Vol. 6, No. 2 (1972), pp. 165–182.

9. Jean O'Barr, *Third World Women: Factors in Their Changing Status* (Durham, 1975). A major exception is Barbara Ward (ed.), *Women in the New Asia* (Paris: UNESCO, 1963).

10. Ester Boserup, *Woman's Role in Economic Development* (London: Allen & Unwin, 1970).

11. Irene Tinker and Michele B. Bramson, *Women and World Development* (Washington, 1976).

12. Jaquette, *Women in Politics.*

13. Deborah Pellow, *Women in Accra* (Algonac, Mich.: Reference Publications, 1977).

14. Kathleen H. Merriam, "The Impact of Modern Secular Education Upon

Egyptian Women's Participation in Public Life" (Paper presented at the 1976 annual Middle East Studies Association meeting); and Mark Tessler and Linda Hawkins, "Gender and Personal Efficacy in Developing Countries" (Paper presented at the 1979 annual Middle East Studies Association meeting).

15. See, for example, Fred Hayward, "Correlates of National Political Integration: The Case of Ghana," *Comparative Political Studies* Vol. 7 (July 1974), pp. 165–192; John Holm, *Dimensions of Mass Involvement in Botswana Politics: A Test of Alternative Theories* (Beverly Hills, Calif.: Sage Publications, 1974); Inkeles, "Participant Citizenship"; Joseph Kahl, *The Measurement of Modernism* (Austin: University of Texas Press, 1968); Daniel Lerner, *The Passing of Traditional Society* (New York, 1958); Norman Nie, G. Bingham Powell, Jr., and Kenneth Prewitt, "Social Structure and Political Participation: Developmental Relationships," *American Political Science Review* Vol. 63 (June and September 1969), pp. 361–378 and 808–832; and Mark Tessler, "The Application of Western Theories and Methods of Political Participation to a Single-Party North African State," *Comparative Political Studies* Vol. 5 (July 1972), pp. 175–191.

16. See, for example, Almond and Verba, *The Civic Culture;* Robert Lane, *Political Life* (New York, 1959); and Lester W. Milbrath, *Political Participation* (Chicago: Rand McNally, 1965).

17. Alex Inkeles and David H. Smith, *Becoming Modern* (Cambridge, Mass.: Harvard University Press, 1974), p. 224.

18. See, for example, Boserup, *Woman's Role;* Jaquette, *Women in Politics;* and Tinker and Bramson, *Women and World Development.*

19. Mark Tessler, "Political Generations," in Russell Stone and John Simmons (eds.), *Change in Tunisia* (Albany: State University of N.Y. Press, 1976).

20. This point is forcefully made in the dependency theory literature. See, for example, Andre Gunder-Frank, *Capitalism and Underdevelopment in Kenya* (Berkeley, 1974).

21. Robert Melson and Howard Wolpe, "Modernization and the Politics of Communalism: A Theoretical Perspective," *The American Political Science Review* Vol. 64 (December 1970), pp. 1112–1130; John A. Armstrong, "Mobilized and Proletarian Diasporas," *The American Political Science Review* Vol. 70 (July 1976), pp. 393–408; and Mark Tessler, Linda Hawkins, and Jutta Parsons, "Minorities in Retreat: The Jews of the Maghreb," in R. D. McLaurin (ed.), *The Political Role of Minorities in the Middle East* (New York, 1979).

22. See, for example, Robert A. LeVine, "Political Socialization and Culture Change," in Clifford Geertz (ed.), *Old Societies and New States* (New York: Free Press of Glencoe, 1963); and Bill and Hardgrave, *Comparative Politics.*

23. For an extended discussion of the nature and possible consequences of variations in regime orientation, see Tessler and Freeman, "Regime Orientation and Participant Citizenship."

24. There have been a number of excellent case studies evaluating specific mobilization-oriented single-party regimes. See, for example, Nicholas Hopkins, *Popular Government in an African Town* (Chicago: University of Chicago Press, 1972); Clyde Ingle, *From Village to State in Tanzania* (Ithaca, N.Y.: Cornell University Press, 1972); James B. Mayfield, *Rural Politics in Nasser's Egypt* (Austin: University of Texas Press, 1971); and Lars Rudebeck, *Party and People: A Study of Political Change in Tunisia* (New York, 1967). In general, however, these studies suggest that all regimes have had both successes and failures and, more importantly, their focus has rarely been on political attitudes at the individual level. There have also been a few studies contrasting countries with

varying degrees of commitment to political mobilization. See, for example, Philip Foster and Aristide Zolberg (eds.), *Ghana and the Ivory Coast* (Chicago: University of Chicago Press, 1971). Again, however, these studies provide little systematic evidence about the impact of political programs on individual attitudes.

25. See, for example, Charles Micaud, *Tunisia: The Politics of Modernization* (New York: F. A. Praeger, 1964); Charles Micaud, "Leadership and Development: The Case of Tunisia," *Comparative Politics* Vol. 2 (July 1969), pp. 468–484; Clement Henry Moore, *Tunisia Since Independence* (Berkeley: University of Calif. Press, 1965); Rudebeck, *Party and People;* and Mark Tessler, William O'Barr, and David Spain, *Tradition and Identity in Changing Africa* (New York: Harper & Row, 1973), pp. 193–302.

26. John Entelis, "Ideological Change and an Emerging Counter-Culture in Tunisian Politics," *Journal of Modern African Studies* Vol. 12 (September 1974), pp. 543–568; Elbaki Hermassi, *Leadership and National Development in North Africa* (Berkeley: University of Calif. Press, 1972); Mark Tessler, "Single-Party Rule in Tunisia," *Common Ground* (AUFS) Vol. 2 (October 1976), pp. 55–64; Mark Tessler, "Women's Emancipation in Tunisia," in Lois Beck and Nikki Keddie (eds.), *Women in the Muslim World* (Cambridge, Mass.: Harvard University Press, 1978); and Abdelkader Zghal, "The Reactivation of Tradition in a Post-Traditional Society," in S. N. Eisenstadt (ed.), *Post-Traditional Societies* (New York, 1972).

27. Mark Tessler, "Cultural Modernity: Evidence from Tunisia," *Social Science Quarterly* Vol. 52 (September 1971), pp. 290–308; Mark Tessler, "Problems of Measurement in Comparative Research: Perspectives from an African Survey," *Social Science Information* Vol. 12 (December 1973), pp. 29–43; Mark Tessler, "Response Set and Interviewer Bias," in William M. O'Barr, David H. Spain, and Mark A. Tessler (eds.), *Survey Research in Africa* (Evanston, Ill.: Northwestern University Press, 1973).

28. The references cited in the preceding note describe the approach to establishing measurement reliability and validity that was followed in the present study. Detailed evidence of the validity and reliability of the present measure of participant citizenship is to be found in Tessler and Freeman, "Regime Orientation and Participant Citizenship."

29. Mark Tessler, "The Application of Western Theories," and Jean O'Barr, "Studying Political Participation in Rural Africa," in O'Barr, Spain, and Tessler, *Survey Research in Africa* ((Evanston, 1973).

30. See, for example, Ethel Albert, "Women of Burundi," in Denise Paulme (ed.), *Women of Tropical Africa* (Berkeley, 1971); June Nash and Helen Safa (eds.), *Sex and Class in Latin America* (New York: Praeger, 1976); and Kathleen Newland, *Women in Politics* (Washington: Worldwatch Institute, 1975).

Part IV

A New Arab Order?

13
Rich and Poor in the New Arab Order

Malcolm H. Kerr

I

The 1970s are likely to go down in history as the decade in which the Arabs missed the boat. At a time when fate dropped in their laps a spectacular opportunity to tackle their massive development requirements and build Arab unity on the basis of fruitful economic cooperation, the Arab leaders instead merely established new patterns of wastefulness and political rivalry. The scandalous expenditure of many billions of dollars each year on useless construction projects in Saudi Arabia, and the unceasing orgy of killing and destruction in Lebanon, are the twin hallmarks of their failure. It is noteworthy that these two operations are both "joint ventures" in which the Arab world as a whole actively participates, collaboratively in the one case, combatively in the other; and in both cases parties in the outside world are major participants also, fellow-builders, as it were, of the new Arab order.

It is not an exaggeration to speak of a "new Arab order," on the social, economic, and political levels alike. Born of the twentyfold rise in oil prices between 1970 and 1981, the new order reflects a common process of structural change that all the Arab states have entered into during the past decade. We can easily enough identify the engine of change on each level.

On the social level it is the massive migration of manpower to the oil states, a phenomenon with consequences of fundamental importance to the sending and receiving countries alike. On the economic level it is the accumulation of financial assets in the oil states, their availability for circulation throughout the region, and the consequent distorting effects on the economic structure and policy of every non-oil state. On the political level it is the new belief that power grows, not out of the barrel of a gun nor out of the appeal of a revolutionary leader or movement, but out of an ample state treasury and the possibilities this

Reprinted with permission from *Journal of Arab Affairs* 1, no. 1 (1981):1–26. Copyright 1981 by the Middle East Research Group, Inc.

provides for the cultivation and manipulation of clients. On all three levels of change, the "new order" has meant new mechanisms binding the Arab world to the West: the exchange of persons on an unprecedented scale; a great upsurge in commercial transactions; and a new perception by Western governments, for good or ill, of their strategic stake in Saudi Arabia and the Gulf.

In a way it may seem paradoxical to speak of a new Arab order, inasmuch as the oil boom has accentuated the contrasts between the oil-rich and the oil-poor states. Most of the oil is located in the most underpopulated, backward, isolated Arab countries, such as Saudi Arabia, Kuwait, the United Arab Emirates, and Libya. Other countries such as Egypt, Jordan, Lebanon, Syria, and Tunisia possess what the oil states lack—manpower, industry, education, etc.—but are short of money. In some ways these contrasts complicate the prospects for economic and political integration between the two sets of states, yet the accumulation of revenues in the oil countries has inevitably stimulated a great acceleration in the interactions between them and the others, thus making the Arab world more of a "system" in the proper sense of the word than before. What the new Arab order emphatically does not signify is that Arab life is more orderly, or that the long-term prospects for the progress of Arab society are better. The new order has brought new problems, such as the twin scandals of construction in Saudi Arabia and destruction in Lebanon mentioned above, and it signifies that these problems belong to all the Arabs in common. A third problem area, which will be of primary interest to us in this essay, is that of development—or misdevelopment—in the non-oil states as they struggle to cope with life in the shadow of their wealthy neighbors.

This essay is not the place to discuss the Lebanese tragedy at any length. Suffice it to say that whereas, in the old days, Lebanon was permitted to prosper because the Arab states gave it their blessing as a mutually convenient haven of sanity, now it suffers because those same states have found it convenient to fight their battles there. The Arabs have designated Lebanon as a kind of preserve in which to unleash all their demons of madness, while transferring their instincts for tolerance and mutual advantage to Saudi Arabia and the Gulf.

This is not by chance. The Arabs do not act alone in either place, and in both cases an underlying issue affecting their behavior is the future of their relations with the outside industrialized world. How will the oil boom affect these relations? Will the interests of doing immensely profitable business with the West progressively overshadow the traditional political conflicts over Israel and Palestine, strategic hegemony and the Cold War? Will the Arab world, representative of the Third World as a whole, evolve from its past preoccupations with ideological questions of nationalism, freedom, social progress, and international equality, to a new depoliticized focus on selling oil and spending money? In important ways, this question is what the "joint ventures" of Saudi

Arabia and Lebanon are all about. They are part of the same picture, that of the new Arab order.

Saudi Arabia and the other oil-rich states are, of course, the fulcrum of the new Arab order—socially, economically, politically. They are the home of the golden goose, and it is natural that outsiders behave circumspectly with regard to them: for whereas they used to go to Lebanon for refuge and relaxation, they now go to the Gulf to make money, not in competition but in cooperation with each other—and with a host of outsiders. Our theme in this essay is to consider the oil states not as autonomous societies but as inter-Arab and international institutions of convenience—institutions which, however, have been grievously misused by international and Arab commercial and political elites, primarily at the expense of the populations of the larger and poorer Arab states where the serious business of development ought to be going on. But the price the latter are paying is heavily disguised since not only their own elites, but also a liberal sprinkling of their ordinary citizens, are part of the game.

The unspoken "conspiracy" that govens the appalling pattern of wasteful expenditure in the oil states is, of course, a worldwide one, and the dominant partners are the giant industrial firms of the U.S., Europe, Japan, and Korea that help the local governments plan the projects, and win multibillion dollar contracts. But the interesting point is that the conspiracy is, in fact, almost universal, and there is no one to oppose it. The pattern of expenditure may be wildly wasteful, and mass human needs may be neglected, but politically and economically there is no contest. In the oil monarchies themselves, it goes without saying that every project and every transaction enriches local parties; those who are left out are scattered and unorganized, and there is always room to expand the pyramid of privilege. Equally obvious, Western governments as well as businesses welcome the massive recycling of petrodollars that comes with expenditures on airports, office complexes, petrochemical plants, and lavish military facilities and weaponry—however useless—in the oil states.

It is true, perhaps, that young men returning with university degrees from abroad, and some traditional religious dignitaries at home, may be scandalized by the corruption, waste, and immorality inherent in the spending process. But there are many opportunities for them to be co-opted as partners into it, one way or another: the young graduates can build and manage hotel swimming pools and videotape distribution centers, and the religious dignitaries can nourish their status by closing them down. Whatever qualms the more conservative Saudis have about the social disadvantages of breakneck expenditure, they have had no discernible success in slowing it down. It may be—who can tell?—that the attack on the Grand Mosque in Mecca in 1979 presaged a mass Iranian-style puritanical revolution that will destroy the whole pattern one day. But the very character of the Mecca uprising—a bizarre suicidal operation carried out by utopian zealots—serves all the more to remind us of the absence of any normally identifiable and organizable social sector in Saudi Arabia that can be expected to provide countervailing pressure against the current spending policies, or against the regime itself.[1]

In addition to interests in the oil states and the industrialized world, there is a third leg to the triangle of conspiracy to waste oil revenues. This lies in the neighboring non-oil Arab states, the "poor cousins" whose own collective interest in receiving large-scale financing and joining with the oil states in well-coordinated development planning has been the principal victim of the conspiracy. In short, thanks to their structure of leadership and interests, the non-oil states join in the conspiracy against themselves.

There is nothing mysterious or illogical about this. Naturally enough, the effects of the oil boom on the non-oil societies in the Arab world have been such as to deepen and perpetuate the already existing lines of privilege and profit in the oil states themselves. The oil boom has offered a tremendous outlet for surplus labor across the Arab world, from unskilled rural migrants to the most highly trained professionals: the brain drain that used to flow exclusively in the direction of Europe and North America now moves, in large part, to the Gulf, not in search of a new life but of four or five years' salary savings with which to return home to Egypt or Jordan or Tunisia and invest in a better future. The existing local commercial opportunities—real estate, banking, importing, retailing, and tourism—are immensely enhanced by the availability of private Saudi and Gulf capital in search of quick profit. The governments of the non-oil states realize the easy advantage of seeking miscellaneous loans and gifts by ingratiating the oil regimes, rather than threatening or browbeating them as Egypt's Nasir and the Syrian Ba'thists used to do, or promoting arduous, long-term (ultimately probably frustrating) campaigns to negotiate the reform of inter-Arab economic relationships for the sake of balanced development. Moreover, some of these governments have had some good reason, and much professional advice from the International Monetary Fund (IMF), the World Bank, the United States Treasury, their own Ministers of Finance, and others, to move in the direction of *laissez faire.*

The upshot has been that for better or worse, almost all the non-oil states, including Egypt, Syria, Jordan, Sudan, North Yemen, and Tunisia, have followed economic policies in the 1970s pointing in a basically similar direction: that of liberalization, or, in Arabic, *al-infitah.* Despite considerable variations of detail from one country to another, everywhere the *infitah* has included measures to relax central controls over the economy so as to facilitate the entrance of foreign capital, the productive investment of domestic capital, and the movement of domestic labor to the oil-producing neighbors.

Meanwhile, the economic liberalization has been accompanied in most cases with a political counterpart: the revival of certain conservative interests at home, closer and more deferential relations with the oil states (especially Saudi Arabia), and similar relations with the industrialized states (especially the U.S.). Together, the economic and political liberalizations have been the means by which the capital-poor states have adapted themselves to the oil boom. In the process, they have in certain respects become replicas of the oil states, the products also of a kind of "conspiracy" of domestic and international interests, built around the circulation of considerable new wealth, a construction boom, new large-scale government contracts for the improvement of infrastructure, and a vast upsurge in local demand for luxury imports of all kinds.

As in the oil states, this is a "conspiracy" in which there are few audible voices of dissent. Even though plenty of people are poorly served in the end by what is happening—the civil servant or school teacher confronting inflation, the laboring and lower-middle classes facing housing and transport shortages, the scarcity of certain subsidized consumer staples, the decline of the quality of public education, the emigration en masse of people with skills and expertise—nonetheless opposition is scattered and muffled. For one thing, the benefits of economic liberalization, and particularly of labor migration, cut very broadly across class lines. Every family in every town and village in the non-oil states is likely to have its husband or sons, or at least its cousins, working in one of the oil states and accumulating savings in which the family will share. Roughly a million North Yemenis—half the labor force—are in Saudi Arabia. For another thing, opportunities for temporary emigration in large numbers constitute an important safety valve for disaffected individuals. While the Yemenis are overwhelmingly nonpolitical workmen, the estimated one and a half to two million Egyptians abroad, who include 15–20 percent of the labor force, comprise a high proportion of university graduates whose attitudes toward their own government are much more likely to be independent and critical. A final influence against political opposition in the non-oil states is the expansion of individual opportunities in commerce and careers, as a consequence of the expanding circulation of money and the opening up of the private sector: even without emigrating, one can hope more than before that something will turn up.

To some extent, the susceptibility of certain non-oil states to pressures in favor of *al-infitah* can be traced to factors that preceded the oil boom or were unrelated to it. The era of socialism and radical reformism in Egypt, Syria, Tunisia, and elsewhere in the 1960s was, after all, based on rather fragile cultural, social, ideological, and institutional foundations, as many studies have shown. Already before 1973 certain domestic changes had occurred in several states which served to prepare their governments to respond quickly to the sudden quadrupling of oil prices. In Egypt, Sadat had succeeded Nasir and imprisoned Ali Sabry and his leftist associates; in Syria, Asad had ousted the ideological militants of the Salah Jedid faction of the Ba'th Party; in Tunisia, Bourguiba had deposed Ahmed Ben Salah from his position as economic czar, and cut short his collectivist experiments. Well before 1973 there was a new readiness in each of these countries to loosen some of the controls, attract foreign capital, and encourage the underemployed domestic labor force to migrate to Libya and the Gulf.

Yet these budding changes before 1973 were nothing compared to what followed, for the oil boom offered the governments of the poor states far more than they had ever dreamed: a quantum increase in labor migration and remittances, a lavish scale of private investment by citizens of the oil states in the non-oil ones, and the flow of intergovernmental aid and investment in amounts far exceeding previous foreign aid from the great powers. Moreover one would not be a substitute but a supplement to the other, for an Egypt or a Tunisia lubricated with Arab petrodollars would become a much more eligible trading partner and investment area for the Western countries than before.

In any case, whatever the relative importance of internal and external factors pressing the non-oil states toward *al-infitah,* the combination was strong enough to sweep aside all sorts of institutional and ideological obstacles, and to deal a devastating blow to the prospects of socialist economics and revolutionary political activity. Considering the long list of failures and illusions of the Arab Left, this may have been no loss in itself. Unfortunately, the way things turned out, an equally devastating blow was dealt to prospects for balance, planning, and coordination in the economics of all states of the region, even those under more moderate and pragmatic governments.

II

In the remainder of this essay we shall consider the case of Egypt as a significant measure of the response of the non-oil states to the oil boom, and of the evolution of their roles within the new Arab order. Egypt is the largest and in some ways the most advanced Arab state, yet also one of the poorest in mass living standards and most urgently in need of cashing in on the opportunities for development created by the accumulation of fabulous riches in brother Arab states.

Broadly speaking, Egypt has moved toward a greater resemblance to some of the oil states in her economic and political life. The emphasis in the national economy has shifted from agriculture and manufacturing—pushed strongly during the Nasir years—to commercial activities that capitalize on the existence of new money in circulation. The political leadership has become a kind of family affair, dominated by a patrimonial figure and his entourage. The foreign policy is heavily based on the principle of catering to the political leadership, the business tycoons, and the film stars of the Western world.

Despite the announced philosophy of *al-infitah* in Egypt, which preaches the liberation of domestic as well as foreign investment potential for the development of productive enterprise, in fact the areas of activity into which the new Egyptian entrepreneurial class has moved—real estate, tourist services, luxury imports, etc.—are ones that do little to build up the productive capacities of the country. Nor do the foreign investors with which the domestic interests associate themselves (notably Saudis and Kuwaitis) have a different tendency.[2] As long as *al-infitah* continues, however, these activities should be profitable for those involved; thus they will constitute an important interest group well placed to press for the prolongation of the policy even if it is not paying off for the nation as a whole, and to convince the government that the present state of affairs is actually quite satisfactory. Here is a phenomenon that precisely mirrors a counterpart situation in Saudi Arabia, where a large class of commercial operators has a vested interest in the expanding economy. Commercial expanison, it is argued in Egypt, spells the country's salvation.

Superficially at least, such an argument is not hard to make. The rate of growth in the GNP—around 9 percent in 1980; the improvement in the balance of payments; the ever growing revenues from American aid, the Suez Canal, tourism, and the remittances of Egyptians working the Gulf; the appearance of new prosperity in downtown Cairo, with its construction boom, the October bridge and the traffic flyovers, the imported goods for sale, the slightly improved telephone system—all this suggests at face value that things are getting better. In some respects they are. But it encourages the government to settle for overall improvements in the national accounts, to ignore problems of productivity and income distribution, and, in the assurance that more windfall revenues are always on the horizon, to adopt a rather casual attitude toward the intractable problems of basic reform. One analyst has compared this attitude to that of the governments of the oil-rich states: despite Egypt's poverty she is run like a rentier state, along with relying on windfalls, with the difference that her windfalls come from outside the country rather than inside.[3]

In some ways a system of this sort is reminiscent of Lebanon prior to the civil war; in others, it is more like Iran before the revolution. The comparison with Lebanon stems from the inordinate emphasis on commercial activities as the backbone of the economy: importing and retailing of consumer goods, banking, business services, real estate, and tourism. In addition, as in Lebanon, there is the low priority attached by the government to the level or quality of social services and the reliance on private education, private medical care, etc., by those who can afford it. There is the same lack of attention to the needs of rural areas and provincial towns (despite President Sadat's fondness for alluding to the cultural values of rural life). There is the same effort by the regime to cultivate the good will and protection of the Western powers, as well as the tolerance of militant states in the region, by building up the country's reputation as an international commercial entrepot, political sanctuary, playground, and all-round facility.

There are, of course, many differences between Lebanon and Egypt which preclude a really systematic effort by the Egyptian government to seek to adopt the Lebanese role—although it does appear to pursue it, however unconsciously, to an unhealthy extent. The most obvious difference is that Lebanon's ability to play the role in the past depended vitally on the fact that, like Switzerland, she was a neutral country within the region with a small, compromise-minded population of diverse communities, background, and political orientation and without external ambitions; thus she was more easily accepted by the others as a common convenience. For Egypt, with the Arab world's largest population, industrial base, and military forces, the Lebanese role is incompatible with her national stature and strategic interests.

On the domestic, economic, and social levels there are other differences that have received perhaps less recognition from the government. The traditional Arab-Islamic culture of the great majority of Egyptians does not make them plausible candidates to acquire, or encourage in their midst, the cosmopolitan, mercantile, polyglot personality of Levantinism. Furthermore, while the purveying of commercial services to the region brought considerable prosperity to Lebanon, it cannot sustain an economy of the size of Egypt's. Even in Lebanon, it eventually failed to serve the larger society well: the poorer communities, excluded from participation, came to pose a social and political challenge to the system as they camped in the "belt of misery" on the outskirts of Beirut. So also in Egypt, where a much smaller proportion of the population can hope to benefit from the new commercialism, the accentuation of social inequality may eventually erode the political passivity of the country's great mass of urban migrants.

Comparison with Iran presents a rather different case. It stems first of all from the phenomenon of rapid and poorly controlled growth, coming largely from sources of income accruing to the government rather than to private individuals (in Egypt's case, revenues from oil, the Suez Canal, and foreign aid), which the government at least ostensibly tries to direct toward investment in industry, agriculture, and infrastructure. It does so, however, in an improvised manner and in cooperation with a new class of private entrepreneurs largely of the regime's own making: favored individuals and foreign interests who learn to capitalize on their connections with those in power and, of course, to cut them in on the deal. The reason the planning is so poor in such a system is that the rationalization of a modernizing, industrializing economy is not the controlling consideration: rather, it is the appearance of great progress and activity, represented simply by a rapid rise in GNP, the prosperity of a growing new upper class, and the very visible integration of the country into the world economy. Again as in the Lebanese case, a high rate of inflation and an increasing degree of inequality between social classes are obvious consequences.

These economic features of the Iranian model have certain political accompaniments. The bureaucracy is more than ever a dumping ground for unusable high school and university graduates, but presiding over it is a new class of technocrats who, in turn, are politically subservient to the political leadership. There is a built-in ambivalence between the bureaucracy and the technocracy: together they nominally represent the interest of management and supervision of a growing modern economy, but with the emphasis on appearance rather than reality, on private deals rather than national development; it is always easy for both bureaucrats and technocrats to be bypassed by those above them. Of course, the bureaucracy-technocracy syndrome was already a phenomenon in the socialist Egypt of Nasir, but with the difference that in those days, for the political leadership and for many individuals employed within the apparatus, concrete national purposes really were important.

Another feature of the Iranian model is militarization. Egypt had already been militarized under Nasir and, according to various presidential declarations, was supposed to undergo a measure of demilitarization after the peace treaty with Israel. In the following year both the rhetoric and the military budget shifted and it became clear that the importance of the armed forces was destined to grow rather than shrink. This is because the attention devoted to these forces was not a function of national defense needs but of the political preoccupations of the regime: close relations with the new weapons supplier, the United States; the adoption of a forceful posture toward certain neighbors (Libya, Ethiopia); and, presumably, a desire to cultivate the loyalty of the generals and colonels on whom the life of the regime depends.

Finally, the Iranian model presents the figure of the patrimonial leader, with striking implications for Egypt. The patrimonial leader holds the system together through a network of personal loyalties centered on himself, with the object of building up patronage, power, and control. The dispensing of favors, the manipulation of clients, the rotation of officeholders, the keeping of one's own counsel on vital matters, the primary reliance on confidants whose membership in the inner circle is unrelated to any official status, the cultivation of a whole mythology of omnipotence, omniscience, benevolence, unanimous popularity—all these are essential ingredients of the cult of patrimonialism.

The patrimonial syndrome is traditionally associated with an hereditary monarchy but is by no means limited to it. More important, the syndrome is more successfully associated with a static society and static economic resources than with a situation of flux and rapid change. When the resources to be passed around are limited, then everything has its steady value, and the personalities to be manipulated are more or less stable as well, so that the game is more easily controlled. The introduction of sweeping and unfamiliar changes, as in the Iranian case in the 1960s and 1970s or, to some extent, in the Egyptian case today, threatens to throw the game into confusion by inserting the element of uncertainty. It is thus not surprising that the demise of Shah Mohammed Reza Pahlavi, some 37 years after he ascended the throne, came several years after the sudden rise of oil prices had pumped additional billions of dollars into his nation's economic and social bloodstream. For the patrimonial form of leadership fits poorly with rapid economic change, demands for planning, rationalization, delegation of authority, and transformation of social and political relationships. No doubt the Shah, spending a few weeks in Morocco after his fall, was in a position to compare some interesting notes with King Hassan II, still on *his* throne and still presiding over a comparatively stagnant economy.

But Egypt is different in many ways from Iran, and President Sadat is different from the Shah, since he maintains a more realistic human touch with his populace and with the outside world: he visits his village, he attends the mosque, he wears a safari suit, he gives extemporaneous speeches to his people on television. While his economy has not exactly been inundated with wealth *a l'iranienne,* his people are generally better educated and his government better institutionalized than those of the Shah, and he treats them accordingly with more respect. He does not rule by terror. His religious establishment is cooperative, and lays no claim in the Shi'ite fashion either to martyrdom or to theocratic primacy.

But these are differences of secondary importance, not essential substance. The similarities are probably of greater significance: the one-man rule, the manufacturing of unanimous support, the promise of great days, the reliance on an inner circle and the manipulation of the regular state administration, the shuffling of cabinet ministers in and out of office, the disregard of expertise and reasoned counsel, the scorning of facts and figures and the preference for illusory grand schemes, the hobnobbing with world leaders, the cultivation of generals, the fondness for ornate uniforms worthy of banana republic dictators, all the while preaching nostalgia for the village life of simplicity: all this adds up to a picture remarkably close to that of the Shah. Add to this the rapid changes in the Egyptian economy, in which fortunes are being made, inflation is rampant, and some traditional livelihoods and values are being abruptly undermined, plus the sudden and unrestrained Americanization of everything in Egyptian life from foreign policy to consumption habits, and one can hardly grant President Sadat the right to complacency.

Overall, in the long run Egypt under Sadat appears headed for an accumulation of social strains and tensions—but the rate, and the medium-term political effect is an open question. On the economic front the prospects are for several years of very rapid growth, followed by a leveling-off in the long run with risk of stagnation as certain rapid-growth sectors of the economy exhaust their potential for further expansion. These sectors include the Suez Canal, oil production, tourism, remittances, and the construction boom. There is a limit to what can be expected from them. Consider for instance the case of oil, of which Egypt is a modest net exporter. The doubling of the price by OPEC in 1979–80 was a great boon to Egypt, enabling her to record a favorable balance of payments in 1981 for the first time since the 1950s. Yet, according to current projections of the Egyptian Ministry of Petroleum, in the absence of new major discoveries, the country's rising rate of consumption will catch up with production by 1985 and she will once again become a net importer of this ever-more-costly commodity.

Or again, consider the case of workers' remittances, next to oil the largest hard-currency earner for Egypt. Forecasts differ regarding the likelihood that the employment of Egyptian labor in the oil states will hold up in the future. A study by two staff economists at the World Bank suggests that Egyptian labor will continue to be indispensable to Saudi Arabia at least in its present level for many years.[4] This may or may not prove correct. A more gloomy opinion circulating freely in some circles in Cairo and the Gulf is that Egyptian skills and expertise have been earning less respect of late than before, and that there is a growing preference to employ Westerners (even at higher salaries) in their place. This guesstimate reflects an almost universal belief in Egypt that the standards of higher education in the country are in a stage of alarming decline.

Be that as it may, there is some reason to anticipate that before many years, sustained advances in Egypt's economy must be fueled by the expansion of agriculture and industry, sectors that the Open Door Policy purports to encourage but has failed to do during its first half-dozen years.

What then might Egypt look like by the year 2000 assuming a continuation of the present regime under Sadat or a natural successor, and assuming a relatively optimistic projection of continued expansion of the economy at the rate of five percent per year? A population of 60 to 65 million can be imagined with a per capita income of $500-600 in 1980 prices (up from $350 in 1980), a population in the greater Cairo area of 18 million, a booming tourist industry, a continuing but moderately reduced exportation of manpower to the Gulf, an export-oriented agriculture falling far short of paying for needed food imports, a vestigial oil-extraction industry of negligible importance, a chronically ailing public-sector industrial network, a Western business community of ten to fifteen thousand, and a prosperous system of international banking doing most of its business outside Egypt and repatriating the bulk of its profits abroad. We can also expect a deepening gulf between a large, increasingly cosmopolitan and affluent business-based upper and upper-middle class, inhabiting a smart, new, well-paved cleaned-up downtown Cairo with a skyline of hotels and office skyscrapers, and an ever-growing mass of underemployed and disaffected wretches inhabiting one of the world's largest slums, watched carefully by the police and the army. Presiding over it all will be a nominally constitutional, thinly veiled, tough-minded dictatorship, Brazilian style, supported by the senior military commanders in the background.

This is the optimistic scenario. The more pessimistic projection is that it would not survive until the year 2000, for the beneficiaries of such a system may find their position undermined as time passes. According to the Lebanese mercantile model the problem is the lack of real productivity in the system, hence its inability to sustain rising levels of mass employment and consumption, and also the lack of central direction. The system might survive for many years, however, and it might require an external catalyst (like the Palestinian problem in Lebanon) to bring on a crisis.

According to the Iranian patrimonial model, on the other hand, the problem is mass alienation from the social dislocations and repression that result from the megalomania of the ruler. To the extent that Egypt follows in the footsteps of either or both of these models, the future does not bode very well for the long run. The gaps between rich and poor may become too glaring, the challenge to traditional values too degrading, the costs of propping up the level of living of the upper classes too exorbitant, the tools of repression too inadequate. Even if the system survives the century, it will not be a showcase of success.

III

Throughout the non-oil-rich states of the Middle East, the oil boom and *al-infitah* have resulted in fuller employment, rapidly rising national income, and expanding sectors of construction and commercial activity. Other effects have included high inflation, accentuated maldistribution of income, agricultural decline, food shortages, labor shortages, and an overall distortion of development priorities. Local manufactures have been overwhelmed by more efficiently produced foreign imports. Public services—education, transport, low-cost housing—have suffered.

Some of these adverse effects seem bizarre when we consider that the starting point in the process was an increase in the supply of money in the Arab community as a whole, available, presumably, both for regional development and for universally improved living standards. After all, as some experts on welfare in the United States have remarked for many years, what the poor most conspicuously lack is money. One would have thought that in a country as well endowed with skills and as short of money as Egypt, the advent of an extra three or four billion dollars a year would serve to put the country on its feet. But this assumption overlooks the possibility that shortage of money may not be the chief traditional deficiency in Arab development, and that priorities are more likely to be misplaced when easy money is on hand than when it is not.[5]

Nonetheless, there is no doubt that in all the non-oil countries the need for infusions of capital is real enough. In the Egyptian case, in fact, this is an old story, for Egypt has faced balance-of-payments problems ever since the exhaustion of her sterling reserves in the 1950s. In the 1950s and 1960s Nasir conducted an incessant campaign to muster contributions from the Soviet Union, the United States, and others to finance his ambitious development programs. After the 1967 defeat by Israel he was obliged to negotiate for aid from the Arab oil monarchs, to compensate for the loss of the Suez Canal revenues and to re-equip his armed forces.

But the access to Arab oil money in the 1970s and, prospectively, in the 1980s has had much more dramatic implications. The amount of money potentially available is unimaginably greater than anything received in the past, and because it comes from within the Arab family there is some reason to imagine that the donors may prove more responsive to Egypt's particular needs and requests than others have been. Moreover, with their need for Egyptian manpower and, in some instances, Egypt's political cooperation, the relationship has an aspect of healthy mutuality.

However, the mutuality is less than complete, and so is the good will. On the Egyptian side there has been a pointed conviction that the oil states bore Egypt a heavy moral obligation because of her sacrifices in the wars against Israel. In fact, during the four years that followed the 1973 war, assistance committed to Egypt by the Gulf states of Saudi Arabia, Kuwait, the United Arab Emirates, and Qatar totalled no less than $6.5 billion, conservatively estimated.[6] This was a large sum, although it fell far short of what the "Arab Marshall Plan," sometimes spoken of in Egyptian official circles, might have entailed. More than a few Egyptians have expressed the belief that the intention of the Gulf states was to give Egypt just enough to keep her and the Sadat regime alive, but not enough to restore her previous strength and potential for Arab leadership.

Meanwhile, on the side of the Gulf states there has been a widespread feeling that no amount of aid would satisfy Egypt or rescue her crumbling economy; and there has also been plenty of anger at Sadat and his government for abandoning the struggle against the Arabs' common enemy.

Egypt's readiness to cultivate the Saudi connection carries a number of crucial implications. Saudi Arabia is not just another Arab country: it is the citadel of Islamic orthodoxy, and it is governed by men whose political outlook is highly conservative. Moreover, their consant preoccupation in Arab affairs has been a defensive one: how to fend off threats and challenges from other parties who are more sophisticated, better armed, better manned, and better organized than themselves, and who are jealous of their wealth. Beyond this, the Saudis are well aware of the extent to which their security, finances, and growing infrastructure depend on the preservation of a cooperative relationship with the U.S. and Euorpe—a condition not always compatible with the requirements of inter-Arab politics.

How the Saudi leaders deal with Egypt, therefore, how ready they are to meet her needs, or to rely on her to meet theirs, must depend on their calculation of Egyptian intentions and of the practical long-term consequences of a closely cooperative relationship. How strong do they really want Egypt to become? How economically healthy and independent? To what extent are they willing to see Egypt regain political influence in the Arab world? How confident are they that with their own recent accumulation of wealth, they can hold their own in inter-Arab politics and control the political consequences of their distribution of aid?

The answers to these questions have been considerably complicated by two events of recent years: the Egyptian-Israeli peace treaty of 1979 and the Iraqi invasion of Iran in 1980. Both of these events illustrated the ambiguity as well as the vulnerability of Saudi Arabia's political, strategic, and economic interests.

Sadat's initiative and the Saudi response to it suggested that some of the new images of petrodollar politics in the mid-1970s were in need of correction. It had become fashionable to point to the growing diplomatic ascendancy of Saudi Arabia, and to the helplessness of Egypt. Not only had the Saudis come into the possession of enormous financial assets, but they seemed to show considerable skill at using them in the international arena, building up their credit, their reputation for probity, and their leadership in a discreet way—with the industrialized world, the Third World, and in the Middle East. If money talks, as surely it must when there are billions of it, the Saudi leaders seemed to have the knack of making it speak authoritatively in a whisper. Egypt, it was said, was Saudi Arabia's completely dependent client, and Riyadh held a clear veto over Cairo's foreign and domestic policies. Ditto for Jordan, Sudan, and North Yemen. Syria may have been somewhat less beholden but was still considered very responsive. Even Southern Yemen and Somalia had been (more or less) bought off.

Sadat showed that all this was a faulty view of the situation. His trips to Jerusalem and Camp David, and his negotiation of a virtually undisguised separate peace with Israel, took no account whatever of Saudi interests. Angry as the Saudis undoubtedly were with Sadat for presenting them and the other Arab states with a *fait accompli,* it was not to their advantage to seek Sadat's overthrow and replacement by unknown elements or to deal destructive blows at the Egyptian economy. Their relationship with Egypt passed from that of a close partnership to that of a divorced couple who keep in touch and are "still friends." Egypt might be officially quarantined from the Arab system, but her weight and her interests were not altogether excluded from the Arab states' calculations.

While the Saudi government joined in the general Arab political boycott of Egypt, and in the cancellation of governmental aid and investment programs, they took the lead in seeing to it that transport and communication links were kept open, the employment of Egyptian workers in other Arab countries continued, and the large deposits of Arab oil-rich governments in Egyptian banks left intact.

Was this the old story, familiar everywhere between patrons and clients, of the tail wagging the dog? Or was this an indication that Sadat sensed an alternative to Saudi handouts: a new commercial and political connection with the United States and Israel, plus a spectrum of private investors from the Middle East and elsewhere? The lesson emerges, in any case, that the hegemony of mere money, unsupported by manpower, cultural attainments, military strength, or industrial development, may be something of a mirage.

The Iraqi-Iranian war added something further to this lesson, for it served to remind the Saudis of their vulnerability in the face of ambitious and militarily more powerful neighbors, and therefore of their need for something other than Iraqi good will and forbearance to protect them. To defend their interests in the long run, they would need support from other Arab parties capable to some extent of offsetting Iraq's bid for military and political predominance in the region. Logic dictated, therefore, that somehow a way should be found to restore the bonds of legitimate partnership with Egypt, without offending Iraq or other Arab parties in the process.

Thus the new order of inter-Arab alignments appears to be one, not in which the old Egyptian hegemony is replaced with Saudi or Iraqi leadership, but in which all states in the region find themselves in flux, groping somewhat inconclusively for stable positions within a multipolar equilibrium. In this new system, as Ali Dessouki tells us, we may expect an increasing tendency of governments to separate economic and political considerations in their relations with each other, following a new pragmatism in place of mercurial sentiment or inflexible ideology; and we may expect that, in spite of the great need of the non-oil-exporting countries for aid and investment from their neighbors, the reciprocal nature of the ties will be better recognized.

Whatever the course of events between Egypt and Israel or in other conflict situations in the Middle East in coming years, the drama of Egypt's bid to prosper in the shadow of the Gulf states will continue to be poignant. This bid promises to be a test case for many other Third World countries whose developmental processes have until now been blocked. The accumulating wealth of the OPEC states can be to their benefit or their expense, depending on policies the oil rulers decide to follow. A beneficial strategy would aim at regional integration and the industrial and agricultural development of have-not neighbors; it would seek to put a lid on wastefulness within the oil states' own processes of development, and it would seek to minimize the practice of placing financial surpluses in the Western money market rather than in Third World projects where they are most needed and, in fact, potentially most profitable.

The failure of the 1970s—all too likely to be perpetuated through the 1980s—is perhaps more clearly recognizable today with a little hindsight that it was predictable ten years ago, and perhaps there is nothing surprising in it. After all, few would argue that the United States would have successfully industrialized in the past century and a half simply by virtue of the discovery of oil in Texas and Oklahoma, and by the freewheeling activities of the barefoot millionaires in those territories who had been fortunate enough to own the lucky plots of real estate. Nor did neighboring Indians or Mexicans profit greatly from the occasion, although some consequently found employment. Oil discoveries in the U.S. fit into a context of an already expanding, integrated, technologically advancing, agriculturally self-sufficient national economy.

The Arabs have not been so lucky, neither the rich ones nor the poor ones. Still, their own future is up to them, for there will be no substitute for their own collective self-help: as long as they permit the vast nest-egg of money within their lands to be treated by the world (and by themselves) as an excuse for "Saturday night fever," an escape from the real world of development headaches and a shortcut to national success, they can expect plenty of eventual disappointment. It has become commonplace in the oil states to acknowledge that oil is a dwindling resource, that in time it will be gone. So too will the opportunity it offers for constructive cooperation between those who have it and those who don't, for economic integration and political statesmanship.

Notes

I am indebted for many of the ideas in this article to various collaborators in the volume *Rich and Poor States in the Middle East: Egypt and the New Arab Order,* edited by Malcolm H. Kerr and El Sayed Yassin, published in 1982 by Westview Press. Portions of this article are adapted from my own introductory and concluding chapters in the volume.

1. For an excellent recent review and interpretation of the dilemmas of development in Saudi Arabia, see Eric Rouleau, "L'Arabie Saoudite: paradis ou poudrière?," *Le Monde,* April 29–May 4, 1981.

2. For a negative assessment of foreign investment potential in the Egyptian economy under the open door policy see Ali El-Gritly, *Khamsa wa 'ashrun 'aman: dirasa tahliliya lil-siyasa al-iqtisadiya fi misr, 1952–1977* ["Twenty-five years: an analytical study of economic policy in Egypt, 1952–1977"] (Cairo: al-Hai'a al-misriya al-'amma lil-kitab, 1977), p. 288.

3. Marie Christiane Aulas, "La provocante 'modernisation' de l'economie egyptienne," *Le Monde Diplomatique,* March 1979, pp. 6–7.

4. Naiem Sherbiny and Ismail Serageldin, "Expatriate Labor and Economic Growth: Saudi Demand for Egyptian Labor," in Kerr and Yassin, eds., *op. cit.*

5. This point is well elaborated by Galal A. Amin, *The Modernization of Poverty* (Leiden: Brill Press, 1974).

6. This includes bilateral aid commitments of $4.7 billion from the Gulf Organization for the Development of Egypt, but excludes loans from the various development funds, unannounced *ad hoc* gifts arranged between rulers, and deposits by Gulf governments in Egyptian banks. See United Nations Conference on Trade and Development, "Financial Solidarity for Development: Efforts and Institutions of the Members of OPEC," January 1979; and *Al-Nahar Arab Report and Memo,* 23 April 1979, both cited in Jake Wien, *Saudi-Egyptian Relations: the Political and Military Dimensions of Saudi Financial Aid Flows to Egypt* (Rand Corporation, P-6327, 1980), pp. 47–50.

14 Images of the New Social Order

Saad Eddin Ibrahim

Arab society has known three major modes of living: desert, countryside, and town. One way of gauging social change is to monitor over time what happens in each of these three modes of living. The six images of change we sketch below cover the spectrum of Arab human ecology. The first image, the mechanized Bedouin, is central to the present-day desert mode of living. The two images of lumpen capitalists, as well as the veiled medical student and the angry Muslim militant, are typically urban images. The Egyptian peasant outside the Nile Valley is an outgrowth of the rural mode of living.

Each of the six images is symptomatic of structural changes in Arab society. A change is defined here as "structural" if it entails qualitative rather than merely quantitative alteration in values, norms, attitudes, relations, or behavioral patterns.[1]

The Mechanized Bedouin

Nomadism is one of the oldest life-styles in the Arab World.[2] The fact that over 80 percent of the area is desert, arid, and with very little rainfall gave rise to nomadic pastoral life for a segment of Arab population—the Bedouins. All the country states of the Arab World have a Bedouin component in their population. But it is in Saudi Arabia, the Gulf States, southwestern Iraq, the Syrian desert, Libya, Sudan, and Somalia that Bedouin population exceeds 10 percent of the total. The 1977 Saudi census estimates their number at about 1.9 million or 25 percent of the kingdom's total official population.

The main social organization of the Bedouins is made up of the tribe (*kabila*) and its subsegments (*'ashirah, batn,* and *fakhz*). Their habitat is the desert, their shelter is animal-hair tents, and their means of sustenance are camel or sheep herds. Their value system emphasizes primordial loyalty to the kinship group, communalism, courage, and hospitality. In sum, the traditional image of the nomadic Bedouin for the last few millenia has been a tent, a herd, a horse, a sword, a primordial value system, and constant roaming in the desert. This combination of elements made for a successful system of adaptation to a harsh environment. It also set the Bedouin life-style aside in sharp distinction from the two sedentary life-styles of Arab society, the rural and the urban.

This nomadic life-style, which had resisted any marked alteration for thousands of years, is now undergoing major changes. In the early days of oil exploration in the late 1930s, Bedouins began to work first as guides for American oil companies and then as unskilled laborers. Some of them were trained to drive and maintain trucks. Some began to purchase secondhand pickup trucks from the Arabian-American Oil Company (ARAMCO).[3] It was a new status symbol for the few during the 1950s and 1960s. But in the last ten years the truck and other types of motor vehicles have become a "tent-hold" item. Now they are the functional equivalent of baggage camels and horses. Trucks are used to haul water, to transport flocks of sheep from one grazing site to another, and to oversee camel herding over a wide expanse of desert.

The motor vehicle has had a tremendous effect on the life of the Bedouins. It has opened up new cultural and economic vistas to the nomads. Now they go to cities more often; they listen to the radio all the time while roaming the desert; and they deal with car agents, mechanics, electricians, and gasoline dealers.

The increasing use of trucks in the desert has been accompanied by other equally dramatic changes in the infrastructure basic to the exploitation of the desert. Both government and oil companies developed underground water resources by drilling deep wells. As a result, the nomad's patterns of grazing and time cycles have markedly changed. Now they can stay longer, especially in the summer, in one site close to waterheads. They have also learned to share water sources with other tribes, since the wells are not tribally dug or owned. These two developments have inspired the government to offer the nomads educational, social, and health services during the summer season. The services delivery program is known as the Summer Campaign and has expanded steadily since 1977 to cover the entire kingdom. The government is planting, and in fact building into the Summer Campaigns, the seeds of sedentarization of the Saudi Bedouins. The location of the school, the mosque, and the clinic around a deep water well gives the nomadic tribes a point of reference and an incentive to settle. Other enticements are constantly offered.[4]

Underlying the interest of the government in settling the nomads is the serious shortage of manpower in Saudi Arabia—a problem that is discussed in more than one place in this volume. The Saudi nomadic Bedouins and the Saudi women are the two major untapped sources of badly needed indigenous manpower. While it may be quite a time before the puritanical Saudi mores allow the tapping of womanpower, the nomads are readily accessible.

Efforts to incorporate nomads into modern sectors of the Saudi society have succeeded in only two areas: working in the oil fields and enlisting in the Saudi National Guard.[5] In both cases, however, the individual Bedouin remains strongly committed to his tribe and to its nomadic life-style. He shuttles back and forth between the two subcultures for some years, then often gets married, retires from the modern sector, and settles back into the nomadic life-style along with the rest of his clan or tribe. Of course, some may opt for permanent sedentary life, but this is still the exception.

Reverting back to a nomadic life-style, however, is not going back to traditional nomadism. The tent, the camel, the sheep, the horse, and the sword are all still there. But cascading over them are the truck, the radio, and the machine gun. The Bedouins still move around the vast Arabian desert. But they linger longer at each site; and when they decide to move from one site to another it is now much faster. The herd is still the Bedouins' major economic base—for milk, meat, hair, transport, and as a medium of exchange. But now it is supplemented by cash money from wages and salaries obtained from working in the oil fields or as national guardsmen. The traditional Bedouin diet of milk, dates, and meat has been supplemented by Uncle Ben's Converted Rice and canned food.

Oil and the wealth spilling over from it have affected the Bedouins in still another way. Camels are now bred as luxury and sport items. The Royal Family and the Saudi upper stratum have gone heavily into camel racing in recent years. The Bedouins have, in turn, made a sizeable profit from the new sport. A good race camel may sell for as much as $15,000.

The Saudi Bedouins, like other groups in the Arab World, have been touched deeply by oil and its chain effects. We noted here some of the obvious consequences. No doubt there are other consequences that remain latent. Also, like other groups the Bedouins are silently struggling to preserve a way of life in the face of new technologies, new modes of production, and new economic forces. In this dialectical interplay, the outcome evolves as a synthesis of sorts. Thus modern technology, symbolized by the motor vehicle, is used to preserve a traditional way of life: herding and roaming the desert. Likewise, a traditional means of sustenance, the camel, has turned from an imperative for survival into a means of luxury sport. Cash provides a link between the desert grazing sites and the city's modern sports arena.

In his reaction to modern occupations, the Bedouin again has been selective. When asked by this researcher about which occupations they would like to see their children engaged in (other than herding), the majority picked military ones—with air force pilots at the top of the list. Commanding things or people appeals to the Bedouins. We suspect that their choice is not without relevance to their traditional value system. If courage, chivalry, and constant moving are part of the Bedouins' normative system, then commanding an air force supersonic fighter seems to come very close. Commanding a tank, an armored vehicle, or a truck still reflects the same normative system. Little wonder, therefore, that most of the Bedouins who opted for modern occupations ended up in the Saudi Army, National Guard, or as truck drivers. In this sense, the Bedouins have avoided the sharp dichotomous choices which may otherwise negate one another. Phrased differently, the Bedouins have picked from the arsenal of modernity those items that could be wed to, or even enhance, their traditions. This is not to suggest that such synthesis has always been smooth or without its share of strain. There are signs of increased divorce, alcoholism, and drug use among the younger generation of Bedouins who shuttle back and forth between the two subcultures. There is also a growing restlessness and defiance of traditional authority. But all of these signs are still too limited in scope and frequency to draw any firm conclusions.

Lumpen Capitalists: The Saudi Entrepreneur[6]

Another image of a changing social order in the Arab World is that of the new Saudi entrepreneur. Most oil countries—mainly Saudi Arabia and Kuwait—have had a traditional commercial class equivalent to the Bazarries in Iran and the Khan Khalili merchants in Egypt. Unlike Iran under the Shah, these traditional merchants in Arab oil countries are thriving, having expanded their activities and diversified their merchandise. But along with them a new class of entrepreneurs has evolved. Their frame of reference is international and they deal with governments and multinational corporations. Their activities do not fit readily into the customary categories of entrepreneurs under modern capitalism, nor in those of traditional merchants. These new Saudi entrepreneurs are not fruitfully productive; nor are they completely parasitic. But they could be anything in between. Unlike the typical Western counterpart, the Saudi entrepreneur does not take any risk and loses hardly any of his capital. In fact he may undertake his role without much or any capital to start with. Nevertheless he is always assured of making a profit.

Abdullah is a typical new Saudi entrepreneur.[7] His profile and mode of operation are illustrative of the entire class. A native of one of central Najd's tribes, Abdullah completed his secondary education in Saudi Arabia. He was to go to Egypt for his college education in the early 1960s. But deteriorating relations between the kingdom and Nasser's Egypt resulted in his being sent to the United States instead. After a crash course in English in Texas, Abdullah enrolled in one of the West Coast universities where he obtained a B.A. in social science. He returned to Saudi Arabia and served for two years as a civil servant, then was sent back to the United States to obtain an M.A. degree in planning and public administration. Upon completing this mission he joined the then newly established Ministry of Planning. Along with other Western-educated Saudi technocrats, he presided over the drawing up of the first two five-year plans for the kingdom's social and economic development. Soon after, Abdullah resigned from his government post; at the age of 34 he started a "private company." This undertaking was a "conglomerate" right from the beginning. Its first brochure indicated that the company dealt with and intended to engage in import-export; feasibility studies for private and public institutions; consulting in engineering management and social services delivery systems; construction of roads, public buildings, housing, power and water stations; and building of hotels, hospitals, and supermarkets. In brief, there was hardly an area of "hard-" or "software" activities that was not covered by the company's charter. In less than five years of operation, Abdullah and his partners were all multimillionaires. The miracle of this phenomenal "success" becomes the more startling as we learn that the "conglomerate" began with the equivalent of $50,000 as capital, a four-room villa donated by one of the five partners as a temporary headquarters, a telephone, a telex hookup, two typists, and Abdullah as the only fulltime member out of the five. With this skeleton staff, the company handled several hundred million dollars' worth of government contracts. Their initial business included the building of primary schools, an airport, two feeder roads, welfare community centers, and seven huge studies for various ministries. All of the company's business in the first five years was with the Saudi government.

The story of Abdullah is that of several thousand Saudis who are seen at home in flying white robes, quite vigilant about the kingdom's traditions and Islamic rituals. They are the same jetsetters in Pierre Cardin business suits making multimillion-dollar deals in Paris, London, and New York or spending hundreds of thousands in gambling casinos in Monaco and Las Vegas.

The "secret" of success for the new Saudi entrepreneur is the accident of geology (oil), education, government service, and the economic boom in the 1970s. Since there is no risk, the only thing that differentiates one entrepreneur from another is his ability to assemble a "group" as partners in a private company. The ideal group consists of individuals who are blood relatives or close friends but who are strategically located in Saudi social and governmental structures.[8] Because the state is the number one spender, it follows that most profitable business must be transacted with the government. It helps if one or more of the partners is in the government and in on the planning of the next five years' projects. They would have valuable and advance information as well as easy access to former technocratic colleagues or even former subordinates who by that time would be making the decisions. It is also imperative for the group to have at least one high-ranking connection for political coverage in times of crisis. Most successful groups have a link with a member of the Royal Family.

The Saudi entrepreneur is masterful in the art of subcontracting. The indigenous Saudi partners do not actually do much beyond securing the big contract. Every task called for by the latter, whether it is major or minor, is farmed out to subcontractors from the Arab World and more often from places as far off as South Korea and the United States. But in all cases, the Saudi entrepreneur ends up with a handsome profit. The profit is hard to evaluate in terms of a percentage "return on investment" for there is usually little or no seed capital invested to begin with.

This is not to suggest that the Saudi entrepreneur is entirely a parasite, reaping profit without work or appropriating the surplus value from some overexploited proletariat. In fact, he does perform a socioeconomic role which for lack of a better term we have called "lumpen capitalist."[9] He assembles partners and information. He establishes contacts with the outside world and secures political coverage inside Saudi Arabia. All these combined elements make for a bulldozer-like group to get things done in the Saudi environment. The latter contains a lot of rough, unpaved, and somewhat barren terrain in which only a bulldozer can operate.[10]

The new Saudi entrepreneur is a modern, educated individual reacting to the oil boom and to the tremendous wealth flowing from it. He deeply feels and perceives himself as performing a useful role in building Saudi Arabia. He may not argue the fact that he is overbuilding himself in the process, nor would he argue that his returns are a long way out of proportion with his actual performance.

He is a cultural broker par excellence as much as he is a business intermediary. He interprets the Saudi sociopolitical environment to the outside world and vice versa. The interpretation does not have to be accurate or objective but it always enhances the service of his vested interests. He realizes that the high premium on this cultural brokerage is temporary and will not last beyond the oil. Shrewdness and opportunism are the educated Saudis' responses to the glut of oil wealth.

Lumpen Capitalists: The Sponsor (*al-kafil*)[11]

A third image of the oil-based social order is that of *al-kafil,* literally meaning the sponsor. He is usually a native of an urban area of an underpopulated oil-producing Arab country, i.e., Saudi Arabia, Kuwait, the United Arab Emirates, Qatar, or Libya. The combination of wealth, manpower shortage, and indigenous native fear of outsiders has coalesced to produce this most peculiar socioeconomic role—*al-kafil.*

Despite the Arab League economic agreements and labor charters,[12] most oil-rich Arab countries have enacted stringent migration and labor laws that blatantly discriminate against non-natives, including those from other Arab countries. With the exception of Iraq and Algeria, free travel (e.g., tourism) into oil-rich countries is not allowed. Travel has to be for work, official business, family visit, or pilgrimage (as in the case of Saudi Arabia). For all those seeking employment, there should be a contract and/or a sponsor as a prerequisite for obtaining visa, residence, and work permit. When the employer is the state, it acts as an impersonal organizational sponsor. But it is in the private and informal sectors that the class of individual sponsors emerges full-blown as a novelty of oil-based societies.

Abu-Hamad[13] is a typical example of the *kafil.* I encountered him during a mission for a UN agency in Saudi Arabia. Abu-Hamad was an official driver for that agency's office in Riyadh. The ostensible goal of the mission was to help in the upgrading of native Saudi manpower through literacy and vocational training programs. It was not unnatural, therefore, to strike up a conversation with the mission's driver on the subject of education. This was made easier by Abu-Hamad, who was quite inquisitive and an eager conversant with his guests. Abu-Hamad, as it turned out, was an illiterate in his late 40s, a third generation sedentarized Bedouin, married, and with five children, all of whom were in school. One of the interesting things about him was his belief in the value of education for his children but not at all for himself. As we presented him with the prospect of our opening accelerated adult literacy classes and asked him if he would join some evenings every week, his response was an emphatic but argumentative, "No." For one thing, Abu-Hamad was quite busy and satisifed with his life. He pointed out that he had inquired about how much money each person in the UN mission was making and had learned, to his satisfaction, that the head of the mission with a Ph.D. (at least 20 years of formal education) and several years of experience was making less money than he was earning himself from various sources. It turned out that Abu-Hamad was a *kafil.* Chauffeuring a UN car was just something to do, since driving was the only skill he had. The salary he received from it was a minute part of his total income. The bulk of his earnings was derived from two grocery stores, a toy store, a garage, a barbershop, and a tailoring shop, but he was neither able to perform nor willing to learn any of the skills involved in these enterprises. He hired others to do the work. To be more precise, others may have approached him to be their *kafil.*

A non-Saudi cannot by law, initiate or fully own a business in Saudi Arabia. Thus a Syrian tailor or an Egyptian mechanic wishing to open a shop must find a Saudi sponsor as a partner. Abu-Hamad was a partner to or a full owner-employer of Egyptians, Palestinians, Syrians, Lebanese, Yemenis, and Pakistanis. These other nationals put up the capital, the skills, and the labor. He gave them only the legal coverage by lending his fingerprint (later his signature) to contractual arrangements to obtain licensing. In return, Abu-Hamad (a very pious and fair man) was getting 50 percent of the profit. He and those sponsored by him (*makfulin*) were quite happy with the arrangement. Other more greedy *kafils* may appropriate as much as 80 percent of the profit for the same legal coverage.

The institution of the *kafil* has several other variations. In one activist version, a *kafil* may travel around the neighboring countries, recruit people of various skills, and set them up in appropriate enterprises as employees of his or as partners. A *kafil* may simply import labor and then retail it out to other local employers for a percentage of their wages. In the least activist version, a *kafil* may lend his signature to enable potential workers from other countries to come to Saudi Arabia. They would be on their own until they found employment, and would then pay their *kafil* a fee.

The *kafil,* of course, has some vague legal responsibility vis-à-vis both the government and the sponsored (*al-makful*). He may be held accountable for the public behavior of those sponsored by him. The *kafil* often keeps with him the passport and all traveling documents of those individuals whom he sponsors. Thus they cannot travel in or out of the country or work for anyone else without his consent. In other words, the *kafil* not only extracts a substantial profit from the sponsored ones, but he also controls them almost completely while they are in his country.

In its stark and extreme form, this "human trade" comes very close to what might be called "temporary slavery." The local legal codes are entirely on the side of the *kafil.* He has the right to terminate the employment of, or partnership with, a sponsored person at will. He can demand his deportation at any time. While these rights of a *kafil* are occasionally abused, the bulk of the transactions carried out under this institution are mutually beneficial, although far from being equal.

Like the other two images of the new social order, the *kafil* is a by-product of the change in substructure of the oil-rich Arab countries. The vast oil revenues, the skyrocketing public spending, the construction boom, the mounting demand for labor, and the limited supply of indigenous manpower have made it imperative to import labor. But it is not free labor flow in response to strict supply and demand. A noneconomic variable intervenes in the process—the sociopolitical fear of being overwhelmed by outsiders. That fear reflects itself in migration, labor, business, and property laws, which lopsidedly favor the natives and discriminate against outsiders. It is this intricate chain of causation, triggered by oil, that has given rise to the *kafil.*

The *kafil* is a shrewd native with little or no formal education, responding to his environment. In recent years, this environment has contained financial, human, and legal elements which he uses to his advantage. Not every native is a *kafil;* but enough in oil-rich countries are doing it to make them a distinct social formation. The *kafils,* like the new entrepreneurs discussed earlier, are performing a role and getting a substantial profit in the process. But since the role is not productively well defined, and since the profit is way out of proportion with any effort exerted by the *kafils,* we have also termed them as part of a "lumpen capitalist" group.

The Egyptian Peasant Outside the Nile Valley[14]

Moving over to the other side of the wealth divide in the Arab World, we also observe several images of the new social order. A visitor flying into Cairo's International Airport, say, from the mid-1970s on, is usually struck by the sight of thousands of Egyptian peasants crowding the place—arriving, departing, or mostly saying farewell to or welcoming relatives and friends. The visitor would readily observe that most of the village folk are using this mode of transportation for the first time. Their noise level, the amount and type of baggage, and the mixture of bewilderment and excitement indicate the peasants' unfamiliarity with the flying subculture. Most of the peasants are oil-country bound. Like other groups before them (high and medium level manpower), they are seeking work and fortune elsewhere outside the Nile Valley.

The migration of Egyptian peasants puts an end to a lingering stereotype of the Egyptians as the most sedentary of all Arabs. The stereotype was not so very inaccurate. Compared to their Syrian, Lebanese, Yemeni, Tunisian, Algerian, and Moroccan counterparts, Egyptians were indeed the least migratory Arabs. There were socio-ecological reasons for this oversedentarization of Egyptians, which we need not go into. Suffice it to say that like other hydraulic societies, Egyptians derived a reasonable subsistence livelihood from river-irrigated agricultural land in the Valley and the Delta. Over thousands of years, a symbiosis developed between man, land, river, and central authority. The continuity of this equilibrium was contingent upon the peasant's relationship to the land—as tiller and producer of value—some of which was to be appropriated by the central authority.[15]

The fact that Egypt's population has doubled several times in the last 200 years (from 5 million in 1800, to 10 million in 1900, to 42 million in 1980) without any corresponding expansion of agricultural land (the latter grew only from 5 to 7 million acres in 200 years) meant a collapse of the millennial symbiosis. The mounting population pressure meant an increasing number of landless and poor peasants every year. The early reaction of the dispossessed was to stream into Egypt's urban areas; but in the last ten years, other younger generations of dispossessed Egyptians have discovered new outlets: the oil countries.

Serag is a typical case. Born in a Delta village to a small farmer as one of six children, he was sent to work for a village notable at the age of 8. He grew up close to the children of his employer, who were all at school. At the age of 18, he was drafted into the army and was caught up in the aftermath of the 1967 war. Serag was kept in the army until November 1974. He was one of those who crossed the Canal, and as an infantryman he participated in tank battles, using shoulder-carried antitank missile launchers. At the age of 26 he returned to the village, ready to get married and start a family. His former patron, the village notable, had died, and the household was scattered among heirs, most of them absentee. His own father had grown poorer and had sold the half acre he had once owned to pay for the marriages of two of the daughters. Serag left the village after two months and went to Alexandria, where one of the sons of his former employer was now living and teaching at the university. He asked the son to help him find a job; he offered to drive his car. While the son could have used a chauffeur, since he and his wife were working and had two school age children and possessed only one car, the young assistant professor could not afford Serag's salary and upkeep in the city. However, norms of hospitality, paternalism, and dictates of status prevented the son from turning his back on Serag. He let Serag work for him as a chauffeur at LE10 per month (about $15). Everyone was happy with the arrangement, since the assistant professor could now do extra work outside the university for additional income. Several months later, however, the arrangement was threatened as the professor learned that his request for secondment to the University of Riyadh had been approved and that he was to leave for Saudi Arabia within a few weeks. Serag implored the professor to take him too. The professor gave Serag a generous bonus and promised to find him a job in Saudi Arabia and then send for him. To Serag's surprise, within a few weeks he received a letter from the professor and a contract from a wealthy Saudi to work for him as a chauffeur.

Within ten days Serag got his travel papers and visa organized and was airborne for the first time in his life, bound for Saudi Arabia. He immediately started on his new job at SR500 a month (LE100; $150), in addition to free room and board. Serag was elated. He was saving virtually all his salary. In six months he was given three weeks off to go and visit his family. Arriving in the village in bright new clothes, carrying a radio-cassette combination for his elderly father and other assorted gifts for everyone in the family, Serag was the talk of the village for several weeks. People came in droves to greet him and possibly to make sure that what they had heard about his fortunes was really true. More important, many of the young well-wishers whispered in Serag's ear their hope of being helped by him to go to Saudi Arabia. Upon returning, Serag in fact began actively to seek employment for three of his brothers and his two brothers-in-law, and within the year he managed to secure contracts for all five of them. He then began to help other more distant friends and relatives.

In the summer of 1979, I enumerated the number of peasants from Serag's village who were in Saudi Arabia and the Gulf. The figure was 174—all aided by Serag in less than four years. Equally significant is the fact that other villagers began to seek to migrate to other Arab and non-Arab countries. The same enumeration in 1979 showed that about 150 persons from the same village were scattered among Lebanon, Jordan, Syria, and Iraq (their relatives did not know their exact locations)[16] and about 30 were reported to be in Libya. Six villagers were in Milan, Italy. All in all, about 360 peasants from the village were outside their habitat in the Nile Valley for the first time in their lives and possibly in the history of the village. Actually, except for the very few pilgrims every now and then, no one from that village is known ever to have left Egypt or, say, traveled in an airplane, until the early 1960s.

The case of Serag and his village is not uncommon among the other peasants of the 4,000 Egyptian villages. What these migrant workers do abroad is virtually any work they can find. Those among them who acquire skills while serving in the army end up with jobs that pay more—such as drivers, mechanics, electricians, or welders. Most of them, however, work in construction or service jobs. Surprisingly, very few are employed as farm workers in Saudi Arabia, where their Yemeni counterparts seem to have had an earlier start.

Virtually all peasants working abroad save money. The use pattern of their savings indicates that their money goes into marriage of self or close kin, gifts, purchase of land, building of new houses, and investing in tractors, flour mills, and irrigation pumps. Television sets, refrigerators, and gas stoves began to make their appearance in most villages immediately after their electrification. Many of the peasant migrants perceive their work sojourn as temporary. If the migrant is married, he leaves his wife and children in the village, either with his parents or in an independent household close to that of either his or her parents. He would send money periodically to his parents and his wife.

Many of these migrants have effected a marked change in the village class structure. In the 1950s and 1960s, education for the villagers was the fastest path of upward social mobility. Now it is migration to a rich Arab country that counts as the best mechanism. Many children of the poverty-stricken landless peasants are now well off, in the middle or upper-middle stratum of their village. They are intermarrying with families that, no more than ten or fifteen years ago, would only have hired them as farm workers, like young Serag.

The Veiled Medical Student

Another image that strikes the visitor to Cairo in the last decade is the sight of veiled and semiveiled women in the streets and public places. Especially noteworthy is the scene at the Kasr al-Aini Bridge on the Nile, between the Meridien Hotel and the Manial Palace. Here, dozens of young college women are seen crossing at the stop light on their way to Cairo University's Medical School. What is unusual about these women is the fact that quite a few of them are veiled.

For centuries the veil had come to symbolize the "oppression" of Muslim Arab women and their inferior status. In the early 1920s, a feminist leader, Hoda Sha'rawy, led a women's movement seeking greater equality.[17] One of its first acts of defiance was the unveiling—an act that came to symbolize their determination to be emancipated.

The movement did succeed in modifying family and personal laws in 1927, obtaining more rights for women in education, the professions, and state employment.

The 1952 revolution pushed further the cause of women's rights, granting them the vote and the right to run for public office (in other words, political equality with men) in the 1956 constitution. By then the veil had nearly disappeared from major urban areas (it had never existed in rural areas on any noticeable scale). The march of women's emancipation still had a long way to go, but it was proceeding steadily. The number of girls enrolled in primary schools jumped from fewer than 300,000 in 1952 to over 1.6 million in 1976, a 530 percent increase. On the university level the increase was even more dramatic—from fewer than 10,000 in 1952 to more than 153,000 in 1976, an increase of more than 1500 percent in a quarter of a century. Women were appointed as cabinet members,[18] ambassadors, heads of corporations, and several were elected to the People's Assembly (Egypt's parliament).

Why then, all of a sudden, has the veil reappeared? And why especially among one of society's most educated sectors—urban college women? What does it mean for the cause of women's rights—does it represent a setback? Where does the whole phenomenon fit in the new emerging social order of the Arab World?

Ilham is a case in point.[19] At the age of 21 she was in her third year of medical school. Ilham is the second among five children born to a middle-class family in Mansoura, a Delta town. Her father was college educated, with a B.S. in accounting, and for twenty years has been a government employee in the Taxes Department (Internal Revenue). Her mother had only a few years of formal education. Ilham was the first female on both sides of her parents' families to go to college. When interviewed, she recounted her parents' eagerness and encouragement to excel in her studies at secondary school. She was always at the top of her class—something that inspired her and her parents to think of medical school and becoming a doctor. The first hurdle toward this goal was passing the statewide examination with high grades (*magmu'a*). To most Egyptian families, the year of this examination is a long nightmare. If there is a son or daughter preparing for it, the whole household is often put on a "war footing." The state of top emergency is justified to most middle-class Egyptian families, since future career prospects of their children are contingent upon this single examination (*thanawiyya 'amma*). Ilham made it with flying colors; her grades entitled her to the top medical school (that of Cairo University) in that year.[20] And even though she could have enrolled in the medical school at Mansoura University (her home town), she and her family opted for the best.

At the age of 18, Ilham moved to Cairo, full of excitement mixed with apprehension. This was her first experience of being on her own, away from her family. She secured a room in the women's dormitory at Cairo University. The mix of people she came across every day in the dormitory, the classroom, the bus, and in the street was quite bewildering. Most of all she had a difficult time relating to some of her classmates, who seemed to have more money, better clothes and broader experience. They knew more about life, sex, love, dating, and drinking. Some of them were heavily made up, smoked, and even went with men in their cars. Ilham reported that she was frightened as some of her classmates tried to draw her into their kind of circles. Until then, she was unveiled, wore modern clothes, had been a moviegoer with her family, and had read romantic novels. Nevertheless, the kind of life she was being enticed to join in Cairo sent waves of fear through her veins. She thought to herself that not only was she unable to do what the "other" women were doing, but in her heart she also condemned their behavior.

It was about the fourth month of her first year when she had an encounter that put her mind at rest. On the bus from Mansoura to Cairo, after the midyear recess, she sat next to another woman who was veiled. After a short while she noticed the veiled woman picking up a book to read—it was a college chemistry book. Ilham struck up a conversation with her seatmate. She was curious as to why the other was veiled if she was at college, sitting with men in the same classroom. Her companion told her that she was appalled by the behavior of some of the women in Cairo, disapproved of their display of expensive clothes and their disregard for "our values" and Islamic traditions. She insinuated to Ilham that some of these "decadent girls" might even be prostitutes, catering to wealthy tourists from oil countries. She knew some of them were from modest families and could not afford the kind of clothes they wore to school. Ilham was dumbfounded by these "revelations." Her traveling companion concluded by stating that she had decided to veil in order to set herself apart from the decadent crowd. Since her veiling, she prayed more regularly with some of her veiled friends and she studied much better. Ilham was very impressed. A week later she went back to Mansoura with all her modern, but modest, wardrobe and told her family of her decision to veil. Her parents, to her surprise, disapproved of the idea. Her two younger brothers protested vehemently that she would look odd and that they would be teased by their friends in the neighborhood. She finally settled the argument by tearfully sobbing that she did not want to be thought of as a prostitute to wealthy oil tourists in Cairo. Without really knowing for sure, she asserted that some of her classmates were just that, whereupon her parents and brothers fell silent, and concurred with her decision.

In her own account Ilham did not mention anything that was strictly political behind her decision to veil. But when asked about her views regarding some of the politically oriented religious groups on campus, she readily declared her support of their goals, i.e., the application of Islamic *Shari'a* to all spheres of life. She voted for their candidates in student elections and would marry one of them if proposed to. What about working outside the home? Yes, she would if her husband approved and if it did not conflict with her duty as a wife and mother.

Ilham and thousands like her in Egypt and elsewhere in the northern tier of the Arab World (Lebanon, Syria, Jordan, Tunisia, Morocco, Algeria) are enigmatic to outside observers, as well as to many of their fellow countrymen. For they are not old or middle-aged traditional women. They are young and highly educated. They are veiling by their own volition—and in many cases against their parents' wishes.[21] Is the veil a setback to modernity? Here we must submit that some of the Western social science categories do break down—or at least are rendered irrelevant. For if modernity means unveiling, fashionable clothes, mixing freely with the opposite sex, and dating, then Ilham and thousands like her would represent a setback to the cause of "modernity." If modernity, on the other hand, means learning of modern science, technology, and the humanities, and if it means commitment and preparation for a career outside the home, then Ilham and her like are quite "modern."

Here it may be useful to distinguish between imposed and volitional veiling; e.g., between, say, Saudi college women and their Egyptian counterparts. Educated women choosing to veil seem to be conveying a symbolic message, like anyone else who opts for a particular style or appearance.[22] They are asserting one or more of the following: an authentic identity vis-à-vis imitations of Western styles of life, disapproval of what seem to them decadent and corrupt practices in society, warding off costly effects of currently high inflation by avoiding conspicuous clothing, and establishing good (i.e., moral) reputations.

The veiled medical student represents a complicated response to a complicated world around her—a world over which she has no control. That world includes an influx of foreigners, oil wealth, expensive consumer goods, high inflation, and "alien" life-styles. Despite her superb achievements in examinations, she finds herself overwhelmed, estranged, and insignificant in a big, impersonal urban world. Clinging to a "heritage" seems to restore her feeling of worth, protect her against the unknown, and lessen the alienation she feels. In a curious way, like the Saudi Bedouins, Egyptian veiled medical students are quite selective vis-à-vis the "modernity bag." They take out of it science, technology, and commitment to professional careers. They leave out the rest. They feel and firmly believe that what they have selected is consistent with their "heritage," "Islamic tradition," and "authenticity (*asalah*)." It is their way of imposing a semblance of order on an otherwise chaotic world.

The Angry Muslim Militant

The male counterparts of the veiled college women are the young Muslim militants. This is an image mostly of college-educated, bearded, angry men. It is an image that has dominated the world's mass media since the Iranian revolution and especially since the seizure of the

American Embassy and some fifty hostages in Tehran in November 1979. But insiders to the Arab and Middle East area had seen the genesis of this image much earlier. In Egypt, at least, it dates back to the aftermath of the 1967 defeat of Arab regimes at the hands of Israel. Many area observers sensed a resurgence of religiosity, which in the beginning was quite amorphous, mystical, retreatist, or superstitious.[23] Even Egypt's defeated regime sensed the phenomenon and attempted to exploit it to its own advantage.[24]

But as the decade of the sixties drew to an end, the amorphous religiosity was beginning to take shape, to harden at the edges, and to develop nuclear cores. We began to hear of organized Muslim groups on university campuses calling for the assertion of the Islamic faith and for exorcising Egypt and the Arab World of all imported ideologies and foreign influence. These beginnings coincided with Sadat's succession to power following the death of President Nasser. In the best traditions of Egyptian rulers, Sadat, too, sought to exploit this new spirit among the young. He needed some balancing popular base to counterweigh Nasserists and leftists, who were perceived as a serious challenge to his leadership. To him and his media, "imported ideology and influence" were synonymous with socialism and the Soviet Union. But little did Sadat know that these very Muslim groups would be even more hostile to his own ideological alternatives: the "Open Door Policy," accommodation with Israel, and alignment with the West and especially the United States.

The fact was driven home to the regime in a bloody coup d'etat attempt in April 1974, only six months after the October War, which was hailed as an Arab triumph. Sadat was still riding high in popularity and was being proclaimed by his media as the "redeemer-hero." The plot was carried out by a group known as the Islamic Liberation Organization and invariably called in the Arab media the Technical Military Academy Group (henceforth MA).[25] It was so called because their scheme for taking over started with occupation of the academy and seizure of its arsenal. The group was to march from there to the Arab Socialist Union (ASU), where President Sadat and the rest of Egypt's ruling elite were scheduled for a major state function. The attempt was foiled, but only after scores of militants, army, and security men had fallen dead and many more were injured.

From then on, the regime has been violently confronted by one Islamic group after another. Names of groups such as Al-Jihad (Holy War), Jund Allah (Soldiers of God), Jama'at al-Muslimin (the Muslim Group), and Jama'at al-Takfir w'al-Hijra (Repentance and Holy Flight, henceforth RHF), among others, began to be known to the public as they clashed with the authorities.[26] The spread of Islamic militancy was dramatically highlighted by the clash of July 1977, when the RHF group kidnapped and executed one of Sadat's former cabinet ministers for religious endowment (*al-Awqaf*), Sheikh Ahmad Hassan al-Dhahabi.[27] In the aftermath of gun battles, arrests, trials, and execution of its leaders, it was revealed that the RHF was 3,000 to 5,000 strong, tightly organized, and spread out all over the country.[28] Muslim candidates swept student elections in all of Egypt's universities after 1976,[29] a fact that prompted President Sadat to dissolve Egypt's student unions by a presidential decree in the summer of 1979.

The two Muslim publications *Al-Da'wa* and *Al-I'tisam* have been widely read. After the virtual banning of all leftist publications, the two Muslim monthly magazines have been the only serious opposition papers—critical of Sadat's internal and external policies, especially of his peace treaty with Israel and his relationship with the United States and the deposed Shah of Iran.

Who are the Muslim militants? Why have they appeared at this point in time? Would they amount to anything similar to what happened in Iran? These and other relevant questions cannot be fully answered here. There are other detailed treatments of the subject.[30] Our interest is confined to sketching this emergent image of a new Arab social order.

Tallal is a bona fide Muslim militant.[31] He was one of the leading figures in one of the attempted coups d'etat. He was tried and sentenced to death along with other leading members of his group, but because of his young age (he was 21 years old at the time), his sentence was commuted to life imprisonment. He was interviewed along with other militants in prison between 1977 and 1979.

Tallal, the oldest of four children, was born in a small town to a small middle-class family. His father, a civil servant with a college education, was constantly trying his hand at poetry and novel writing but never achieved national fame. His mother had only a few years of education and was a devoted housewife. Both parents were born in a rural village, but the mother, more so than the father, retained her village manners and values. Tallal grew up in a house full of books and around friends of his father who traded political and literary ideas. But he acquired a strong dose of religion and tradition from his mother. As in most middle-class families, Tallal was continuously encouraged to achieve scholastically. In the *thanawiyya 'amma* (the statewide examination at the end of secondary school education), he obtained high grades, enabling him to enroll in the prestigious Faculty of Engineering at Alexandria University at the age of 17.

Tallal recalled that even though he was successful at studying, achieving was not his prime concern. When the 1967 defeat occurred, he was only 15 years old, but he asserts that he was politically conscious and was deeply shocked by the defeat. He remembers that he retreated to his room for several days, oscillating between weeping, reflecting, meditating, and sleeping, but hardly eating or talking to anyone. His mother, worried about his state, urged him to take a bath, pray, and read some Quran. He finally did, and to his surprise, felt an overwhelming sense of peace sweeping over him. He had read and memorized Quranic verses for school homework before, but this time Tallal felt quite different. The verses had a penetrating meaning that addressed him, his crisis, and that of his nation directly. Tallal was a "reborn" Muslim. He knew there and then that the Quran contained all the Truth, and wondered why he and others had not realized that before. He kept his discovery to himself for a while. Meanwhile his mother was quite pleased with Tallal's emergence from his room, his strong appetite, and his readiness to go out of the house again.

Tallal's first outing was ten days after the defeat. He went with his father to a nearby city to attend a political rally in which one of Nasser's top aides was to be the main speaker. Tallal recalls that he used to love and believe in Nasser but that he was utterly bewildered when he heard the speaker stating to the audience that the Arabs had not been defeated in the war. The speaker asserted that the ultimate aim of Israel and American imperialism was to depose Nasser or destroy him; and because Nasser and other progressive regimes were still in power, the enemies' conspiracy was foiled. Tallal did not believe the speaker and was plagued by an instant doubt when the audience, including his father, applauded the speaker. He remained bewildered for the next two years, taking his comfort in praying and reading the Quran.

It was at Alexandria University, as a freshman, that Tallal's bewilderment came to an end. There, Tallal was living away from his family for the first time. In the college mosque, the fellow next to him approached him with the customary handshake following a prayer. In the process he introduced himself and struck up a conversation with Tallal. This was the beginning of Tallal's initiation into Islamic militancy, for he was invited by his fellow prayermate to attend a lecture on campus about the struggle against Zionism. The speaker, it turned out, was a bearded fellow student from a neighboring faculty. His approach to the topic appealed to Tallal—Zionism, Communism, and Capitalism are all enemies of Islam and the Muslims; the only way to fight them back is to adhere to the Quran and the Sunna. The speaker recalled the brilliant fighting of the Muslim Brothers against the Jews in 1948, which (according to the speaker and Tallal's retelling of it) was the only effective effort to have almost rid the Palestinians of the "Jewish gangs," had it not been for the Arab governments' betrayal—especially that of Egypt, which stabbed the Muslim Brotherhood in the back while they were fighting. Everybody cheered and Tallal found himself this time applauding with the audience. He began to read avidly about the Muslim Brothers.

Tallal was recruited shortly after. His enthusiasm and devotion to the group made him, within a year, part of the inner core leadership. Their objective was to rid the Muslim World of all corrupt regimes, in order to reinstate the Islamic *Shari'a.* In 1974 they felt that Sadat had gone too far in selling out to the West and Israel, and something must be done about it. Thus they staged their coup, which, of course, did not succeed.

Tallal and many of his generation are quite angry at the present social order. Their outrage often takes the form of premature confrontation with the regime. Sometimes they realize that such confrontation will not bring the government down. But as they put it, "It is an outrage for God" (*ghadhbah lil-Allah*). For them it is "propaganda by deed," which can only lead to martyrdom or victory, and both are readily embraceable.

When the militants are persuaded to spell out their ideology, attitudes, and feelings, the listener comes away with an overall clear impression of what they are against but with only a vague, though colorful, impression of what they would do if they were in power. They have deep-seated hostility toward the West, Communism, and Israel. Any ruler who deals with or befriends any of them would be betraying Islam. Excessive wealth, extravagance, severe poverty, exploitation, and usury have no place in a truly Muslim society. They disapprove of nearly all the regimes in the Arab and Muslim Worlds. They attribute many of the decadent aspects of behavior in Egypt either to Western influence or to the squandering of oil money, and they firmly believe that should "true Islam" be implemented, Egypt and the Muslim World would be independent, free, prosperous, just, and righteous societies.[32]

The Muslim militants are mostly like Ilham, the veiled medical student. They come from the middle and lower-middle classes, they are of rural or small-town backgrounds, and they are high achievers and quite intelligent. But they find themselves living in a complicated cosmopolitan world to which they cannot relate and with which they cannot cope. Their talents and energies are neither properly rewarded nor fully recognized by the system. They and their families feel squeezed economically by high inflation. They are startled by the tremendous wealth around them, but anguished as they cannnot have a fair share while seeing it being so conspicuously wasted. Their class has always been the reservoir of patriotism: their parents and grandparents fought for independence. But they see their homeland again being trampled upon by what they consider neocolonialism; i.e., the influx of foreigners, multinational corporations, and corrupt ways of life.

The angry Muslim militants of Egypt have their counterparts in Syria, Tunisia, among the Palestinians, and even in Saudi Arabia. At the core they are nationalists, socialists, and anticolonialists, but they do not use these terms because of their former association. Their quest for authenticity, dignity, equality, and independence is now couched in Islamic terms. An earlier generation of young militants couched the same quest in Arab Nationalist terms; two generations earlier it was mostly couched in Egyptian patriotic terms.

Other Images of Change

The six images sketched above are by no means the only ones marking the Arab landscape. Other images of the new social order include that of the Palestinian being transformed from a wretched refugee into a guerrilla fighter. The psychological impact of this image is probably far more important than its military or geopolitical bearings in shaping the new Arab social order. The decade of the seventies sensed the turbulence that the Palestinian freedom fighter could cause—in Israel, the Arab World itself, and on the global stage. The raids in occupied Palestine, the street fighting in Amman,[33] the assassination in the Cairo Sheraton Hotel,[34] the attack in Munich at the Olympic Games,[35] addressing the world from the United Nations,[36] the civil war in Lebanon, fighting the Syrians,[37] raising the Palestinian flag on the Israeli Mission building in Tehran,[38] and numerous other acts of defiance or assertion have not gained the Palestinians an inch of their usurped land. But they have driven the message home, loud and clear—to oil producers and oil consumers, to rich Arabs and poor Arabs, to Israeli and Diaspora Jews—that no peace or stability would last before their situation is redressed. The presence of so many Palestinians in the fragile Gulf States, so close to the main oil arteries of the West, makes their message quite credible. The dilemma of the Gulf States is their heavy dependence on Palestinian manpower and at the same time their fear of what these very Palestinians might do should any of the rulers follow in the footsteps of President Sadat.

Another image is that of the embattled Lebanese trying to survive while the state is withering away—or more accurately while one state is proliferating into several. The implications of the Lebanese civil war, however, go far beyond the anguish and individual human tragedies. The war has blown open the entire issue of ethnic and minority groups in all countries in the area. Of course, the Kurds and the South Sudanese had fought for years earlier. But bloody and protracted as they may have been, the battles were on the cultural borderland of the Arab World, and religion was not basically at issue. With Lebanon, the conflict has been much closer to the heart of the Arab homeland. Religious and communal differences were deliberately contrived and drummed up.

Israel, all major Arab states, and the two superpowers were implicated. The whole ethnic question is definitely going to be raised in all neighboring Arab countries, Syria, Jordan, and Egypt included. Indications in both Syria and Egypt show that ethnic tension is already turning into incidents of overt conflict.[39] The flaring up of the Lebanese civil war is, therefore, symptomatic of one aspect of the new Arab social order: diversifiers and primordial forces are at work against political and cultural unifiers that were in full swing during Nasser's years.

All the above images of the new social order have several interlinking threads. One such major thread is the oil syndrome; i.e., the raw material, the energy issue, the money, the geopolitics, and the manpower movement. If any of these images were not a direct function of the oil syndrome, then the syndrome has been somehow affected by them. The mechanized nomad, the Saudi entrepreneur, the *kafil,* the Egyptian peasant out of the Nile Valley—all are direct resultants of the oil syndrome. The other images of change have been indirectly affected by oil. Reveiling and Islamic militancy are both reactions to a multitude of things, among them high inflation, conspicuous consumption, and behavioral patterns brought about by the oil syndrome. Curiously enough, the latter's impact on Islamic militancy is double-tiered, the second being the fact that most militant groups relied heavily on the dues of members and sympathizers working in oil-rich countries.[40] Also some of the Muslim militants from Egypt were active members of the group that seized the Grand Mosque in Mecca in December 1979.[41] The Palestinian Resistance generally and the Palestine Liberation Organization (PLO) in particular rely heavily for financial support on donations and dues from Palestinians working in oil countries. It was rumored that in the Lebanese civil war, oil money found its way to the various factions in the fighting.

In brief, oil, through the movement of money and manpower across the state borders of the Arab World, has been felt in a thousand and one ways. . . .

Notes

1. On the concept of "structural change" see Lincoln Gordon, *The Growth Policies and the International Order* (New York: McGraw Hill, 1979), pp. 7–11; Fred Hirsch, *Social Limits to Growth* (Cambridge: Harvard University Press, 1976).

2. This account of the mechanized Bedouin is based primarily on the author's field work on the Saudi nomads in 1976 and 1977. Some of the findings of this field work were reported in S. E. Ibrahim and D. P. Cole, *Saudi Arabian Bedouin* (Cairo: AUC's *Cairo Papers in Social Science* Vol. One, Monograph Five, April 1978). See also D. Cole, *Nomads of the Nomads* (Chicago: Aldine, 1975).

3. D. Cole, "Bedouins of the Oil Fields," in *Natural History* magazine (November 1973).

4. Additional enticements include land grants and loans to build permanent housing, better and periodic veterinary services for their herds. But such incentives are by no means universal all over the kingdom. They have been tried on a limited scale in the Haradh Project in the southwestern part of the kingdom.

5. The Saudi National Guard is a full-fledged military organization, equipped with artillery and armored tanks, as well as light arms. It is distinct from and believed to be a counterweight of the regular Saudi armed forces. The size of the National Guard was estimated at 35,000 and the army at 45,000 in 1978. See the *Military Balance 1977/78* (London: Inst. for Strategic Studies); J. T. Cummings et al., "Military Expenditure and Manpower Requirements in the Arabian Peninsula," *Arab Studies Quarterly* Vol. 2, No. 1 (1980), pp. 38–49.

6. This section is based on in-depth interviews and field observations conducted by the author during 1977 and 1978.

7. All proper names in this account are fictitious.

8. For an empathetic view of the new Saudi entrepreneur see Marwan Ghandour, "The Leader-Entrepreneur in the Private Sector," in the proceedings of a conference on Leadership and Development in the Arab World sponsored

by the Faculty of Arts, American University of Beirut (10–14 Dec. 1979).

9. We owe the coining of this term to a discussion with Professor Charles Issawi of Princeton University.

10. M. Ghandour, "The Leader-Entrepreneur," p. 10.

11. This account is based on the author's field observations in Saudi Arabia in 1977 and 1978.

12. These include the Arab Economic Unity Agreement (1957) and the Arab Common Market Agreement (1964), both of which call for freedom of capital and labor movements across Arab boundaries.

13. All proper names are fictitious.

14. This account is based on the author's field observations in the course of his research on income distribution and social mobility, the findings of which are reported in a forthcoming volume: see Robert Tignor and Gouda Abdel-Khalek (eds.), *Income Distribution in Egypt.*

15. For more details on this relationship see Ibrahm 'Amer, *The Land and Peasant* [Arabic] (Cairo: 1964); Ahmed Ezzat 'Abdul-Karim et al., *Land and Peasant in Egypt Through the Ages* [Arabic] (Cairo: The Egyptian Historical Society, 1974); Muhammed Shafique Ghourbal, *The Formation of Egypt* [Arabic] (Cairo: Al-Nahdha al-Misriyya Book Co., 1957); Nazih N. M. Ayubi, *Bureaucracy and Politics in Contemporary Egypt* (London: Ithaca Press, 1980), pp. 77–156; and Talcott Parsons, *Societies: An Evolutionary and Comparative Perspective* (Englewood Cliffs, N.J.: Prentice-Hall, 1966).

16. Because of inter-Arab strains following the Camp David Accords, air travel between Egypt and most rejectionist Arab states (Iraq, Syria, Libya, and Algeria) was disrupted. Egyptians going to those countries had to detour via Lebanon, Jordan, or Greece. Some ended up staying as transients, especially in Jordan and Lebanon.

17. For more details on this pioneer movement see Lois Beck and Nikki Keddie (eds.), *Women in the Muslim World* (Cambridge: Harvard University Press, 1979), especially the selections by Afaf Lutfi al-Sayyid Marsot, "The Revolutionary Gentlewomen in Egypt," and Thomas Philips, "Feminism and Nationalist Politics in Egypt."

18. The first woman cabinet member was appointed in 1960, but the first woman deputy was elected four years earlier (1956).

19. Proper names are fictitious. The account of this role-model is based on the author's field research on Islamic Revivalist Movements (1977–1979), which was sponsored by Egypt's National Centre for Sociological and Criminological Research.

20. Unlike the American college system, students are assigned to their majors—including professional schools such as medicine, law, engineering, and business—in their first (freshman) year. Their assignment depends strictly on their grades rather than on their own wishes. Of course, a student with very high grades can choose any major requiring his grade level or less. This system was instituted in the early days of the Revolution to ensure universal justice in college admissions, whereas previously they depended in part on connections (*wasta*).

21. For a discussion on this issue of the reappearance of the veil in Egypt, see John A. Williams, "A Return to the Veil in Egypt," *Middle East Review* Vol. XI, No. 3 (Spring 1978).

22. Here the situation may be analogous to that described by Frantz Fanon of the Algerian women to whom veiling was an integral part of their assertion of national and cultural identity. When they were encouraged by the colonialist

French to unveil, Algerian women clung to the veil as a symbol of resistance. However, when the national struggle required that they unveil to infiltrate French quarters and plant explosives, they readily unveiled. See Frantz Fanon, *A Dying Colonialism* (New York: Monthly Review Press, 1965), pp. 35–67.

23. Note for example the mass hysteria among Muslims and Copts alike over the appearance of the Virgin Mary as a pure light above a small Coptic church in the Cairo suburb of Zeitoun, just a few months after the 1967 defeat. The Arab Socialist Union and Egypt's major newspaper *Al-Ahram* jumped in and proceeded to drum up a religious frenzy among the population.

24. When President Nasser, who was an avowed secularist, said in a major speech after the defeat of 1967 "that religion should play a more important role in the society," the broken hero was greeted by an exceptionally enthusiastic roar of applause. See Nazih Ayubi, "The Political Revival of Islam: The Case of Egypt," *mimeo.,* 1980, p. 17. President Sadat, in his turn, upon taking power, declared that he was committed to building a society based on Science and Faith (*al-'Ilm w al-Iman*). He made a point of being photographed by the media every Friday saying his prayers.

25. For details on this group see Saad E. Ibrahim, "Anatomy of Egypt's Militant Islamic Groups," *International Journal of Middle East Studies* (November 1980), pp. 423–453.

26. For details see Note 25 above.

27. For factual details of these events see *Al-Ahram,* 15–19 July 1977.

28. For details about this group in terms of ideology, organization, leadership, and strategy see Saad E. Ibrahim, "Anatomy of Egypt's Militant Groups," *op. cit.*

29. The 1978 student elections at Alexandria University illustrate this point. "Candidates of Islamic associations won on the various faculties as follows: 60 out of 60 in Medical School; 60 out of 60 in Engineering; 47 out of 48 in Agriculture; 42 out of 48 in Pharmacy; 43 out of 60 in the College of Science, and 44 out of 48 in Law School." See Ali Dessouki, "The Resurgence of Islamic Movements in Egypt," *mimeo.,* 1979, p. 4.

30. See for example: Bernard Lewis, "The Return of Islam," *Commentary* (January 1976), pp. 34–49; John Williams, "A Return to the Veil in Egypt," *op. cit.;* R. S. Humphreys, "Islam and Political Values in Saudi Arabia, Egypt and Syria," *Middle East Journal* Vol. 33, No. 1 (Winter 1979); Israel Altman, "Islamic Movements in Egypt," *The Jerusalem Quarterly* Vol. 3, No. 10 (Winter 1979); Ali Dessouki, "The Resurgence of Islamic Movements," *op. cit.;* Nazih Ayubi, "The Political Revival of Islam," *op. cit.;* Hrair Dekmejian, "The Anatomy of Islamic Revival and the Search for Islamic Alternatives," *Middle East Journal* Vol. 34, No. 1 (Winter 1980), pp. 1–12.

31. Proper names are fictitious. The account of this role-model is based on the author's research on Islamic revivalist movements in Egypt.

32. For more militants' ideology see Saad E. Ibrahim, "Anatomy of Egypt's Militant," *op. cit.*

33. The reference here is to the fighting between King Hussein's armed forces and the Palestinian Resistance in September 1970, known usually as Black September.

34. The reference is to the assassination of Jordan's Prime Minister in the Cairo Sheraton on 28 November 1971. The assassins were two young Palestinians, said to be members of the clandestine Black September Organization. The Prime Minister, Wasfi al-Tal, was assassinated for his role in massacring Palestinians in the 1970 fighting in Jordan. See *Arab Reports and Records*

(henceforth ARR), 16–30 November 1971, p. 600.

35. The attack by members of the Black September took place on 5 September 1972 in Munich; 11 Israeli athletes, 5 Palestinian guerrillas, and one West German policeman were killed. *ARR,* 1–15 September 1972, p. 437.

36. The reference is to the UN invitation to Yasser Arafat (chief of the PLO) to address the General Assembly on 13 November 1974. This was the first time ever for a representative of the Palestinian Resistance to be recognized by and invited to speak to a UN organization.

37. The Lebanese Civil War flared up in April 1975 when right-wing armed militia attacked a bus carrying Palestinians and killed and wounded about 40 of them. The war went on and off throughout the rest of 1975, 1976, and part of 1977. Syrian troops became involved in 1976, ostensibly to put an end to the fighting, but ending up in clashes with the Palestinian Resistance, which by that time had been fully committed on the side of the Lebanese Leftists and patriotic forces.

38. The reference is to Yasser Arafat's historic visit to Ayatollah Khomeini in February 1979, only a few days after the latter's triumphant return to his country as the leader of the Islamic Iranian Revolution. See *ARR,* 28 February 1979, p. 1.

39. In Syria, the government of President Assad has been attacked on grounds that it is lopsidedly an Alawite minority regime controlling and oppressing the Sunni majority (80 percent) of the population. See *ARR,* 1978–80, for details of violent clashes, bombings, and assassinations. The Syrian government in its turn blamed these incidents on the Muslim Brotherhood and described that organization as right-wing fanatics. In Egypt, rising tension between some Coptic and Muslim groups in the last three years has prompted the government and the People's Assembly to form several investigating committees, the last of which was in May 1980. President Sadat himself was obliged to address the issue of religious strife publicly for the first time in a major speech on 15 May 1980. See *Al-Ahram,* 16 May 1980.

40. This fact was revealed during the interrogation and trials of the Technical Military Academy Group in 1974 and the Repentance and Holy Flight Group in 1977. See *ARR,* 11–16 July and 1–15 Aug. 1977.

41. The Saudi authorities announced that among those arrested, tried and executed were five Egyptians.

15
Reflections on a New Arab Order

Fouad Ajami

I

Al-infitah, or the "open door" economy in Egypt, is a stepchild of the 1973 oil revolution and it bears its mark: faith in technology, a belief in new possibilities and bloated expectations. Its harvest has been wild rents, land speculations, inflation, and corruption.[1]

In the states at the periphery of the oil revolution, it was reasoned that shackled economies could not compete in the new regional order. It was best that they seize on new opportunities. Their answer was typically bureaucratic: scrap yesterday's laws, ease the state hold on the economy, change to symbols of the new political order. There were state elites anxious to make the transition to the new climate and to break out of the bureaucratic mold. But the doctrinaire distinction between public and private sectors breaks down far easier than the faithful imagine.

The public sector of one era becomes the private sector of the next: The classic case is Mexico—a country whose revolution and its outcome bear more than a superficial resemblance to the Egyptian case. Access to state power provided an opportunity for capital accumulation and extremely valuable experience in mastering the rules of the game. Then the official classes plunge into the private market: The fervor they once displayed for planning and state intervention was channelled into the private market. Official experience thus became the base for a new career in the private sector.

In Egypt, since October 1973, there has been an elite personnel shift of considerable magnitude from the public sector to the private sector. Some of those who made the shift are among Egypt's most powerful and prominent figures. An Egyptian businessman describes the new competition in the marketplace this way: "The market is now full of former prominent officials; two former prime ministers in addition to

Originaly titled "Retreat from Economic Nationalism: the Political Economy of Sadat's Egypt." Reprinted with permission from *Journal of Arab Affairs* 1, no. 1 (1981):27–52.

twenty-two former ministers and tens of former heads of public sector companies, deputy ministers, and governors."[2]

The Egyptian response to the era of petrodollars was a rush to demonstrate a break with the populist interlude. Thus in 1975, the Egyptian bureaucracy reported with great pride that 102 laws had been enacted to create a new economic order. The legislation covered the full range of economic activities: Law 43, the centerpiece, paved the way for foreign investors and gave a generous set of provisions and exceptions; Ministerial Decision number 1058 liberalized import laws, and the import sector was shifted to an open licensing system; banking, which had been nationalized, was thrown open to foreign banks resulting in 25 new banking ventures; foreign exchange transactions were shifted from the official market to the parallel market. Most of the crucial legislation was enacted in 1974/75 at the height of the euphoria with the post–October 1973 order. A little later there had to be an intensification of liberalization. The logic was more of the same. The proponents of *al-infitah* would repeatedly persist in their view that "capital is cowardly," that there had to be more incentive for foreign interests and "hidden local capital." Indeed it was the mandate of one cabinet headed by Prime Minister Abdul Aziz Hijazi to implement the open door economic policy and, when that failed, the task fell to Mamduh Salem—a man with a background in the police services, a former Governor of Alexandria—to achieve what Hijazi's government had failed to do. In President Sadat's words, "Mamduh Salem is today blowing up all the rules and obstacles that impede the freedom of economic affairs." To the proponents of *al-infitah,* intervention by the state was an obstacle, and all obstacles were to be removed.

The relentless attack against the state in the Egyptian liberalizers' arsenal was due, in part, to an unwillingness to pay the public costs of the political order. It was also a bit of political and cultural mimicry—an attempt to be more Western than the West—that reflects an inability to understand the rules of the game in the Organization of Economic Cooperation and Development (OECD) countries. The result is a "more royalist than the King" kind of situation. While OECD countries regulate their economies, those who wish to appeal to the West urge dismantling of many of the economic functions and responsibilities of the state. And in the aftermath of the October war the proponents of the new policy based their arguments not only on a vastly changed regional and international configuration, but also on the widely perceived failure of what passed for socialism.

When one reviews the voluminous debate on *al-infitah* and the broader questions of basic economic choices, one is struck by a curious simplification of economic issues: Economic conditions seem to be of two kinds, *infitah* (opening) and *ingilaq* (closure). Egypt tried the latter, and it presumably failed; thus it was time to go for an overhauling of the system. In the proponents' depiction of the issues, to oppose *al-infitah* is to fall prey to a "fear complex." This fits in with the interesting psychologizing of politics in Sadat's Egypt. Politics reduces itself to the search for identity, and all of Nasir's policies are explained by his "complexes," which President Sadat always refers to but generously refuses to reveal. The "fear complex" appears in President Sadat's *October Paper* (April 1974), in which he observed, "The world after 1973 is not the way it was before: Egypt is strong to rid itself of the "fear complex" vis-à-vis the outside world."[3]

The political process that brought about the "102 legislative changes" maintained throughout that it was Egypt's laws that stood between the country and access to foreign capital. Here and there dissident voices were heard, but the bureaucracy and the interest that pushed those legislators were locked into that proposition. Behind liberalization stood the prestige of the presidency: the authority of President Sadat's *October Paper* and his promise of a new era of prosperity. And, in an authoritarian political setting, the interests that favored the new policy had their way. The would-be regulated (multinationals, their domestic representatives) helped to make the basic economic policies; the bureaucrats, who were generally entrusted with regulation, had a different mandate in the Egyptian case: that of "blowing up" the rules and promoting the interests of the regulated.

Thus the Investment and Free Zone Authority (whose domain covers foreign investments and joint ventures) was never seen as a regulatory agency. Its task was to "package" the country to pave the way for the foreign investor. Bureaucracies being what they are, the Investment and Free Zone Authority became a domain from which careers could be advanced by those who placed their bets on the new economic policy. Predictably the Authority sought to show its diligent pursuit of its defined objectives. Consider the following introduction to its glossy brochure (printed in Beirut, as if to underscore the impact of the open door economy on local industry):

> The General Authority for Investment and Free Zones has embarked on its new task on the 14th of October 1972 by convening the first meeting of its Board of Directors. Since that day, and until the end of December 1977, the Board held 45 meetings in which they approved 534 projects to be set up in land and in the private free zones. The project's capital amounts to LE 2132, at first estimation. The Board of Public Free Zones approved 206 other projects whose capital amounts to LE 208 million. . . .[4]

The word "approve" gives away the tactic of the proponents of *al-infitah,* as they held out the promise of massive foreign investment awaiting a favorable political climate. Thus in 1974, it was announced that LE 500 million were approved, while the actual committed capital was only LE 383,000 or, in other words, less than 1 percent of approved projects. In the same vein, former Prime Minister Mamduh Salem announced in 1975 that one of the achievements of his government had been the approval of 349 projects with a capital of LE 390 million and that another 150 projects had been under study. Some of this was wishful thinking; some was a deliberate effort to suggest that a new and bright future beckoned for Egypt.

The fundamental policy of *al-infitah* was made by the regulated and by its direct beneficiaries. Its basic pillar was the dismantling of state regulation. All the workshops (the Legal and Economic Aspects of Foreign Investment held in October 1975, the Exchange Control and Open Door Policy held in April 1976, the Banking Control and Open Door Policy held in December 1976, and, finally, the Workshop on Proposed Changes to Law 43 held in February 1977) were dominated by an unexamined faith in the efficiency of the market. All ritually recommended that primacy should be assigned to removing state barriers. What is immediately evident in all these meetings is the absence of not only those who might favor different economic choices but even those members of the bureaucracy—i.e., Ministry of Industry officials—who might be committed to a measure of economic nationalism and might have had a vested interest in protecting local industry. The Egyptian officials present at these meetings were invariably the same individuals who were representatives of the Investment Authority, as well as those of the Ministry of Economy and Economic Cooperation. The officials of the Ministry of Industry, not to mention the representatives of affected labor unions, were shut out of the process. Lopsided and pliant majorities in parliament then ratified the key decisions. In none of the workshops were questions of distribution and welfare seriously raised. The reigning economic philosophy can be discerned from the recommendations made.[5] For example, the Workshop on Legal and Economic Aspects of Foreign Investment recommended that:

> . . . the structure of relative prices be thoroughly examined and attention be given to the task of making market prices in Egypt more nearly reflect social costs and benefits. . . . It is recognized that private foreign and private domestic investment respond much more to market prices than to direct decisions by the government. It is also noted that public companies are being given more freedom to respond to market incentives. It is therefore necessary that the same review of the relative price structure in Egypt be undertaken that will lead to proposals that make market prices more nearly reflect social costs and benefits.[6]

Behind this tortured verbiage was the familiar call upon the state to "rationalize" things by terminating subsidies—an added bit of pressure to that applied by the International Monetary Fund (IMF) and the Arab oil states. More of the same emerges from the Workshop on Banking Laws that was attended by virtually the entire foreign banking sector. This time the issue was the convertibility of the Egyptian pound and the exchange rates. It was "recognized" by the participants that there was a "movement to greater reliance on the private sector and the market mechanism." It was concluded that the "current exchange rate policy was a major obstacle, perhaps the major obstacle to private investment entering Egypt." That too was the position underscored by the Workshop on Exchange Control and the Open Door Policy that recommended floating the Egyptian pound and shifting imports from the official to the parallel rates: "It was appreciated that the open door policy represented

> a marked shift in development strategy from that prevailing over the two decades prior to the early 1970s. This shift from the old to the new imposed a variety of demands on the policy maker to effect this transition. At the same time there was a lack of data and full comprehension of how the economy . . . would function as new policies were introduced.[7]

One could go on with this, but the cumulative message is clear. It adds up to a fairly powerful lobby with no countervailing powers. That this lobby's arguments are neither compelling nor fully thought out makes no difference whatsoever. The business interests were (naturally) pushing for the most favorable terms they could get and they invariably came up with the very laws under which they were supposed to operate. The state bureaucracy went along.

The vital changes in foreign investment laws drawn up by a workshop of foreign executives, investment lawyers, and officials of the Ministry of Economy were known to the business community long before they were submitted to parliament. *Egypt Report,* a newsletter published by investment lawyer Ahmad Shalkany, had summarized the changes for its subscribers in February 1977—more tax exemptions, more favorable exchange rates, and no limits on the repatriation of profits. Mr. Shalkany had attended the meetings that came up with the new legislation. He and other lawyers in his firm (which represents and advises foreign enterprises) lobbied for the most generous of exemptions, in effect for the total absence of state regulation. Mr. Shalkany's newsletter asserted that it was "believed" that the "introduction of these amendments will remove the obstacles that have hindered the flow of investments into Egypt up to the present time and create the appropriate investment atmosphere in the Arab Republic of Egypt."[8]

None of this shows a firm understanding of the nature of international political economy, or the dynamics of foreign investment decisions and how they are made. The real problems are wished away; faith is at work. There is an incapacity to realize that economic nationalism asserts itself in countries of conventional "leftist" ideology like Algeria and "rightist" ones like Brazil. Having gambled with great exuberance and certitude on the flood of investment awaiting the dismantling of socialism that supposedly frightened away the foreign investor, the proponents of *al-infitah* held on to their faith, in the face of sobering evidence to the contrary.

Some independent members of the parliament, such as Khaled

Moheiddin, questioned the excessive faith in *al-infitah*. He rightly noted that the experience of Third World countries confirmed that foreign investment was directly correlated with the level of domestic savings and that the critical questions for Egypt were its savings rate, the reform of its infrastructure, and a serious plan for the economy. Unless these were tackled, foreign investors would stay away. The few who would come in would do so in sectors of the economy—banking, consulting firms, fast food chains—that failed to address the basic needs of the society.[9] The relentlessly independent Muhammad Hilmi Murad focused on the generous tax exemptions which were not only unfair but were also the wrong issue. He observed that:

> Foreign investors do not avoid a particular country or invest there because of taxes. Taxes are one factor among many; it is the overall health of an economy that sways the foreign investor. How does Egypt intend to maintain its economy while it erodes its tax base? How will the economy as a whole function when foreign investors have privileges not extended to the Egyptian investor? If foreign investment laws were passed to bring in international technology and capital, then why allow foreign insurance companies to come in when their previous record indicates that they "accumulate domestic savings to serve foreign economies?[10]

Of course the "official" position had many defenders, as shown by the views of two members of parliament. One, Dr. Gamal Uteifi, a deputy speaker, the other, Kamal Mustapha Murad, a former "Free Officer." In defense of the open door policy, Uteifi reveals its sources of inspiration. Returning from a trip to Singapore, Thailand, Indonesia, and the Philippines—countries which are flooded by foreign investment—he informed his colleagues that Egypt is amply qualified to attract foreign investments, adding:

> In reality the problem that faced foreign investment in Egypt is providing the right atmosphere that guarantees security for those investments. Now that we have finished our quick comparisons . . . we have concluded that Egypt is totally prepared for foreign investment; more prepared than any other country. Let us remind the foreign investor of the fate of foreign investments in Ethiopia, Portugal, Pakistan and in many Latin American countries which are subject to daily disturbances and military coups.[11]

Egypt's comparative advantage then is its stability. That Uteifi uses the "New Society" of President Marcos, the Indonesian "New Order," and the atypical case of Singapore as examples of what Egypt should pursue may tell us a great deal about the conception of equity and its fate in the post-October 1973 order. The journey that Uteifi took to these countries left no deep impression on him. The troubles of Indonesia and the Philippines, their scale of corruption and inequity, and the political repression it takes to secure and maintain these orders do not appear in Uteifi's testimony. Nor is there a serious sustained inquiry into the relevance of Singapore to Egypt's needs. There is only the overworked reference to the security of the investor, to his need for the right guarantees.

If Uteifi, a thoughtful, educated legislator, lets the issue of equity fall by the wayside, Kamal Mustapha Murad's position is yet more extreme. Here we see a pre–New Deal kind of logic at work and we confront the purposes to which *al-infitah* was put. For Murad, and for many others like him, *al-infitah* served as a way of attacking any limits on the freedom of capital and the rights of property. There should be no limits on profit margins; the state should go for maximum exemptions, for in doing so it would unleash "hidden local capital." He added:

> What was applied in the 1960s cannot be applied now for we are in the second half of the 1970s and we should not speak the language of twenty years ago but the language of the time. . . . Capital is abundant around us and the annual surplus in the oil states is US $50 billion . . . . I ask the members to approve this plan and as soon as possible for the Consultative Group meeting in Paris needs such a law. . . . The press services are awaiting an approval.[12]

Between Egypt and prosperity stand some "formalities," to use Murad's term—and the legislation of the 1960s. Dismantle those and all would be well. Hidden local capital and surplus petrodollars would solve Egypt's problems. The extent of the wisdom about economic affairs was evident in parliament on another occasion when the import laws were being scrutinized. As a proponent of liberalization put it: "The door should be opened for all to import and export as they wish. . . . We will see that prices will go down and that there will be no deviations."

Selecting such passages may seem unkind, but they demonstrate the manner in which the open door policy had been formulated and defended. This policy promised salvation to an impoverished society that had been through some very difficult times. Its proponents depicted an external environment of plenty that was Egypt's for the asking if only the "anachronistic" policies of yesterday were pushed aside. At this juncture, both domestic Egyptian interests and foreign economic interests converged. For the former there were new opportunities; for the latter the stakes in Egypt were more substantial than the Egyptian market itself. At stake was the health of the international monetary system, the stability of the Middle Eastern order, and Egypt's unique place in the Arab system. In the aftermath of the October war, the fight between the Arab oil states and the oil-less ones had been over for some time and was concluded after 1967 in favor of the former. Egypt's repudiation of its previous radicalism and its adoption of a pro-American policy stood as the clearest embodiment of that victory.

The promises extended to Egypt by President Richard Nixon, by his Treasury Secretary, William Simon, by David Rockefeller, by the Shah of Iran, and by Saudi Arabia, all of whom had inputs into the new policy, were part of a larger game. The particularities of the Egyptian case were of little interest to them. Nor were welfare and distribution high priority items to the Shah of Iran or to William Simon or to the decision makers in Saudi Arabia. But the motives of foreign interests were only one side of the equation. To the global and regional pull, there was a powerful, domestic push. No society is a helpless pawn of others; this much at least could be said of a post-colonial world. Even poor vulnerable states make their own choices. Third World nationalism may have failed to deliver all that was pinned on it, but it has placed a great deal of sovereignty within the state and thus it has undermined the view of Third World states buffeted by winds and pressures beyond their control.

We have already sketched the arguments of the proponents of the open door policy in the troubles and developments of the late 1960s. More yet can be learned about the open door economic policy (both its social base and welfare consequences) through a different route: the lists of investors in the companies authorized by the Foreign Investment codes and published in *Al Waga'i al Misriyya* (Egyptian Facts) and *Al Jarida al Rasmiyya* (The Official Gazette).[13] A thorough analysis (more systematic than the one attempted here) of these lists may yield significant data about the insights into elite linkages, private/public sector relations, and the relation between international commerce and state elites. The lists substantiate the "merging" of the pre-1952 political order. Some old pre-1952 families reemerge; new ones who worked through the Egyptian state after 1952 rise to the top. The lists thus confirm a "restoration" of sorts combined with the rise of a new class through access to state power. . . .

II

There is, however, a public price to be paid for the private success stories. The large commissions earned by the higher echelons of the state bureaucracy bring public ruin in their train. They either deliver the society into the shackles of foreign dependence or they end up jeopardizing the productive wages of a national economy by eroding its industrial base with a flood of imports. Large commissions require grandiose, costly projects—while the development needs of a poor society call upon more modest, basic undertakings. Moreover, there are noneconomic kinds of costs associated with large commissions. Engendering as they do a sense of unfairness about how the economic game is played, about the balance between the toil of the many and the good luck of the few, commissions (and bribes) either invite rebellion and ruin of the kind that recently played themselves out in Iran and Lebanon, or simply perpetuate stagnation and decline.

But the system has an excuse: The system will come through and cleanse itself. What Egyptians refer to as *Nazahat al-Hukm* (the integritiy of the political process) has become one of the main political issues in recent years. The "model" supplied by the comings and goings in the oil states was bound to spill into Egypt; it ruptured previous limits and encouraged the men in power to go for big stakes. It has always been difficult to practice austerity in a climate where others can hoard and flaunt what they have. None of the attempts to pin corruption on particular cultures, on things like national character, are very persuasive. What matters is the *situation* in which men find themselves. Private enrichment is a wholly understandable response to the demise of the public order. It takes political will to instill discipline (always relative, always vulnerable to some violations) in a political order. These have not been in abundant supply in Arab polities of late; this may be one of the prime political casualties of the era of petrodollars in the Arab world.

If the aim of social and economic thought is to establish a country in the world community, to define its existential and political predicament, then all these grandiose projects merely foster thin illusions making it possible for the few to escape Egypt's troubles into some imaginary land. Under the Khedive Ismael (1863–1879), the dream was to make Egypt part of Europe. Some of the proponents of *al-infitah* aspire to no less and act out their own version of progress, their own version of what Europe and America are all about—in total defiance of the accumulated wisdom about development and the options open to poor societies in the world system.

Consider some of the debris: One of the most prestigious and grandiose projects is a tunnel under the Suez Canal. The *Economist's* detailed analysis of this 100 million dollar project reads in part:

> Immensely sophisticated and largely untested, digging equipment was brought from West Germany; simpler and more labor intensive methods might have suited the Egyptians better. Egyptian steel from Helwan was not strong enough to line the tunnel. Concrete segments were used instead, but it turned out that these had to be made from imported, not Egyptian cement.
>
> Fatal accidents, including the electrocution of a number of distinguished Egyptian engineers, have dogged the project. Mr. Sadat proposes to use the equipment to build two more tunnels under the canal. When engineers wonder at how such space-age stuff can be moved, the President speaks of the pyramids.[14]

But beyond such projects as this lies a more fundamental issue: the old question of domestic industrialization, imports versus manufactures and a national position in the world economic system. The real danger of the open door policy is its impact on local industry, and from this on native welfare and employment.[15]

In the end, it is within the strictures of a moderate version of economic nationalism—which underpins this analysis—that the open door economy is faulted. The case for economic sovereignty should not be an absolute since, in our world, that is an impossible goal to aim at. But one does not have to be an uncompromising Gaullist to note the negative costs of the scale of dependency in Egypt now. Two things can be singled out: the impact upon national industry—hence upon employment and mass consumption—and the subordination of an economy to the dictates of others. First the question of industry.

With the severe ecological limits on its agriculture, the search for a viable industrial base has been a powerful, almost instinctive, theme in contemporary Egyptian history. This was Muhammad Ali's quest until it was thwarted by European power in 1841; it was also the dream of Tala'at Harb and the Bank Misr group under British occupation in the 1920s and the 1930s. The "Free Officers" regime was heir to the same tradition. The slogan "from the needle to the rocket" expressed the ambition of giving Egypt a viable industrial base. Sadat's *October Paper* continued in the same vein.[16] The case for the open door economic policy rested on Egypt's need for more effective, less cumbersome access to outside capital and technology. The proponents of the new policy looked toward the markets of the Gulf states: Not only would an industrial boom satisfy Egyptian needs, Egypt would also become an "export platform"—combining outside technology with cheap Egyptian labor.

A sophisticated industrial base requires considerable time to develop. In addition it calls for a good deal of social discipline and a willingness to save, all at a time of intense global competition for markets.

The quick-kill mentality that dominated the post–October 1973 order ruled out the possibility of such an industrial transformation. Nor were the outside markets easy to penetrate. The abundance of capital in the Gulf states, the hungry competition for those markets by OECD exporters, the kinds of technologies that Saudi Arabia and Kuwait were importing, reduced the Egyptian scheme to another of the aborted dreams entertained after 1973 by those who were convinced that a new world was in the making.

Thus the laws passed to enable Egypt to capture outside markets reduced themselves to what should have been an easy thing to predict, an "import mania" in the Egyptian market, a steady undermining of much of what had been accomplished in Egyptian industry after two decades of systematic bias in favor of industrialization. The relentless attacks against the public sector had done their job. The political consensus essential to protect native industrialization was undermined, and the result amounted to a change in the country's view of its economic possibilities. Egypt would generate hard currency through the export of its labor to the Arab states, from tourism, the Suez Canal, and foreign aid. In return it would rely on imports. Strategically placed elites would conduct the transactions. They would hide behind laissez-faire ideology presumed to be at work in rich, capitalist societies. They would also invite those who could not be absorbed in the agriculture sector to emigrate: make their fortunes elsewhere and return to engage in trade, open a boutique or a travel agency. Yesterday's populist experiment had stacked the bureaucracy and the public segment. Armed with what they depicted to be the dismal record of the populist experiment, *the "liberalizers" came back with no policy at all, only an attack on yesterday's populism and its inefficiency.*

The bias in favor of industry has been replaced with a bias in favor of the importer. This more accurately reflects the superior political resources of the importers and the middlemen and their proximity to political power. As Issam Rifaat, a seasoned analyst at *Al Ahram al Iqtisadi* observes, the tariff structure is "killing" local industry: "It has changed from an instrument of protection for infant industry to an instrument for burying the public sector. In several key industries the tax on raw materials is 10–30% of value while finished products are subject to a tax of 5%. The import tax on finished generators is 2% but 35% on raw materials, and spare parts; 12% on tractors but 17% on spare parts; 20% on light bulbs but 30% on raw materials."[17]

Among the abundant examples of industries in trouble as a result of the unrestricted import laws passed in the 1974–1976 period are the tire, textile, plastics, and paper industries to name a few.[18] The banking sector has not fared any better; foreign banks which were brought in to help finance investments have ended up engaging in regular banking transactions and diverting Egyptian savings outside the country.

A mere two years after the formation of the new economic policy, the lines became increasingly drawn between cheaper imports and local manufactures. The political process favored the former. But that victory can be short-lived. As local and national capitalists, who once hailed the open-door policy, began to suffer its consequences and as sympathetic intellectuals took note, defection from the new policy commenced. We see this in the position of the Egyptian Federation of Industries whose president, Hamed Habib, came out against the hasty import laws favored by other sectors of the bureaucracy. Local industry, he warned, was being undermined by a number of factors: (1) the import laws; (2) smuggling from the free zones; (3) the "import complex" which drives those with purchasing power to buy foreign goods as a badge of their own cosmopolitanism and sophistication; (4) the loss of East European and Soviet markets.

The concern with cultural integrity, always most intimately felt by the intelligentsia, has caused many to take a second look at the open door policy. The editors and staff of the influential *Al Ahram al Iqtisadi* who once hailed the new policy appear to have joined its critics—gently and with great caution for they are part of the country's official media. In a bitter and sarcastic commentary written in early 1976, its editor-in-chief Lutfi Abdul Azim expressed cultural and economic grievances that the new policy will have to address if it is to avert a dismal fate. He said:

> The open door policy has been such a remarkable success because there is plenty of German, Dutch, and Danish beer on the market and plenty of foreign cigarettes on the sidewalks. The open door policy should be welcomed for there is an abundance of Kentucky Fried Chicken and foreign fast foods changing the habits of the average Egyptian from eating *ful* [fava beans] to hamburger; plenty of elegant foreign-made cars relieving the crisis of transportation.[19]

The same editor also commented on the food riots of January 1977. Here his themes were the "new consumer society," and the place of the poor masses in it; the alienation from an order which flaunts such waste and wealth in the midst of suffering. He took issue with the regime's statement on the riots as an "uprising of thieves" and a "communist conspiracy." Abdul Azim's view was no doubt held by the majority of Egypt's intelligentsia. He stated:

> Few individuals were actively engaged in looting and burning but there was a "silent majority" that stood by and did not care. There is an "economic apartheid" between a new class that hoards all the opportunities and the vast majority of the people. Why should the average person care whether the casinos on the road to the Pyramids were burned when he hears that a belly dancer makes in one evening what it takes a wage earner a period of five years to earn?[20]

III

Eventually, ruinous and hasty economic policies have to be paid for. In Egypt and other Third World societies caught in the debt trap (Peru, Zaire, Turkey, to name a few), the result will be to sacrifice their economic autonomy. In country after country, the "politics of credit-worthiness" has more to say about the actual conduct of policy than any ideological exhortations. The crisis of foreign debts brings in its train new forms of intervention and dependence: forms that the nationalist leaders did not foresee a generation ago. Subscribing to a primacy of politics, the first generation leaders sought the trappings of statehood. Today those trappings are there but sovereignty turns out to be an empty shell. This is the way a British economist puts it:

> Access to the higher credit tranches in the IMF is only obtained at the cost of the effective elimination of the economic independence of the borrowing countries. This is true of an industrialized country like Britain as it is for a peripheral country like Mauritius; in both cases internally determined economic priorities must give way to those established by the need to bring the balance of payments into equilibrium and to repay international credit when it falls due.[21]

The medicine that the IMF recommends can be tough to take. In Peru, Turkey, and Egypt, IMF guidelines had to be enforced by calling out the army. IMF guidelines were behind the Egyptian government's decision to halve its food subsidies in January of 1977. This decision sparked a popular upheaval which was suppressed with a loss of seventy-nine lives. A U.S. Senate Foreign Relations Committee report noted the connection between IMF guidelines and the grim game of governance in a situation of scarcity and constraints.[22]

In defense, the IMF can point to the fact that it "confines its conditions to broad economic aggregates," that it does not "dictate details of taxes and spending" and that "the way individual governments choose to meet its conditions reveals much more about them than it does about the IMF."[23] There is no doubt that there is a great deal of merit to this view, but realities within Third World societies almost invariably dictate the typical way adjustments are made: at the expense of the poor. As an Egyptian minister explained the decision to cut food subsidies: "Last year we had a budget deficit of over $2 billion. Of the four key budget items—military, investment, subsidies, and debt service—it was decided that the subsidies were the most expendable item."[24]

The relative political weakness of the poor and the ideology of "market pricing" constitute a vicious circle. Subsidies seem expendable because those who benefit from them are disorganized and those in power are sure of the efficacy of the medicine they propose. Caught between those who wanted to phase out the subsidies and the angry Egyptian masses who finally drew a line for their rulers in the January 1977 riots, the Egyptian government retreated and called on the U.S. to make "the IMF give way."[25] The president's strength lay in his weakness: If pushed too far, his regime might collapse.[26]

It is clear from the above that much of Egypt's economic strategy, along with its highly unpredictable and fluctuating foreign policy, has been a dangerous trapeze act dependent on an American net to keep the act from turning into disaster. The post–October 1973 Egyptian order exaggerated what others would and could do for Egypt while at the same time it underestimated what the donors would ask for in return.

Ideologically the open door policy was wrapped in the garb of "Westernization." But men and societies removed from the West rarely seem to understand what is at work in the world they wish to emulate. There is a massive gap between the free-for-all capitalism defended in Egypt and what obtains in today's international political economy. The "open" trading system created in the post–World War II years broke down in 1971. This fact is fully understood in OECD countries. As the McCracken report states:

> This potential for rapid growth would not have been realized . . . had it not been for the favorable economic climate created by governments—first by their assumption of responsibility for the achievement of high employment, and second through their commitment to economic inte-

gration in the framework of an open, multilateral system for international trade and payments.[27]

This is not the first or last time that incantations in non-Western societies about progress and Westernization sharply differ from realities in the West.

IV

Great expectations often culminate in bitterness and recriminations. The "generous Arab brothers" of 1974 and 1975 became, in the words of a writer for the Egyptian daily *Al Akhbar,* "shoeless goatherds"[28] only two years later. Whether the recriminations once visited on the Russian and then on the oil states eventually come to be visited on the U.S. remains to be seen. In today's international system, nations either pay their own way or they fall behind. In this milieu they make all kinds of "adjustments" to decline and stagnation. While powerful groups help themselves to public resources, many of the gifted emigrate to other lands. Despair sets in and the dominant order abandons any serious commitment to public welfare.

Albert Hirschman's work, *Exit, Voice and Loyalty,* is depictive of one ominous Egyptian response to politico-economic decline, the emigration of some of Egypt's most gifted youth.[29] Choking off the voice option, the Egyptian order has been encouraging the exit option with negative consequences for the quality of the social order and for mass loyalty to the society at large. In one informal survey of university students, nearly 85% expressed a desire to leave Egypt upon graduation.[30] This trend set in after the 1967 war; it turned into mass exodus after 1973. The pull of oil wealth was one factor; but there were domestic factors as well. In Egypt as elsewhere emigration buys off a measure of stability by removing from the system potential dissidents; but it also removes from the society those who would have been more likely to resort to the voice option and to make some contribution to the public interest.

Traditionally Egypt was a society whose inhabitants were reluctant to venture to other lands. It possessed the stability of an agrarian order where men stayed, normatively and physically, at home. It was only in the past decade or so that mass emigration became a widespread Egyptian phenomenon. The private gains are easy to document but the public costs to productivity and social stability, though harder to specify, are surely considerable. There is the shortage of skilled manpower felt in critical Egyptian industries; there is the cost in productivity that results from those biding their time, waiting to leave. As Adel Husayn wrote: "It could be said that he who has not emigrated is preparing to do so; that is, he considers himself in transit and we can imagine the impact of such a phenomenon upon his productivity."[31] States can, as Hirschman argues, make it tempting for their citizens to stay at home. He adds: "Social justice, too, may be a public good; individuals may find it enjoyable to live in a society where income distribution is comparatively egalitarian."[32] It then follows that a high level of inequality is an invitation to some to pick up and go elsewhere.

Whatever its ideological shortcomings, the Egyptian order made the effort under 'Abd al-Nasir. The radicalism that moved it may have been accidental—reflecting the personality of the ruler; the rise of new classes sensing new possibilities; the intransigence of an old order; the pressure of a global system that pushed the experiment further than the Egyptian custodians may have initially intended. Then things took the turn depicted here and there was the resurgence of the old conservative sensibility about inequality: the kind that lives in all societies and more so in old civilizations that witness the rise and passing of all sorts of claims, the emergence and fading of movements that set out to change the world and then succumb to it.

In a thoughtful analysis of the Egyptian experiment, Lewis Awad writes that the Egyptian revolution has "aged," that it needs a new social contract, a new sense of what it is dedicated to.[33] The prospects for "stalled societies"[34] such as Egypt are grim unless they can somehow confront what Barrington Moore has aptly called the "appalling costs of stagnation."[35]

Notes

Paper originally prepared for the Income Distribution Project of the Research Program in Development Studies at Princeton University. My debt to the project and its participants is immense. I wish to note in particular the help of Gouda Abdel Khalek, Ali Dessouki, Saad Ibrahim, John P. Lewis, Robert Tignor, and John Waterbury. In this project as in other pursuits Henry Bienen's help and encouragement were critical.

1. See for example an interesting description of the post–October 1973 situation in Egypt, Mohamed Heikal, *The Sphinx and the Commissar* (New York: Harper & Row, 1978), pp. 261–262.
2. *Al-Ahram,* August 7, 1976.
3. Muhammad Anwar el Sadat, *Waraqat Uktubar* [The October paper], Cairo, 1974.
4. Investment and Free Zones Authority, *Report on the Arab and Foreign Investment Until 31/12/1977,* 1978, p. 3.
5. All the citations are taken from Ford Foundation files on the workshops, available in the Cairo office.
6. Ibid.
7. Ibid.
8. *Egypt Report,* February 1977.
9. See Moheiddin's statement in *Parliamentary Proceedings* (May 10, 1977), pp. 34–36.
10. Ibid., pp. 25–28.
11. Ibid., p. 14.
12. Ibid., p. 24.
13. The sources for the new investors lists are *Al Waga'i al Misriyya* [Egyptian

Facts] and *Al Jarida al Rasmiyya* [The Official Gazette]. For the 1961/1962 list, I used those reproduced by Mahmoud Murad, *Who Ruled Egypt?* (Cairo, 1975).

14. *The Economist,* July 14, 1979, p. 62.

15. See Robert Gilpin's excellent discussion in his *U.S. Power and the Multinational Corporation* (New York: Basic Books, 1975), particularly pp. 215–262.

16. The October Paper, *op. cit.* pp. 40–41. Also see *Al Ahram al Iqtisadi,* January 15, 1978; also April 1, 1978.

17. *Al Ahram al Iqtisadi,* April 1, 1978.

18. *Al Ahram,* December 21, 1978.

19. *Al Ahram al Iqtisadi,* February 15, 1976.

20. *Al Ahram al Iqtisadi,* February 1, 1977.

21. E. A. Brett, "The International Monetary Fund, The International Monetary System and the Periphery," *International Foundation for Development Alternatives Dossier 5,* March, 1979 (Nyon, Switzerland), pp. 1–15.

22. U.S. Senate Foreign Relations Committee, Subcommittee on Foreign Economic Policy, *International Debts, The Banks, and U.S. Foreign Policy* (Washington, D.C.: U.S. Government Printing Office, 1977), p. 6.

23. *The Economist,* June 3, 1978, p. 92.

24. *The New York Times,* February 26, 1977.

25. *The Economist,* March 3, 1979, pp. 71–72.

26. *The Economist,* July 14, 1979, pp. 62–64.

27. Paul McCracken and others, *Towards Full Employment and Price Stability,* A Report to the OECD by a Group of Independent Experts, 1977, p. 11.

28. Cited in *The Economist,* October 7, 1978, p. 79.

29. Albert Hirschman, *Exit, Voice and Loyalty* (Cambridge, Mass.: Harvard University Press, 1970).

30. Cited in Adel Husayn, "Petrodollars as an Obstacle to Unity and Complementarity," *al Mustaqbal al Arabi* (Number 5, 1979), p. 28.

31. Ibid. p. 28.

32. Albert Hirschman, "Exit, Voice and the State," *World Politics,* vol. 31, October 1978, pp. 90–107, p. 105.

33. See Lewis Awad's sophisticated and fair-minded assessment of Nasserism, *The Seven Masks of Nasserism* (Beirut, 1976).

34. The concept of "stalled societies" is developed (with emphasis on France) in Michel Crazier's book *The Stalled Society* (New York: Viking Press, 1973).

35. Barrington Moore, Jr. *The Social Origins of Dictatorship and Democracy* (Boston: Beacon Press, 1966).

Contributors

Fouad Ajami is professor of political science at the School of Advanced International Studies, Johns Hopkins University, Washington, D.C.

Lutfy N. Diab is professor of psychology at the American University of Beirut, Lebanon.

Juhaina S. Al-Easa is associate professor of psychology at Qatar University, Doha, Qatar.

Tawfic E. Farah is president of the Middle East Research Group, Inc. of Fresno, California, and editor of its publication, *The Journal of Arab Affairs.*

Fadwa El-Guindi is associate professor of anthropology at the University of California, Los Angeles, California.

Saad Eddin Ibrahim is professor of sociology at the American University in Cairo, Egypt.

Malcolm H. Kerr is president of the American University of Beirut, Lebanon.

Hilal Khashan is assistant professor of political science at King Saud University, Riyadh, Saudi Arabia.

Levon H. Melikian is professor of psychology at Qatar University, Doha, Qatar.

Jean F. O'Barr is professor of political science at Duke University, Durham, North Carolina.

Monte Palmer is professor of political science at Florida State University, Tallahassee, Florida.

Edwin T. Prothro is professor of psychology at the American University of Beirut, Lebanon.

Faisal Al-Salem is associate professor of political science at Kuwait University, Kuwait.

Michael W. Suleiman is professor of political science at Kansas State University, Manhattan, Kansas.

Mark A. Tessler is professor of political science at the University of Wisconsin, Milwaukee, Wisconsin.

Index